E.M.S. Namboodiripad

E.M.S. Namboodiripad

Series Editor
Dr. M.H. Syed

Editor
R.K. Singh **P.K. Choudhry**

hbpl

Himalaya Books Pvt. Ltd.

'Ramdoot', Dr. Bhalerao Marg, Girgaon, Mumbai - 400 004
Tel : (022) 23863863, Fax : (022) 23877178
Email : himpub@vsnl.com

First Edition : 2011

Published by : H.B.P.L.
"Pooja Apartments", 4-B, Murari Lal Street, Ansari Road,
Darya Ganj, New Delhi-110 002
Phones : 23270392, 23278631 Reliance : 30180392 to 396
Fax : 011-23256286 Email : hphdel@vsnl.com

Sole Distributers : HIMALAYA PUBLISHING HOUSE PVT. LTD.

Branch Offices

Mumbai : "Ramdoot", Dr. Bhalerao Marg, Girgaon, Mumbai-400 004.
Phones : 23860170/23863863 Fax : 022-23877178
Email : himpub@vsnl.com
Website : www.himpub.com

Nagpur : Kundanlal Chandak Industrial Estate, Ghat Road, **Nagpur 440-018.**
Phone: 2738731, 3296733 Telefax : 0712-2721215

Bengaluru : No. 16/1 (Old 12/1), 1st Floor, Next to Hotel Highlands,
Madhava Nagar, Race Course Road, **Bengaluru - 560 001.**
Phone : 22281541, 22385461, Telefax: 080-22286611

Hyderabad : No. 3-4-184, Lingampally, Besides Raghavendra Swamy Matham,
Kachiguda, **Hyderabad - 500 027.** Phone: 040-27560041,
27550139, Mobile:- 09848130433 Telefax: 040-27560041

Chennai : No. 85/50, Bazullah Road, T. Nagar, **Chennai - 600 017.**
Phone: 044-28344020, 32463737, 42124860

Pune : No. 527, "Laksha" Apartment, First Floor, Mehunpura,
Shaniwarpeth, (Near Prabhat Theatre), **Pune - 411 030.**
Phone: 020-24496323/24496333/32326733

Lucknow : Jai Baba Bhawan, Near Dr. Sanjiv Awasthi, Church Road,
Kurshi Road, Aliganj, **Lucknow - 226 024.**
Phone: 9305302158, 9415349385

Ahmedabad : No. 114, "SHAIL", 1st Floor, Opp. Madhu Sudan House, C.G.Road,
Navrang Pura, **Ahmedabad – 380 009.**
Phone: 079-26560126, Mobiles: 09327324149,09314679413

Ernakulam : No. 39/104 A, Lakshmi Apartment, Karikkamuri Cross Rd.,
Ernakulam, **Cochin – 682011**, Kerala.
Phone: 0484-2378012, 2378016, Mob.: 09344199799

Bhubaneswar : 5 Station Square, **Bhubaneswar (Orissa) - 751 001.**
Mobile: 9861046007, E-mail:-orissa@himpub.com

Indore : Kesardeep Avenue Extension, 73, Narayan Bagh, Flat No. 302,
IIIrd Floor, Near Humpty Dumpty School, Narayan Bagh,
Indore (M.P.) 452 007 Mobile: 09301386468

Kolkata : 108/4, Beliaghata, Main Road, Near ID Hospital, Opp. SBI Bank
Kolkata - 700 010. Mobile: 09910440956

Printed at : Shri Krishna offset Press Delhi-93

Preface

Biography, is now a form of literature, very much in vogue. In fact, biography is a description or account of someone's life and the times, which is usually published in the form of a book. A biography is more than a mention of personal facts (life, education, work, relationships and death), it also portrays the subject's experience of events. Technically speaking, a work is biographical, if it covers, all of a person's life. Biography writing has a long history. A biography is real. Ancient Greeks developed the biographical tradition, which we have inherited, although until the 5th century AD, when the word 'biographia' first appeared, in Damascius' "Life of Isodorus," biographical pieces were called simply "lives". It is quite likely that the Greeks were drawing on a pre-existing eastern tradition. Certainly Herodotus' "Histories" contains more detailed biographical information on Persian kings and subjects. The earliest surviving pieces, which we would identify as biographical are Isocrates' "Life of Evagoras" and Xenophon's "Life of Agesilaos," both from the fifth century BC. "Parallel Lives" by Plutarch, a Greek writing under the Roman empire, is a series of short biographies of eminent men.

The Golden Age of English biography emerged in late eighteenth century, the century in which the terms "biography" and "autobiography" entered English lexicon. The classic works of the period were Samuel Johnson's "Critical Lives of the Poets" and James Boswell's "Massive Life of Johnson". Generally American biography followed English model. By World War I, cheap hardcover reprints had become popular. The decade of the 1920s witnessed a biographical 'boom'. Later, biographical writings developed a lot and today biographies are written and compiled in the finest form of the genre. In India too, biography, as a form of literature has been evolved, cultivated and polished over the years. Here is an effort to promote this tradition further.

This series of biographies of great men, great women and celebrities in all walks of life is an adventurous academic endeavour, in its own right. A team of researchers and compilers has worked for a good period of time to accomplish the project. For this purpose, hundreds of books by eminent authors and editors have been consulted and referred to. We have benefited from various works, liberally, in order to illustrate and enrich this effort of ours. Present book is devoted to the great personality of Elamkulam Manakkal Sankaran Namboodiripad.

Elamkulam Manakkal Sankaran Namboodiripad, popularly known as EMS, was a prominent Communist leader and the first Chief Minister of Kerala. As the first non-Congress chief minister in independent India, he also became the leader of the first democratically elected communist government in the world. He was renowned as a socialist and a Marxist-theorist. During his college days, he was deeply associated with the Indian National Congress and the Independence Movement. He was a writer and author of several literary works and his book on the history of Kerala is notable. He was one of the founder leaders of Congress Socialist Party. He was also considered to be one of the founders of the Communist Party of India (CPI) in Kerala.

This is a compact and comprehensive account of the above mentioned great life, which is bound to attract the attention of scholars, researchers, students and the general readers alike. Let's hope this humble effort would receive a warm welcome and due applause.

— ***Editors***

Contents

1

An Illustrious Life

Introduction

Great Communist leader, Elamkulam Manakkal Sankaran Namboodiripad, (June 13, 1909 - March 19, 1998), popularly known as E.M.S., was the first Chief Minister of Kerala. As the first non-Congress chief minister in independent India, he became the leader of the first democratically elected communist government in the world. He was renowned as a socialist and a Marxist theorist.

E.M.S. was born on June 13, 1909, as the son of Parameswaran Namboodiripad, at Elamkulam, in Perinthalmanna taluk of the present Malappuram district. In his early years, he was associated with V. T. Bhattathiripad, M. R. Bhattathiripad and many others in the fight against the casteism and conservatism that existed in the Namboothiri community. He became one of the office bearers of Valluvanadu Yogakshema Sabha, an organisation of progressive Namboothiri youth. During his college days, he was deeply associated with the Indian National Congress and Indian Independence Movement.

He was a writer and author of several literary works and his book on the history of Kerala is notable. E.M.S. died on March 19, 1998. He was married to Smt. Arya Antharjanam and had two sons and two daughters.

Early Life and Education

As a young student he was greatly influenced by the speeches and writings of Gokhale. Tilak and Mahatma Gandhi. He was thus attracted towards the freedom movement launched by Mahatma Gandhi in 1920s and 1930s. While he was a student in the B.A. class, he was arrested and sentenced to three years' imprisonment. But he was released in 1933 when Gandhi withdrew the satyagraha movement. He was indeed a true patriot and a secular leader.

While he was in jail at Cannanore, he happened to meet leaders like Kamal Nath Tiwari of the Lahore Conspiracy Case and Sen Gupta, Chakravarti and Acharya of the Anushilan group from Bengal and thus the seeds of the Congress Socialist Party in Kerala were sown at the Cannanore Central Jail. Thus, in 1934, when the Congress Socialist Party was formed at Patna, Namboodiripad became one of its founders and he was elected as one of its Joint-Secretaries. In the same year, he was elected as a Member of the AICC in 1934. The same year he took charge of the office of the Kerala Pradesh Congress Committee and it was under the leadership of the Socialist group, including himself, that the Congress became a mass organisation in his own province.

An Experiment with Marxism

The demise of E.M.S. Namboodiripad shed a pall of a gloom over the cultural arena of Kerala. What makes Kerala a distinct entity with improved human relations has a lot to do with the life and philosophy of E.M.S. The state has become a model for the world in the Physical Quality of Life Index (PQIL). In an interview published in The Hindu (October, 2, 1996), a right-wing economist and former US Ambassador to India specifically mentioned Kerala for its improvement. E.M.S. was born in a traditional Brahmin family but he was never a "flamboyant Brahmin boy" as described by Arundhati Roy. On the contrary, his masterpiece, written and published in 1948, depicted almost all marginalised cultures of Kerala, conferring an equal dignity and status on them. In that book, Keralam Malayalikalude Mathrubhumi (Kerala – the land of Malayalese), he introduced a radical shift in literary criticism.

E.M.S. could produce a method of his own after imbibing the spirit of Marxian methodology and thereby analysed the life and times of Keralites. His endeavour was to achieve an oppression-free existence of mankind. E.M.S. produced such a great work even before the advent of the Western Neo-Marxian materialistic studies. For him, the study of the Kerala culture turned into a kind of culture criticism when modern industrialisation was not even in an embryonic stage in the State. So what is now called culture criticism or cultural materialism was practised by E.M.S. in Kerala even 50 years ago. He introduced not only a materialistic interpretation of culture but also a progressive vision of the developments of the world. Without using the jargons of New Historicism or Post-modernism, E.M.S. could topple the hierarchy of culture and even deconstructed the high/low binary in art and literature. When the dominant ideology of Kerala, stemming from the Sanskritised grammatical structure, propagated the ingenuity of what was written and read in Sanskrit alone, E.M.S. unhesitatingly eulogised even the cultural contributions of the underprivileged. In this respect, his reading of Kumaran Asan's "Duravastha" stands out as unique; it is in contradiction with what Mr. Kancha Illaiah said recently about the politics of the communist parties. Mr. Kancha Ilaiah was in the University of Calicut to deliver a speech at a Dalit seminar. In the inaugural session, he said the Dalits alone could help in their emancipation. What happened in the academic life as well as public sphere in Kerala is different.

> In "Duravastha" there is a stanza ending
>
> "....... left Hindu religion – owing to casteism
>
> rotten itself into Brahmanism".

In the preface, the poet confessed that he was deviating from the poetic tradition and undertaking the inevitable depiction of the "present" ignoring the tradition which preaches that "the past or indirect" themes alone be conceived of in poetry. The poet's lamentation that "Duravastha" is maladroit (vilakshana) compared to his other poems not withstanding the thematic importance shows the extent of hegemony over the language and literature in that period. But, for E.M.S. there was nothing wrong in the poem depicting the most obnoxious casteism. The poet, belonging to an untouchable community, Ezhava (now OBC), himself had a doubt over the structure of the poem as nobody was spared by the ruling ideology. E.M.S., despite his belonging to the Brahmin caste, could question not only the caste discrimination but also the dominant ideological position in considering the structure of art and literature.

For E.M.S. there was no "vilakshana" in "Duravastha" and the poet accordingly undermines the "monopoly of upper caste" in literature. E.M.S. could transcend his subjective barrier (as we would expect) to accept the ridiculing and harsh poetic language against his own caste. He also analysed various literary movements and treated them as the social constructs of a particular period. His way of treating literature was unique as even at that time he could decode them into the products of social praxis. In the study, E.M.S. introduces an entirely new treatment, not only demolishing the distinction between high and low art but also deconstructing the demarcation among art, literature and socio-political issues.

Thanks to the new perspective of E.M.S., there is a wider acceptance of a new sensibility. It is not as simple as we may think to dissolve the ruling ideological encumbrance in the way of cultural exchanges. When Sri Narayana Guru preached the philosophy of one man, one religion and one God, the Ezhava-Thiyya (Other Backward Community) accepted it as they were the immediate beneficiaries of the change. But the Scheduled Castes and upper castes did not pay much attention to the preaching. When the communist party began to work actively to undermine feudalism and E.M.S., as a leader of the movement, preached 'advaita' of the Marxian kind it became acceptable to all except a few feudal landlords.

For the beneficiaries were almost all people belonging to different castes. At that time, there were several upper castes, immediately below Brahmins, who were actually struggling to earn their daily bread. Several sects of upper castes themselves wanted to break their traditional relations with the Brahmanical order. The Brahmins also wanted their own women to breathe a new air of freedom for which an early renaissance movement fought a war within the community.

In short, when a Brahmin Marxist leader preached a change which would benefit the majority of the communities the society in general accepted it because it was in line with their unconscious hierarchical order. Hence, Mr. Kancha Ilaiah is not correct when he says the Dalits must organise themselves into a Dalit-Bahujan Samaj to woo the Dalits. If such an identity crisis exists in Kerala, it may be within the high professional class seeking better promotion and least bothered about its counterparts tolling in villages. In the early 20th century, Kerala witnessed several caste-oriented reform movements.

However, none of them could break the hierarchy of the Brahmanical order as such. On the contrary, the anti-feudal struggles in the villages united the people belonging to different castes. The culmination of the struggle was the victory of the communist party in 1957. It was also an experiment with Marxism because the parliamentary democratic practice was then unknown to the communists of the world. If Kerala had been an independent country, E.M.S. would have paved the way for the whole world reckoning with the new order.

But unfortunately he could not even complete the project of land reform as the Centre Government under the leadership of Nehru dismissed the State Government on fabricated charges. This was like a specter haunting the "law and order" of the hegemonic class and hence it wanted to dissolve the new anti-feudal force. Anyhow, about half of the Kerala society still follows the progressive philosophy propagated by the movement and even the remaining half enjoys the quality of life secured by the Land Reform and Education Bill initiated by E.M.S. ministry of 1957. Above all, the notion of equality, fraternity and freedom prevails in the minds of the people of Kerala. A Dalit in Kerala is no more a Dalit in the sense in which he lives in Tamil Nadu or Karnataka. The same is the case with women.

Although E.M.S. was only one among the leaders of the communist party which led to the progress of the State, he was at the centre of the "new order". He was the man who taught the Keralites how to evolve a methodological shift in every sphere of life by deconstructing the high/low binary in culture. It is an experiment worth taking up wherever there is heterogeneity in culture and hence very much relevant to other States. In a article in The Hindu, Mr. Kancha Ilaiah admonishes the Dalit leaders, asking them to follow the discipline of the communist parties. Actually all those who sincerely wish to evolve an emancipatory force in India should follow the path of Kerala and demolish the hierarchy in the cultural order. In this respect the pioneers of emancipatory movement such as Mr. Kancha Ilaiah and Ms. Gail Omvedt should not fail to see the facts in relation to the actual state of existence in Kerala. In the passing away of E.M.S., Kerala has lost an eminent thinker and revolutionary comparable to Lenin and he left enough material as food for thought, to evolve a strategy of emancipation for tiding over the aporias in the present political scenario. (E.M.S. passed away on 19 march 1998 and this article was published in The Hindu, 30th March 1998).

Nehru's E.M.S Dilemma

In the second general election in 1957 something so startling happened that it instantly became an international sensation. In Kerala — at that time called India's "problem state" by one and all — the undivided Communist Party of India won the state assembly poll, thus becoming the first-ever communist formation anywhere in the world to come to power through a free and fair election. The surprise and excitement over this soon yielded place to worry — more in the outside world than within the country, at least initially.

A professor at Singapore University wrote a learned tome forecasting that Kerala would be for the Indian communists what Yenan was to the Chinese Communist Party. From their bastion in the southwest corner the Indian "Reds" would sweep across their country just as Mao's followers had done in theirs, starting from the caves of Yenan. At Nehru's press conference, a visibly alarmed foreign correspondent asked what he would do if, as seemed likely, the communists won the parliamentary election, too. "If that misfortune overtakes us, we would cope with it. You need not be worried unduly", he replied.

During his election speeches, particularly in Kerala and West Bengal, he had sharply attacked the communists for their penchant for violence and for being "guided from outside". In one these speeches that I covered, he went so far as to declare that the communists were "absolutely and completely out of place in India." But after the electoral verdict in Kerala went in their favour, he took the position expected of him: that he and his government would cooperate with the first non-Congress state government as long as the communist ministry, headed by the much-respected E.M.S. Namboodiripad, acted according to the Constitution. On this score, E.M.S. (as he was popularly known) could not have been more accommodating. In Nehru's own words, the chief minister had "put on the most proper and decorous constitutional clothing". At the Prime Minister's suggestion that plantations owned by foreigners should not be nationalised, E.M.S. retracted from the promise he had made during the election campaign.

However, Nehru's attitude towards Kerala's communist ministry was not shared by several of his senior colleagues in the government and the party, indeed by the entire Congress right wing. Govind Ballabh Pant, Union home minister, was acutely suspicious of communist designs, and immediately sent a "warning" to Trivandrum (now Thiruvananthapuram) against its decision to commute death sentences and release all political prisoners. Even more hostile to the communist ministry was Kerala's governor, K. Ramakrishna Rao, a conservative Congressman. The divergence between the Prime Minister and the right wing increased. Some of the Kerala ministry's actions, such as supporting the plantation workers during their illegal strike displeased even Nehru.

The crunch came, however, over the two main planks of the communist government's essentially moderate agenda. The state assembly passed an Education Bill and a Land Reforms Bill, which touched off a rising tide of opposition to the Namboodiripad government. The church, the Muslim League and the Nair Society all owned a large number of lucrative private schools and colleges as well as large landholdings. They formed a joint front and started a virulent agitation not only to get the controversial bills withdrawn but also to overthrow the communist government. Nehru wanted to resolve these differences through persuasion and the legal process. For example, when the Education Bill reached the president for his assent, he referred it to the Supreme Court for its advisory opinion. The communist ministry denounced this and even criticised the president. This annoyed even Nehru. But he continued to resist suggestions for Central intervention in Kerala. However, the Congress unit in the state had jumped on the joint front's bandwagon despite Nehru's advice to the contrary.

To cut a long and complicated story short, a stage arrived when law and order in Kerela seemed to spin out of control. Violent crowds went on the rampage. The police resorted to firing. Heated rhetoric on both sides escalated. There was absolutely no meeting ground between the communist ministry and the joint front — which rejected Namoodiripad's offer, made on Nehru's advice, of discussion on the entire Education Bill, not just its disputed clauses.

Slowly Nehru came to the conclusion that the only way out of the disastrous situation in Kerala was for Namoodiripad to put the two bills to the test of public opinion and therefore hold fresh elections. To persuade E.M.S. he invited the chief minister to Mashobra near Shimla where he was holidaying. Namboodiripad declined the PM's advice, and argued that to force a fresh election on the only non-Congress government in the country was "discriminatory", and could only lead to the conclusion that this would be the fate of all state governments other than those of the Congress.

Still Nehru remained reluctant to use the Centre's extraordinary powers to get rid of the communist state government even though he was displeased by its ways. However, those who had hitherto failed to make him change his mind gained sudden and substantial strength.

For Indira Gandhi, who had just become Congress president, favoured their point of view. It was she who persuaded her father to overcome his qualms. How sharp the arguments between the two must have been is best indicated by a letter she wrote him on June 20, 1959 while living under the same roof: "Papu... There is no point calling the agitation (in Kerala) communal.

It is communal only in so far as everything in Kerala is communal, including the communists. The communists very cleverly played the Nairs against the Catholics and now are trying to play the Ezhavas against both."

Just over a month later and only four days short of 51 years ago, Kerala went under president's rule. Yet during the tense, prolonged and sometimes bitter confrontation leading to this denouement, there was a hilarious interlude. On the way back home from Mashobra, E.M.S. addressed a press conference in Delhi to explain his point of view. One questioner asked him what the Prime Minister had served him for lunch during their discussions. "Exactly what a good Kashmiri Brahmin should offer a good Namboodiri Brahmin from Kerala: fish, meat and chicken", he replied.

The Farewell

Even as it grieved, Kerala seemed proud. Elankulam Manakkal Sankaran Namboodiripad had lived in the midst of the people of the State – as one among them – till the other day. He was surely the tallest Communist leader India has seen – anti-imperialist and freedom fighter, social reformer, historian, writer, journalist, thinker and theoretician.

As dusk fell on Friday, March 20, as cries of "Lal Salaam, E.M.S.", "E.M.S. is immortal" and so on rent the air, as hundreds wept along with State Chief Minister E.K. Nayanar, as his Communist party colleagues raised their clenched fists, Kerala bid a tearful farewell to its beloved leader in the presence of his family members and national and State leaders. Bharatiya Janata Party president L.K. Advani, sworn in Union Home Minister only the previous day, flew in from New Delhi to pay homage on behalf of the BJP Government at the Centre.

E.M.S. Namboodiripad Lying in State at the Durbar Hall in the State Secretariat in Thiruvananthapuram

A sea of humanity - men and women from all walks of life, a majority of them ordinary workers and peasants - surged at the make-shift barricades erected across the narrow roads leading to the crematorium, climbed nearby walls and trees, to have a last glimpse of their most popular political genius. From early morning, people from all parts of Kerala and even neighbouring Tamil Nadu, and vehicles flying black flags, flooded the city. Everyone had a black badge or a black-bordered picture of E.M.S. pinned on them.

A subdued voice over the microphone repeatedly requesting the crowd not to break through the cordons was the only sound, as the State police presented the ceremonial gun salute to the first democratically-elected Chief Minister of Aikya Keralam, or unified Kerala.

As the party flag was pulled over his face, shrill voices rose again: "Lal Salaam, E.M.S." For a minute, the unseen image of a bespectacled, diminutive man shuffling his way to a microphone, seemed to pervade the air. A large majority of the people there, in their minds, would have even heard him say, with his famous stammer: "sahodaree-sahodaranmare..." (sisters and brothers...).

E.M.S., born as a Namboodiri Brahmin at Elamkulam village in feudal, caste-ridden British Malabar, was consigned to the flames without rituals, but in emotional ceremony.

Thiruvananthapuram was numb with grief from the previous day, when news of his sudden illness and death at a private hospital broke. E.M.S. Namboodiripad died of an undetected lung infection (suspected to be pneumonia) at 3.40 p.m. on March 19, barely hours after he had dictated two articles for the Communist Party of India (Marxist) daily newspaper Desabhimani and replies to a few letters and complained of breathing difficulty, at his rented third-floor apartment at Kamaleswaram.

Last Journey to the Electric Crematorium

His constant companion and personal assistant Venu told Frontline:

"EM had complained of breathing difficulty even while dictating the first article. But when I informed him that Desabhimani needed a second one also before the deadline today, he readily dictated the second one. Later I helped him to the toilet, but he seemed to be in bad shape when he came back. So I called the AKG Centre and the doctor (personal physician Dr. P.P. Joseph) arrived soon. He prescribed some antibiotics.

"Later, when he was making some corrections in the articles, he could not hold his pen properly and the letters were illegible. He took only a handful of rice for lunch, then fell seriously ill. We took him to the hospital, but in the car he slumped forward unusually."

Dr. Joseph said: "He had only slight breathing difficulty when I examined him. Later, in the hospital, the ECG showed only a minor variation. But X-ray of the lungs showed shadows on both sides. His condition worsened and he was soon not responding to medicines. He was on a respirator. Cardiac arrest occurred at 3.40 p.m. Our preliminary conclusion was that he died of pneumonia. But there was no time to confirm."

At 89, E.M.S. had no illness other than mild blood pressure and joint pain, occasional breathing trouble and vertigo, Dr. Joseph, who has been treating him for over two decades, said.

The first of the long queues had formed outside the AKG Centre, the CPI (M)'s State headquarters - where E.M.S. had attended the party's State Secretariat and State Committee meetings continuously for six days from March 9 - even as the body was lying in hospital. All over Kerala, shopkeepers downed shutters spontaneously, flags were lowered, and every street corner announced austerely, in bold black: "E.M.S. is dead."

Cortege Leaving AKG Centre, the State Headquarters of the CPI(M)

The State Assembly concluded its day's session and a special Cabinet meeting later decided to postpone the presentation of the State Budget, scheduled to be presented on March 20, and declare a seven-day State mourning.

Nayanar and Ministers Paloli Mohammed Kutty, T.K. Ramakrishnan and A.C. Shanmukhadas were among those who reached the hospital on hearing that E.M.S.' condition was critical. Within half an hour of his death, the body was taken to the AKG Centre. There was not a dry eye there as Namboodiripad's immediate family members - wife Arya Antarjanam, daughters Malati Damodaran and Radha Guptan, sons E.M. Sreedharan and E.M. Sasi and daughter-in-law Girija - paid their respects and sat beside the body draped in the CPI(M) flag. The unending stream of people to the AKG Centre continued throughout the night, until the police blocked entry at 9 a.m. the next day.

A huge crowd had assembled outside AKG Centre as the body was taken out at 10.25 a.m. on a flower-bedecked open hearse, along a 1.5 km route to the Durbar Hall of the State Secretariat, there to lie in state.

The most touching scenes were witnessed at the Durbar Hall. At no time in the recent history of Kerala has a political leader been honoured by such a huge and spontaneous congregation of mourners. The body lay in state under a huge chandelier. Armed policemen stood with their arms reversed. E.M.S.' family members, State Ministers, party leaders and other dignitaries sat along the sides of the huge hall.

Tens of thousands of people from all sections of Kerala society filed past the departed leader, silently, and sometimes wailing or sobbing loudly. They touched his feet or offered flowers. Some came in wheelchairs. All of them had waited for hours in the hot sun to have a last glimpse of the leader.

Many of them knew E.M.S. personally, one way or the other. A majority had only watched him from afar. There was Paachi, a sweeper who had attended all the meetings addressed by E.M.S. in Thiruvananthapuram from 1957. A group of about 60 people had come from E.M.S.' Elamkulam village. A group of flower merchants brought a huge decorated wreath, with the hammer and sickle symbol on top. All of them had the same expression of incredulity and sadness.

By 1.30 p.m., the national leaders began to arrive. CPI(M) general secretary Harkishan Singh Surjeet, CPI general secretary A.B. Bardhan, CPI(M) Polit Bureau members P. Ramachandran, Prakash Karat and Sitaram Yechuri, CPI(M) leaders from West Bengal Bimal Basu, Binoy Chowdhury and Anil Biswas, Tripura's Finance Minister Badal Chowdhuri, CPI(M) leaders from Tamil Nadu led by N. Sankaraiah, State secretary from Rajasthan Hariram Chauhan, Delhi State secretary Pushpinder Grewal, Karnataka State secretary P. Ramachandra Rao, and CPI(M) Central Committee member Brinda Karat paid emotional tributes to their comrade.

Tamil Nadu Governor M. Fathima Beevi and State leaders including Opposition Leader A.K. Antony and Speaker M. Vijaya Kumar placed wreaths. Wreaths were also laid on behalf of President K.R. Narayanan, Governor Sukhdev Sing Kang, who is away in New Delhi, Prime Minister A.B. Vajpayee and West Bengal Governor K.V. Raghunatha Reddy. Frontline Editor N. Ram laid a wreath and represented The Hindu group of publications at the funeral.

Akg Centre and the Chief Minister's office were flooded with condolence messages. President Narayanan said that with Namboodiripad's death the country has lost a towering personality who made a monumental contribution to the freedom movement and national development. He said that as the architect of India's first land reform measures, Namboodiripad was a man of rare vision, acumen and determination. The President said: "A scholar, historian and journalist, he was above all an educator of the people as well as their leader. Unremittingly, for the last several decades, he analysed the socio-political scene from the firm-rootedness of his intellectual position and enriched Indian political thought to his very last days."

Prime Minister Vajpayee recalled that E.M.S. had brought to politics a sense of commitment and purpose and that he was a champion of the cause of the working classes and the downtrodden.

At the State Secretariat, the queues seemed not to end, and when the doors of the Durbar Hall closed around 4.15 p.m. there were thousands outside who had failed to see their leader one last time. Family members paid their last respects once again.

At 4.30 p.m., the last journey into history began. Outside, the decorated hearse was waiting, with an ocean of people surrounding it. A genuine emotional attachment was perceptible. As the pallbearers came out of the Durbar Hall, the huge lawns of the Secretariat and the main roads around it resounded with the slogan: "Upon time, upon history, we swear: No! No! E.M.S. is not dead; He lives, he lives, he lives within us; He will live through us. Inquilab Zindabad!"

Surjeet, E. Balanandan, Nayanar, V.S. Achuthanandan, S. Ramachandran Pillai, P. Ramachandran, Prakash Karat, Sitaram Yechuri, Binoy Krishna Chowdhuri, Bardhan, CPI(M) State secretary Chadayan Govindan, E.M. Sreedharan and E.M. Sasi sat around the body. A picture of a young E.M.S. smiled from behind the vehicle at the 89 volunteers bearing black and red flags, representing every year of the fruitful life their leader had spent. Ahead, all along the 3 km route to the crematorium, volunteers were showering flowers, inches thick on the road. The pilot vehicle announced to the hundreds who lined the streets, or had climbed buildings and trees to see E.M.S.: "The mortal remains of Comrade E.M.S., the revolutionary leader of a momentous era, the one who made history and walked ahead of it, here, behind this vehicle..."

At the Secretariat

Immediately after the funeral, at a condolence meeting held near the crematorium, Chief Minister Nayanar wept as he recalled the last moments of Namboodiripad. "He was deliberately a man of controversy. His statements were designed to create a flutter and trigger a debate. He did it deliberately, with an intent, not unknowingly. But once his purpose was achieved, EM would suddenly end the debate in a manner he thought best."

Nayanar reminded the huge gathering that E.M.S. was also honest enough to admit his mistakes. "Although he hailed from a traditional Brahmin family of land owners and was tutored in the Vedas, it was his Marxist-Leninist convictions that made him so humane and endeared him as a leader of the toiling masses."

Earlier, recalling his long association with his favourite comrade, Nayanar said in a formal message: "I don't think that anybody has led such a committed and active life like him - a life that was never marred by selfishness."

CPI(M) general secretary Surjeet described E.M.S. as a model for all revolutionaries and noted it was not Kerala alone that was mourning his death, but the entire country. "The Communist movement had produced many great leaders, but E.M.S. is known in all homes of India as a true Communist and patriot... Our association at the top leadership of the party is over 44 years long. When the first breach on the Congress' monopoly on power was made in 1957 in Kerala, he showed a new path to the entire world through the introduction of land reforms. By this very act, he became a leader of national stature."

Advani said that though he differed with the ideology represented by Namboodiripad, he respected his idealism. "His was a total commitment to the cause he believed in and the ideals he subscribed to... Namboodiripad was one of the great personalities of the freedom movement. Although there was nothing much in common between the ideology of Mahatma Gandhi, Sardar Patel or Namboodiripad, who all fought for the country's freedom, there was a lot in common, when it came to their idealism."

Perhaps it was CPI general secretary Bardhan who spoke for all: "It was certainly Namboodiripad's ideology that shaped Kerala the way it is today... The thoughts and writings of E.M.S. have influenced a generation of Communists. We all have read E.M.S. We have listened to E.M.S. We have fought against E.M.S. We have rallied behind E.M.S. We have stood for E.M.S. and stood against him. But we could never ignore E.M.S."

Everything looks the same at the red-tiled, airy E.M.S. study in the third floor rented apartment in Thiruvananthapuram. The shelves full of books, the long cane chair with the blue cushion, the small plywood-topped teapoy where he perched his feet, the table with a reading lamp and hearing aid, a smaller side table full of books and magazines, among them, a copy of the latest issue of Frontline, to which he contributed regularly. One almost expected to hear his usual salutation, as he looked up with his broad smile: "Ah! Frontline!"

Birth Centenary

In the words of a close associate: E.M.S. both a visionary and a communist with a strong practical bent of mind. He had a strong political acumen and at the same time he was a versatile and knowledgeable politician with commendable hold on a vast range of issues. He was brought up in a wealthy and respectable Brahmin family, but he gave up his studies to join the movement for India's independence from the colonial rulers. It was in the 1930s that he established contact with the communist revolutionaries of Bengal and Punjab. The country and generally the world, then was witnessing a turbulent phase that was marked by intense anti-imperialist and anti-fascist struggles. Comrade E.M.S. too was influenced by the intensity of this struggles and he was slowly drifted into the socialist fold and then in the subsequent years started working to build the communist party. His campaign against ill belief and superstitions and prevalent casteist feelings had started even earlier when he undertook the tedious task of reforms among his own family members. He took an exemplary role in building up the communist movement in the state of Kerala.

It was in 1939 itself that he became a part of the parliamentary politics in Kerala. In the early years of the 40's he had to go underground and he went to work with the poor peasants and became a part of them by adopting their lifestyle in a befitting manner. The love and sensitivity that he showed towards the poor peasants remained an intrinsic part of his characteristics for the rest of his life. He was elected to the leadership of the Party from the time since its very first congress in 1943. He made invaluable contribution as a leader of the Party.

In the fifties, when the party was in the midst of an inner-party ideological struggle he played a significant role by guiding the party and insisting on the fact that a communist party should retain its revolutionary characteristics. He was elected Party General Secretary in 1962 when the ideological struggle in the party became intensive. Comrade E.M.S. boldly expressed his opinion in the party, and many a time we had debated on his opinions. I too, had some opinions in the party on ideological issues and later it was decided to incorporate both the opinions into the party fold for elaborate discussions. All of us at that time decided to work together to strengthen the party. After the division of our party in 1964 Comrade E.M.S. took a vital role in building up party organisation and also penning down our party's programme. During his tenure as the general secretary from 1977 to 1992 he contributed commendably to shape up party's political–organisational line.

From the fifties onwards he played an important role at the party centre and gave his vital inputs as part of the collective leadership of various movements. In the subsequent elections in 1957 when Kerala became a full fledged state under the Indian Union, the first communist government under his leadership emerged. It was under his chief ministership the first non-congress government was established in any state of independent India.

While CPM was not successful in West Bengal at 1957 assembly election, Kerala was building a new history under the leadership of Comrade E.M.S. Namboodiripad. For the first time, the people elected a Communist government in the country and reposed on us a new responsibility for the days ahead. I still remember it was the third week of March 1957. As soon as we learnt of the news Kakababu, Comrade Muzaffar Ahmad, immediately sent a telegram to Trivandrum saying, "We have just heard of the success of the Communist Party in Kerala. We congratulate you on behalf of members of the party in West Bengal and all democratic forces in the state." The Communists alone got sixty seats. Independents backed by the Communists got five, PSP nine and the Congress won forty three seats. The total number of seats was 126. Comrade E M S Namboodiripad was elected the legislative Party leader with Achutya Menon as his deputy. E M S became the first Communist chief minister of the country. The other ministers included K. P. Gopalan, T. A. Majid, P. K. Sathan, Joseph Mundaseri, V. R. Krishna Iyer, K. R. Gouri Amma, Dr. A. R. Menon and K. C. George.

On April 7, the party called a meeting at the Kolkata Maidan to celebrate the formation of a Communist government in the country and the gaining of strength of the CPI in Bengal. The rally, which was presided over by Muzaffar Ahmad, began with a famous song which had been written in the memory of the martyrs of Kerala's Malabar district. I proposed a resolution which said, "We have gone one step ahead with the victory of the Communist Party in Kerala. Our congratulations go out to the people of Kerala and we resolve to forge stronger ties among the democratic and peaceful forces in this state in the fight against imperialism."

After taking over as chief minister, E M S introduced a 16-point programme including major land reforms, farmers' rights on their land and growth of the agricultural industry. He also appealed to the industrialists to take an active role in progress of the state's economy. The new government started work in earnest. In a matter of few days, the historic Ordinance which gave agricultural rights to 10 lakhs labourers and five lakhs sharecroppers came into being while one lakh acre of agricultural land was distributed to landless farmers. All political detenus were released. The Kerala government also announced that the police would not be used to break any democratic agitation.

All these were noble efforts, particularly compared with the experience of long Congress regimes earlier. This was a major responsibility; on the one hand the government had to function within the bourgeoisie-zamindar political structure while, on the other hand, the onus was on the government to lend a revolutionary role to the people's struggle.

In 1952, the Communist Party had won 27 of the 60 Lok Sabha constituencies that it had contested while out of the 122 it had contested this time, 29 had been elected. But the number of votes polled for the party had doubled.

The party had formed the government in the state during second general elections by becoming the single largest party. Jawarharlal Nehru was the Prime Minister then, while his daughter, Indira Gandhi, was the president of the AICC. We all know how tirelessly Prime Minister Nehru and his daughter tried to prevent the Communists from coming to power in Kerala. However, they did not succeed.

E. M. S took over as chief minister amid a wave of people's support and encouragement in Kerala. But on July 31, 1959, the President used Article 356 to dismiss the state Assembly.

There were many tactics which were adopted to prevent the Communist ministry from working to a programme. The AICC with Mrs. Gandhi at its helm entered into an unholy alliance with reactionary and opportunistic forces and parties. A disinformation campaign was launched which said that the masses wanted the Kerala government to go. It isn't exactly a top secret that Prime Minister Nehru had called E.M.S. and asked him the resign, dissolve Assembly and call fresh elections. But E.M.S. ignored this pressure tactics and thus the unrelenting efforts to dismiss the Kerala government continued.

The progressive attitude and some of the virtuous Bills on land reforms and the education system had set the cat among the pigeons in Kerala. These steps had come rudely shocked the vested interests in the state. The so-called popular "mass movement" against the Kerala government had not touched the majority of the people of the state because by the time, an agitation to protect the state government had spread throughout the nation. The people's demand was to get the Congress out of Kerala.

When the disinformation campaign failed and the much expected mass movement against the Kerala government did not come by, the Centre resorted to Article 356 and imposed President's rule in Kerala.

On June 6, E.M.S. had come to Calcutta and two lakh people were there to receive him at the Maidan. Women blew conch shells to welcome the first Communist Chief Minister of the country. I was in Delhi when the decision to impose President's rule in Kerala was announced. Bhupesh Gupta and Dinesh Roy were there along with me. We had gone to present a memorandum of grievances against the West Bengal government.

On August 7, a huge rally was taken out which culminated in the Maidan protesting against the action in Kerala. On July 14, a resolution was adopted at the National Council of the CPI which rejected the proposal for re-election in Kerala.

On July 15, 1959 Triguna Sen, journalist Vivekananda Mukherjee, Dr. Paresh Chandra Sen, Satyajit Ray, Susobhan Sarkar, Hemanta Mukherjee, Gopal Chandra Halder, Sambhu Mitra. Mihir Sen, Binoy Ghosh, Asitbaran, Suchitra Mitra, Mrinal Sen, Ritwik Ghatak and other intellectuals like Nandagopal Sengupta appealed to the President and the Prime Minister in which they said, "Those who are unified to oust the Kerala government by unholy means are working to strike at the roots of Indian democracy. We request that such efforts be stopped immediately. "A separate appeal entitled Intervention shall not be allowed in Kerala" was sent to the President by playwright Bijan Bhattarcharya, actor Bhanu Banerjee and scientist B.D. Nag Chowdhury. On July 15, 1959, a letter signed by 17,336 residents of Calcutta was sent to the President carrying the same message.

On July 3, the party's West Bengal state committee held a rally at the Monument which was attended by more than one lakh people. Indrajit Gupta and I spoke on the occasion. I said that the need of the hour was not to get disillusioned but defend the forces of democracy against Congress dictatorship with fortitude and discipline. A strong movement was necessary for this. Amar Bose of the Forward Bloc (Marxist) presided over this rally. On the same day, when the demand to place the Kerala Governor's report in the Lok Sabha was rejected, the majority of the Opposition members staged a walkout. At that time, Dangey was the leader of the Communist Parliamentary Party. On that very day, I was addressing a press conference in Delhi where I placed the views of the West Bengal State Council of the party. It was during this press conference that we got news that the Kerala government had been dismissed.

Shortly before going to Delhi, I had met Dr. Roy. He had told me that he was against the tactics of the Congress in Kerala and that he did not like the way an elected government was being harassed. He had indicated this to the Congress Working Committee. I remember Dr. Roy telling me that it needed a strong hand to run a government. I asked him what he would have done if he had been in E.M.S.'s shoes. The Chief Minister replied, "I would have arrested all the agitators and taken strict administrative steps." Needless to say, we had ourselves been subject to the "strong administrative steps" as suggested by the Chief Minister. Bhupesh Gupta and I went to meet Feroze Gandhi after the press conference. He did not stay in the residence of the Prime Minister at that time and had shifted to one of the flats allotted to parliamentarians on North Avenue. While asking us to sit, Feroze Gandhi said "A murder has been committed today. Democracy has been killed in Kerala." That day, he told us many other stories. That does not require mention here.

However, during this brief tenure the state government embarked on radical land reforms and had taken concrete steps on democratisation of education system and strengthening health facilities and took steps to uphold the rights of workers and farmers. The stand taken by E.M.S. government acted as a torchbearer for future struggle in the history of Indian democracy. He was successfully able to consolidate the struggle both inside and outside of the Parliament. His legendary skills helped in shaping our party's political strategy in the later stages of struggle.

In 1967 assembly elections, non-Congress governments came up in eight states of India, including West Bengal. In Kerala again a non-Congress government was formed under the stewardship of Comrade E.M.S. But unfortunately CPI, a partner of the left withdraw themselves from this government and joined hands with the Congress. Again the non-Congress government in Kerala though destined to fall was able to have an impact by introducing pro-people policies distinct from its predecessors. This invaluable experience helped us immensely while we managed the successful

Left coalition in the State of West Bengal in 1967 and 1969 as part of the United Front government.

Comrade E.M.S. was a glaring example of a communist leader, who showed all the qualities that one communist should have, and he rightfully had earned accolades, nationally and internationally.

Though he was extremely busy to keep his political and organisational commitments, still he managed to find out time to write the history of India from the Marxist point of view. He contributed immensely to Marxist literature. His writings on the history of India's Freedom struggle, trade union movement, and cultural movement are considered to be masterpieces. His fame as an eminent author and as an acclaimed intellectual was spread even beyond the Party circles. His opinions, writings also served as guidelines to our party at some of the important junctures of national politics. Comrade E.M.S. was not only a national leader but also a leader of the international communist movement.

Apart from Party Polit Bureau and central committee meetings we met and exchanged each other's views many a time. His simplicity, exemplary honest behaviour, his life as a communist earned respect of those who came in touch with him. In his death the country has lost a prodigal and idealistic personality.

Comrade E.M.S.'s contribution in all these seven long decades will be a milestone not only for our party but to the entire nation. After 1992 due to illness his movement was restricted to his home state of Kerala though he regularly wrote his opinions about different subjects to various party forums on different issues and was a regular contributor to the party's literary circuit. His ability to study sequentially different issues was another rare attributes of his memorable life.

Obituary

E. M. S. Namboodiripad was the last of India's firebrand Marxist revolutionaries and theoreticians. As head of the world's first elected Communist government in his southern home state of Kerala in the 1950s, "E.M.S." pioneered radical land and educational reforms that are today being duplicated by other states.

It is largely due to his commitment and guidance that the Communist Party of India (Marxist), or CPM, of which he was Politburo member and general secretary for 14 years, has become such a domineering political force, playing a vital role in India's new era of coalition politics. CPM governments are in power in Kerala and in the eastern states of Bengal and Tripura.

Apart from being an astute politician who led the workers' struggle for over six decades, E.M.S. was an author, historian, social commentator and theorist who astutely adopted Marxist and Leninist ideals to Indian conditions. He never repudiated the fundamentals of Marxism, convinced the world would embrace it once again.

His regimen was Spartan. He lived in a small house rented for him by the party in Kerala's capital, Thiruvanthapuram, and, before retiring from active politics in 1991, daily woke at 4.30 a.m. to write articles, dictate pamphlets or a speech. All earnings from his voluminous writings went to the party chest.

He was born in 1909 into an aristocratic upper-caste Brahmin family. A precocious child, at 13 he joined a local society devoted to fighting orthodoxy and the welfare of the untouchables. He organised campaigns for the abolition of bigamy, for inter-caste marriage and remarriage for widows.

As an undergraduate at St. Thomas College at Trichur he joined the Congress Party's struggle for freedom from colonial rule, and a few years later was imprisoned for a year for participating in the Civil Disobedience Movement. He used his imprisonment to educate himself politically and in 1936 was appointed secretary of the Malabar Congress Committee.

In 1939 he joined the Communist Party of India after differences with the Congress over its cooperation with the colonial government for the Second World War. He gave away his valuable inherited properties to the party, whose Central Committee he joined in 1941. After independence in 1947, he went underground for three years, the federal government having banned the Communist Party, which had called for an armed uprising. He carried a reward of 5,000 rupees on his head, an enormous sum at the time.

E.M.S. became the Communist party's Politburo member in 1948 and nine years later, soon after the formation of Kerala state, its chief minister, the world's first Communist ever to be elected to a legislative post. He headed the state for two years before the federal government, terrified of the "Red Scourge", toppled him. But during his short span in office he introduced wide-ranging social, agrarian, economic and educational reforms that eventually turned Kerala into the model state it is today with an impressive per capita income and an enviable literacy rate of 98 per cent - the highest in India.

In 1964 E.M.S. was largely responsible for splitting the Communist party into the hard-line Marxist group, the CPM that was ideologically untainted by "right-wing deviancy". Three years later he once again became Kerala's chief minister, heading a coalition government which fell apart in 1969. As a veteran Commissar he continued to combat bourgeois democracy through weekly columns, pamphlets and erudite, well-argued booklets. He became CPM general secretary in 1977, a post he held for 14 years.

Elamkulam Manakkal Sankaran Namboodiripad, politician: born Kerala, India 1909; Chief Minister of Kerala 1957-59, 1967-69; General Secretary, Communist Party (Marxist), India 1977-91; married (two sons, two daughters); died Thiruvanthapuram, India 19 March 1998.

2

An Eventful Career

Significant Role

During the long-drawn political struggle for independence E.M.S. Namboodiripad played a significant role in the annals of our subcontinent. At a fairly young age, he offered his services for the cause of Swaraj and suffered in jails. He was born in a well-to-do family on 13 June 1909 in the Palghat district of the State of Kerala. His father, Parameswaram Namboodiripad died when Saknaran was a small child. He was a promising student who received his education in Victoria High School at Palghat, Victoria College, Palghat and St. Thomas' College, Trichur.

In Congress

For a few years, Namboodiripad worked as a disciplined worker of the Congress Party and soon his services were recognised when, in 1937, he was elected to the Madras Legislative Assembly on the Congress ticket. Two years before the second global war, he was the Secretary of the Kerala Pradesh Congress Committee. But in 1940, the entire Congress Socialist Party in Kerala turned over to the Communist Party of India. He was elected to the Central Committee of the Communist Party in India in 1943, and was a Member of the Polit Bureau of the Party for several years till its split in 1964.

He was a very fine writer and had written several works having linkage with his socialistic ideology. His *Gandhi and His Ism;* The *Peasant Question in Kerala* and *Kerala: Yesterday, Today and Tomorrow* are well-known works. Besides he wrote several books in Malayalam. In his writings he pleaded the cause of the weaker sections of our society.

He was very simple in his dress and habits. He wore a white *dhoti* and a white shin, just like an average Malayalee. Thus, his identification with a common man was sincere in every respect.

As the Chief Minister of Kerala, he acted well and geared up the administrative machinery towards right channels. He undertook several reforms for peasantry and factory workers: which greatly enhanced their economic status. He undertook several schemes for the educational development of the people of Kerala.

Leader of Congress Socialist Party

In 1934, he was one of the founder leaders of Congress Socialist Party, a socialist wing within the Indian National Congress and was elected as its All India Joint Secretary from 1934 to 1940. During this period he was also elected to the Madras Legislative Assembly (1939).

He remained committed to socialist ideals and his compassion towards the downtrodden working class made him join the ranks of the Communist movement. He was considered to be one of the founders of the Communist Party of India (CPI) in Kerala, for which he had to go in hiding for some time. During the 1962 Sino-Indian war, he was among those leaders who aired China's view on the border issue. When the CPI split in 1964, E.M.S. stood with the Communist Party of India (Marxist) (CPI(M)). He served as a member of the Central Committee and the Politburo of the CPI(M), before becoming its General Secretary in 1977, a designation he held until 1992. He was a member of the party Politburo until his death.

Congress Secretary

Even when he worked as the PCC secretary, E.M.S. had doubts about the effectiveness of Gandhi's peaceful agitations to achieve social revolution and freedom. His meeting with P. Krishna Pillai in the Kozhikode sub jail helped him substantiate his critical outlook regarding Gandhi's vision. The two of them began to work closely together, first as leaders of the Congress Socialist Party and later as leaders of the Communist Party. Organiser Krishna Pillai, legendary mass leader A.K. Gopalan and E.M.S. founded and built the Communist movement in Kerala.

By the end of 1937, E.M.S. was again elected to the PCC but soon right-wing Congress leaders prevented anybody with left leanings to contest the elections to the Madras Legislative Assembly. At a time when many Congress leaders were lured by power and position, E.M.S. and his small group of comrades campaigned to make ordinary workers and peasants politically conscious about social inequities and Communist ideals.

Member of Assembly

E.M.S. was elected to the Madras Provincial Legislative Assembly in a by-election and became a member of the enquiry committee established to study the tenancy relations in the Malabar region in 1939. When the Congress members reached a consensus in favour of the landlords, E.M.S. presented the lone dissenting note in favour of the tenants. This was the harbinger of the most comprehensive land reforms in South Asia for which E.M.S. provided the initiative nearly two decades later.

In 1940, the British Government banned the Communist Party. Communist leaders in Malabar went underground. About his years in hiding, E.M.S. later recalled:

> "April 1940 was a turning point in my life. Seven months had passed since the Second World War began. All of us were engaged in anti-War activities. The party decided we should go into hiding. One night, I left home without telling even my wife. I left her and our one-year-old daughter. Nobody knew for how long a period. It created a lot of tension inside me... in another way it was a happy occasion. For the first time in my life I could establish a heart-to-heart relationship with ordinary people who were not

members of my community - peasants, farm and fish workers, the poor. Until then my relationship with them was only in my mind. It had not touched my heart."

No ordinary Namboodiri would have dared to rub shoulders with the "untouchables", the ordinary farm workers, peasants and their families, eat meat and fish with them and become a part of their lives for days on end. But E.M.S.' work was to be among the lower castes, untouchable labourers and ordinary workers. In his lifetime, E.M.S. was a significant force in the social revolution that transformed Kerala from an obnoxious past when untouchability and unapproachability were practised to the equitable society that it is today.

In 1947, soon after he emerged from hiding, E.M.S. announced the sale of his family estate and donated the handsome proceeds to the Communist Party. The party used this amount to relaunch the defunct Desabhimani as a daily newspaper in 1947 and E.M.S. was made the Editor. Desabhimani, which was first launched in 1942 as a weekly, had been banned by the British.

In his autobiography, E.M.S. said that the changes that he underwent at a personal level were as important as the social changes that he was instrumental in bringing about. He noted, "Although I was born in a family that was at the top of the caste-ridden feudal society, I grew up as a Communist and a party worker who was engaged in ridding society of the evils of casteism and feudalism. I evolved further so as to sell my huge estates and donate the entire proceeds for the party. This is what made me the adopted son of the working class."

In 1957, the world's first elected Communist Government came to power in Kerala. Within a week, the E.M.S.-led Government introduced an ordinance (and later legislation) that fixed an absolute ceiling on the land a family could own and ordered distribution of all excess lands to the landless. It also granted fixity of tenure, freedom from eviction and the benefit of a fair rent to be set by impartial land tribunals. Cultivator-tenants were conferred the right to buy at a modest payment and over a phased period the title deed of the land that they worked. The land rights of unauthorised hutment dwellers were defined.

Vested interests opposed the legislation, which together with the Education Bill passed by the E.M.S. Government created a dramatic change in society. The result was one of the first dismissals of a State Government under Article 356 of the Constitution. This was engineered by Prime Minister Jawaharal Nehru at the behest of his daughter Indira Gandhi who was then the Congress president, alleging a breakdown of law and order in the State.

As required by court, the Act was later replaced by another law which contained the provisions of the earlier Act. Two successive non-Communist Governments did not implement this new law, which was challenged in the court on the grounds that it contravened the fundamental rights. During the second tenure of the Communist Government in 1967-69, the E.M.S. Government placed a new land reform (Amendment) Act before the legislature, which restored and amplified the radical proposals in the Kerala Agrarian Relations Act, 1960. Through major amendments, the land that could be held under ceiling was reduced and the jenmi system abolished. The new Act, the Kerala Land Reforms (Amendment) Act, was passed without a dissenting note in 1969.

E.M.S. was also the architect of Aikya Keralam (unified Kerala) incorporating the erstwhile princely states of Travancore and Cochin and parts of the British Malabar districts. He argued that a division of the country into States should be solely on the basis of language and cultural affinity of the people living in a region, and this was based on the declared policy of his party at that time.

Heading the State Government

During his political career, E.M.S. was defeated only once in the public elections, when he lost to K.P. Kuttikrishnan Nair (the founder leader of Trade Union Movement in India) of the Indian National Congress by a huge margin from the Kozhikode constituency. In 1957, E.M.S. led the Communists to victory in the first election for the state government, making him the first communist leader anywhere to head a popularly elected government. It was also the first time for a regional party anywhere in India to win state elections. On 5 April 1957 he was appointed as the first chief minister of Kerala. His government soon introduced the Land Reform Ordinance and Education Bill. His government was dismissed in 1959 by the Central Government, which invoked the controversial Article 356 of the Indian Constitution following what later became known as 'The Liberation Struggle'. He became the Chief Minister of Kerala for the second time in 1967 as the leader of a seven-party coalition including the Muslim League. This time his tenure lasted for two and a half years.

E.M.S. was the Leader of Opposition in the Kerala Legislative Assembly from 1960 to 1964 and again from 1970 to 1977. He influenced Kerala society by his vision on decentralisation of power and resources (People's Plan), and the Kerala Literacy Movement. He authored several books in English and Malayalam. Chintha Publication, Kerala has published all his books under the title, 'E M S Sanchika'. He was well-known as a journalist as well.

Land Reform Ordinance

The Land Reforms Ordinance was a law in the state of Kerala, India under the E. M. S. Namboodiripad government limiting the amount of land one person could own.

The E.M.S. government was the first communist state government popularly elected to power in India, in the southern state of Kerala. Soon after taking its oath of office, the government introduced the controversial Land Reforms Ordinance, which was later made into an act. This, along with an Education Bill, raised a massive uproar from the landlord classes. The popular slogan for the radical socialists was "the land for tillers", which sent shockwaves through the landlord classes in the country. The ordinance set an absolute ceiling on the land a family could own. The tenants and hut dwellers received a claim in the excess land, on which they had worked for centuries under the feudal system. In addition, the law ensured fixity of tenure and protection from eviction. These ground-breaking measures caused the pre-mature death of the state government, as the central government, under Nehru, used article 356 to dismiss it, alleging the breakdown of law and order. The land reforms in Kerala imparted drastic changes to the political, economic and social outlook.

Education Bill

The Education Bill was introduced in the Kerala assembly by Prof. Joseph Mundasseri, the then education minister for the first elected (1957) Communist Party of India government. This bill was aimed at eradicating the malpractices prevalent in the private sector educational institutions, and attempted to regulate the educational institutions' function, including standardising syllabi and pay structures. The religious organisations along with opposition parties including Indian National Congress started the so called "liberation struggle" to overthrow E. M. S. Namboodiripad government. This bill along with Land Reforms Ordinance and other agricultural legislation imparted drastic changes in Kerala society, and paved the way for the natural death of feudalistic society in Kerala.

The Education Bill sought to regulate appointments and conditions of teachers. Salaries of teachers were to be paid through the treasury. There was a provision of takeover of management of educational institutions, which violated the law. There was no proposal whatsoever for state takeover of the private educational institutions.

Even though the Education Bill failed to pass through the Assembly many of its provisions were later implemented by subsequent governments with amends.

New Police Policy

The Communist government adopted a new police policy and a new approach towards mass organisations and their activities. Even after independence, the Congress government at the Centre and states were following the old colonial approach towards mass organisations and their agitations and struggles. The British colonial rulers considered awareness among the people about their rights and interests, and every effort to organise them as a threat and used police or military force against such efforts by the people. The British viewed all such moves as issues related to law and order and used brutal force to repress them. The bourgeois-landlord governments that came into power after independence faithfully continued the colonial practice and used police and military forces against agitations and struggles of the people. Even while dealing with cases of ordinary crime the police force was notorious for its highhandedness. The police resorted to third degree methods in the investigation of crimes, which became the normal style of the police. The police force was extensively used by the bourgeois-landlord classes to suppress the legitimate struggles of the working people.

The new "police policy" made two important departures from the existing practice. First, it strictly prohibited third degree methods and torture of persons in custody. The police were directed to make investigations strictly in accordance with the provisions of the law. Second, with regard to mass struggles and activities of mass organisations, the police were not allowed to be used in landlord and bourgeois interest to suppress strikes, struggles and agitations of workers, peasants, agricultural workers and other sections of people. Additionally, it was declared that all industrial disputes would be settled through the method of negotiations between employers and employees.

The earlier practice was that all industrial disputes were settled by the police and such issues were treated as law and order problems. The Communist government directed that the Labour Department alone should deal with all such matters.

The intervention of the police was deemed necessary only when there was a violation of law or a crime was committed. The Communist government declared that the struggles of peasants, students, youth, women and others would be dealt with by the civil administration and not by the police. The government gave directives to all its departments to respect civil liberties and democratic rights of all sections of the people. Detention without trial was prohibited against individuals and organisations.

Police Verification in Jobs Stopped

Another important step by the government was stopping the long-standing undemocratic practice of verification of political antecedents of job applicants. Only when the police certified the "good conduct" of an applicant, he or she would be given a job. This practice was used to prevent any member/sympathiser of the Communist Party from getting any job in the government. The Central government had issued a circular that instructed that job applicants who had been associated with the activities of the Communist party or any of its mass organisations should be certified as "persons of bad antecedents" and that their job applications should be automatically rejected. Within weeks after assumption of office, the Communist government declared that the instructions issued by the Central government would be ignored in Kerala and that there would be no police verification of the character and antecedents of job applicants.

Public-Government Relations

The government gave utmost importance to strengthening and expanding relations between the government and the people. Though the Party had formulated its programme for the development of Kerala, the government made efforts to implement those programmes in consultation with the concerned people. The Communist government considered the policy declarations made in the Election Manifesto of the Communist Party as the basis for such consultations. The government gave encouragement to all mass organisations and involved their view on all policy matters.

The Communist government gave great importance to associating people and their representatives in the day-to-day functioning of the administration. The government constituted people's committees to supervise, advise and assess the work of permanent officials in various departments such as food, land revenue, health, education, etc. Political parties – ruling and opposition – as well as mass organisations and interested individuals were included in such committees. It is to be noted here that in many district and local bodies, the Communist Party was a minority, as the representation of the political parties at every level was decided on the basis of the comparative strength of the Party in that region. However, there was no attempt on part of the government to pack these committees with representatives from the Communist party. This was another departure made by the Communist government from the practices of Congress governments. The Congress governments left the day-to-day administration work only to the permanent officials or if at all they associated some people's representatives, they discriminated against the opposition and particularly the Left.

The new policy initiatives of the Communist government were hailed by the common people and naturally opposed by vested interests. These policies highlighted fundamental differences between previous Congress governments that represented the bourgeois-landlord classes and the Communist government that worked for the workers, peasants and common people. This encouraged more people to join mass organisations and to raise their voices. This growing awareness of the common people and their involvement in public life strengthened the democratic polity in Kerala.

Workers' Rights

The Communist government took new initiatives in protecting the rights of the workers. The government found that the main obstacle in the way of a cordial employer-employee atmosphere in industry was that the employers were reluctant to recognise the rights of employees and even if they did recognise, they reduced this recognition to a mere formality. They were reluctant to concede the legitimate demands of the employees with regard to wage and salary scales as well as conditions of work. The government tried to bring a change in the attitude of employers.

The change in the attitude of the employers could facilitate the employees and their organisations taking a position conducive for maintenance of peace in industry. In order to maintain healthy relations between employers and employees and peace in industry, the government introduced the system of tripartite conference comprising of the representatives of trade unions of the employers and of the government at the state level.

The government also constituted individual industry level tripartite conference for maintaining healthy relations between employers and employees for the first time in India. While taking steps to see that the legitimate demands of the employees of both public as well as private sectors were realised, the government also took measures to make the employees realise their vital role in bringing about efficiency in production and management. The government was conscious that it was necessary to create prerequisites for enabling the employees and their organisations to fulfil their responsibilities. To achieve this, the government tried to implement the following measures:

- The employers and the government should recognise all existing unions.

- The government should offer its good offices in bringing about the unity of different unions in those industries where there are more than one union on the principle of "one union in one industry".
- In those industries where such unification of unions is not thought possible, the framework should be laid on the basis of which industrial disputes can be handled. The tripartite conferences should discuss and devise methods to tackle this issue.
- "Works committees" should be organised in every industrial enterprises and they should have wide powers in regulating and controlling the conditions of work in respective industries.
- Management councils should be organised in enterprises in order to help managements in bringing about legitimacy in the enterprises as well as to familiarise the employees with the financial and other problems facing the enterprises. Representatives of employees should be adequately represented in such councils.

The government also took steps to regulate wage and salary scales as well as the working conditions of agricultural labourers, middle class employees including the non-gazetted officers, etc. These measures, to a great extent, improved the employer-employee relations in Kerala.

The government also took initiatives to organise cooperative societies of workers in many areas. Coir, handloom and toddy shops cooperative societies were formed to ensure job security, better wages and service condition for the employees. This was also a new initiative from the state government to protect the interest of the employees.

Major Social Initiatives

The Communist government, alongwith the efforts for increasing production of material goods, took many new initiatives in social sectors. The government gave more attention for democratisation of education and public health systems. The doctors-people ratio was increased under the Communist government. The government took many steps towards improving and expanding public health facilities so that the poorer sections could get a better and free medical care in government-run hospitals.

Another important step was the introduction and adoption of a legislation on education in the Assembly in order to take certain steps for democratising the education system of Kerala. The objective of the Bill was to provide direct payment of salaries to teachers in private education institutions without any deduction by private manager of schools; to curb the power of managers to suspend or dismiss teachers from employment; to fix criteria for the appointment of teachers and other related matters.

Therefore, teachers in private educational institutions could receive the same emoluments as their counterparts in government schools. It was proposed that the right of private managers to own and manage educational institutions would be controlled rather than abolished.

The managers of private educational institutions projected the entire Bill as an attack on their ownership rights. The Christian Church, the Nair Service Society and many other caste and communal organisations unleashed a false propaganda that the Bill was an attack on the right to property, minority rights and a measure to nationalise educational institutions. The propaganda of the Christian church was that if the Bill were adopted, the institutions would be used for Communist propaganda rather than preaching religion. As in the case of Agrarian Relations Bill, the debate on the Education Bill became prolonged and bitter.

Public Distribution System

Kerala was a deficit state in foodgrains production. The creation of a South Food Zone comprising of southern states of Kerala, Tamil Nadu, Karnataka and Andhra Pradesh formed immediately after the formation of the Communist government brought additional problems in procuring rice for distribution in Kerala. The Kerala government asked the Central government either to supply rice from the Central stocks or to enforce control on prices in Andhra Pradesh, so that Kerala could buy rice at controlled rates. The Central government did not do either and washed its hands off all responsibilities for ensuring rice supplies to Kerala.

In order to meet this difficulty created by the Central government, Kerala government took many steps. It tried to procure rice from within and outside the state for distribution. A system of "fair price shops" was introduced for the supply of rice at cheap rates to the needy sections. The number of fair price shops increased to 6,000. In order to select families to whom supplies were to be made, where shops were to be started and to weed out "ghost" ration cards, the government constituted people's food committees comprising of representatives from all major political parties. Such committees were constituted at the taluk, panchayat and other local levels. The task of the state level 'State Food Advisory Committee' was to oversee the working of the whole system. The "fair price shops" system ensured the supply of foodgrains to the needy sections in Kerala and was a great help to the common people. Eventually the activities of the "fair price shops" was extended to other commodities also.

Decentralisation of Powers

The Communist government appointed an Administrative Reforms Committee with the Chief Minister E.M.S. Namboodiripad as Chairman to examine the issue of administrative reforms of which democratic decentralisation was an important element. The Communist government approached the issue of "democratic decentralisation" as democratisation and decentralisation at all levels from the Centre to states and from the states to lower levels of administration down to the panchayats.

On the question of decentralisation of power, the committee considered the issue of whether there should be a two tier or three tier system of panchayati raj in Kerala. This meant whether there should be panchayats below and district council above or should there be an intermediate layer in between. The committee recommended that in the specific situation of Kerala where panchayats are bigger in size with larger populations than elsewhere, there was no need for an intermediate tier and panchayat below and district councils above was suitable for Kerala.

Implementing these recommendations, the government prepared two new Bills for introduction in the Assembly. The first Bill vested in elected panchayats all the functions discharged by revenue and other department officials at the village level. The second Bill proposed to transfer many functions discharged by district officials to an elected district council with an elected President and assisted by a permanent official of the status of a Deputy Collector. These two bills were introduced in the Legislative Assembly but they could not be passed as the Communist government was dismissed by the Central government.

Administration Democratised

Another important aspect examined by the Administrative Reforms Committee related to democratisation of administration, which addressed the relation between the permanent officials, the political leadership of the government, i.e., the ministry and the public. The Administrative Reforms Committee rejected the view that the political leadership of the government should leave the task of day-to-day administration to the permanent officials. As people's representatives, the political leadership should, through the legislature and the ministry, lay down policies while permanent officials had to implement the policy laid down by the political leadership.

The report of the *Administrative Reforms Committee* opined that it was difficult to draw a clear cut line between policy formulation and implementation:

> It is generally said that Ministers are responsible only for framing the policies, and that once the decisions on policies are taken, their implementation should be left to the Civil Servants. This is a 'conventional half-truth', because in Government, ends cannot always be separated from means. 'What should be done' is, of course, policy-making, but how to do it, when to do it and where to do it, are all as much part of policy as of implementation. It is, therefore, difficult to draw a line between policy and implementation and say where one ends and the other begins. Moreover, it is proper implementation that makes policy significant. The Minister, who is constitutionally responsible for all the executive action of his department, has to ensure that the Policy laid down by him is properly implemented.

According to E.M.S., the task of integrating people's control over the administration in the context of day-to-day administration by permanent officials is not easy and it is the responsibility of the political leadership to effectively ensure that. He writes in *The Communist Party in Kerala – Six Decades of Struggle and Advance:*

> This does not mean that ministers and the legislators should interfere in the day-to-day administration which should of course be left to permanent officials who after all have been trained to do the job. The best of the people's representatives cannot be expected to have the training and experience to carry on day-to-day administration. The fact, however, remains that the essence of democracy is the continuing control exercised by the people through their elected representatives on the permanent officials who run the administration. The task is by no means easy to integrate people's control over the administration with day-to-day administration by permanent officials but that is the crux of the democratic political set-up.

E.M.S. was of the firm opinion that in the background of continuing role of the general administrators and the increasing role of specialists, the political leadership of the administration should play a leading role. The general as well as the specialist cadres are expected to serve the people and the people cannot act except through their elected representative. When the political leadership committed any mistake or violated the norms of democracy and decency, there is a safeguard that they have to go to the people every five years.

Incompetent or corrupt persons or persons misusing their authority will be punished by the people in elections. This democratic safeguard is not there in the case of either the general or the specialised administrator and, hence, they should be strictly subordinated to the political leadership of the government.

Reservation Issue

The *Administrative Reforms Committee* considered the question whether reservation in educational institutions and government jobs for Scheduled Castes, Scheduled Tribes and backward communities should continue or be modified or given up. In Kerala, nearly 50 per cent of the jobs were reserved for those sections and the rest of the jobs were thrown open for competition among all sections of the people.

After examining the question from all angles, the committee made the following recommendations: first, the existing system of reservation should continue unchanged for Scheduled Castes and Scheduled Tribes; second, with regard to the backward communities, reservation based on caste or community should be supplemented by an economic criteria and the applicants from families whose annual income was higher than a prescribed level should not be allowed to enjoy the benefits of reservation; and third, surveys should be undertaken after every ten years to find out whether socio-economic, cultural, political conditions of any of the backward communities has sufficiently improved so that they can be taken out of the list of backward communities.

It was the *Administrative Reforms Committee* headed by E.M.S. Namboodiripad which proposed for the first time in India, the exclusion of a well-to-do section from the backward communities from enjoying the benefits of reservation.

The present practice of exclusion of "creamy layer" actually originated from this recommendation. Both the "forward" and the "backward" communities came against the recommendations of the committee and particularly against E.M.S. Namboodiripad. The "forward" communities attacked the report as it recommended the continuation of the reservation system. The "backward" communities attacked the report for introducing an economic criteria for exclusion.

Muslim Minority's Rights

The British colonial rulers considered the Muslims in Malabar (northern part of Kerala) as criminal tribes and used all kinds of repressive methods against them. They were discriminated against in appointments to government jobs. Muslims were not allowed to repair or do maintenance work in mosques or to construct new ones. They had to obtain special permission from the District

Collectors for this purpose. But in the case of other religious believers, they could repair, do maintenance work or construct new places of worship as they like. The discrimination continued even after independence and under Congress governments. The Communist government ended all discriminative practices against the Muslim minorities and provided equal rights with all other religious believers.

Crusade against Corruption

The government took effective steps against corruption, nepotism and inefficiency in the administration with the involvement of people and their organisations. The approach of the government was guided by the understanding that it was the task of every organisation and every individual who was interested in justice being done to raise their voice against every single act of bribery, nepotism and other evils.

The government gave directions to higher authorities to make prompt enquiries and to take appropriate steps against whom such complaints were made. The government also stressed the role of the organisations of government employees to create consciousness among the people and to bring about a corresponding change in the attitude of the government officials.

The government gave strict instructions about the method of functioning and life style of the ministers. The statement of policy announced by E.M.S. Namboodiripad on April 5, 1957 after taking oath as Chief Minister contained the following instructions to the ministers:

> It is necessary to bring about an order and system in the personal life and official activities of the ministers themselves. It will prove a big obstacle in the way of a good and decent administration if the impression is created that their relatives, friends, colleagues in public work, etc. of the ministers can exert a good deal of pressure on them. Each of us will do our best to see that such an impression is not created. This, however, is inadequate. It is equally necessary to

> evolve certain rules of conduct which are clear and capable of strict enforcement in order to get the activities of the ministers. Whatever discussions we hold among ourselves on this question will be made known to the people. At the same time, I request the people to give their advise and suggestions on how this is to be actually implemented.

Review of Performance

The performance of the Communist government and its new approach helped to rally newer sections in support of the government and the Communist party. It is a fact that the Communist party was not able to get majority in Kerala Legislative Assembly in the 1960 elections after the dismissal of the Communist government.

But the election, in another sense, represented a victory for the Communist party and a defeat for the Congress. While the Communist party fought the elections alone, the Congress was supported by all caste, communal and other reactionary forces and parties like the PSP and the Muslim League. The votes of the Communist party increased from 23 lakhs in 1957 elections to 35 lakhs in 1960 elections.

While the Party along with independents supported by it polled 40 per cent of votes in 1957 elections, it polled 44 per cent votes in 1960 elections. The election results showed that the balance of political forces had shifted in favour of the Communist party and against the Congress.

In Kerala, since independence, Congress was the biggest political party in terms of mass support but the election results showed that the Communist party had emerged as the single biggest party in popular vote within a short period. B. T. Ranadive, writing in the *New Age* monthly, March 1960 described this as follows:

> It convincingly showed that notwithstanding the combination of all parties against it, notwithstanding the malicious and slanderous propaganda carried day

> in and day out by more than thirty daily papers against the Party, the Communist Party emerged stronger – much stronger than before in popular estimation.

The formation of the Communist government and its performance strengthened the Communist party and its mass base in Kerala. As Chief Minister of the first Communist government and as leader of the Communist party, the contributions of E.M.S. Namboodiripad both at the theoretical and practical level, will always be cherished.

3

A Great Leader

E.M.S. Namboodiripad said once, "Individuals become leaders only because they serve the people of the country. The minute they start doing something else, the minute they drop their ideals and ideology and work against their party or the people, they cease to be leaders."

E.M.S. was among the rare Indian leaders who abided by this rule through his public life that lasted more than seven decades. His prescient presence as leader, thinker and theoretician played a pre-eminent role in shaping a modern and cohesive Kerala out of its unsettling political and social history. His tireless efforts as an analyst and commentator helped evolve a form of Communism that suited Indian conditions.

In idealism and exhaustive pursuit of ideology, E.M.S. stood out as a model for political India. He thought differently from his contemporaries, lived dangerously to overcome the limitations of his times and worked constantly for the freedom of the individual and society from the clutches of imperialism, feudalism, fanatic casteism and, more recently, abhorrent communalism. Born on June 13, 1909, E.M.S. was the son of Elankulam Manakkal Parameswaran Namboodiripad, a Sanskrit scholar, and Vishnudatta. Theirs was an aristocratic Namboodiri family in Perinthalamanna taluk of the present Malappuram district. E.M.S.

had four sisters and three brothers; two brothers died soon after birth and an older brother had a mental disability. He lost his father at a very early age.

E.M.S. was affectionately called Kunju (the little one). As was the custom, Kunju's early education was at home. He was imparted a rigorous, ritualistic training in Sanskrit language and literature, logic and the scriptures. Later, he was taught Malayalam, Hindi and English. His mother and his Sanskrit teacher, Àgnitratan, influenced him in his early years. It is said that his mother was keen to make him a Sanskrit scholar and wanted him to excel in the anyonyams (vedic recitation contests). This was not to be. Kunju insisted that he be sent to school. About his education at home and his experiences as a schoolboy at Perinthalmanna, E.M.S. recalled later:

> "Even those who completed such a system of education (at home) would not understand the Rig Veda because students were required only to learn by rote the various suktas and not their meaning... I felt I had started a new life when I joined the school. An entirely new atmosphere than what I was used to. Members from all castes and communities were my fellow students and teachers. Learning was not alone but together, in groups of 25 to 30 students."

E.M.S.' earliest struggles were against the feudal system to which he belonged. V.T. Bhattathiripad, M.B. Bhattathiripad and the young revolutionary E.M.S. were responsible for awakening the Namboodiri community to new social realities. Those lower down in the caste hierarchy, such as the Pulaya, Ezhava and Nair communities, had already experienced the stirrings of social change. They launched a journal Unninamboothiri in which E.M.S. published for the first time his progressive ideas - radical for the times.

First Step in Public Life

E.M.S. became an assistant secretary of the Valluvanadu Yogakshema Sabha, an organisation of Namboodiri youth that fought against the retrograde customs in the community. At 16, he became the secretary of the Yogakshema Sabha and campaigned vigorously for liberating Namboodiri women from oppressive customs. In 1931, E.M.S. took the initiative for the first widow remarriage in the Namboodiri community for which he was "ostracised", ineffectively though. He organised picketing at venues where old men tried to marry young girls and collected funds to fight the karanavars, the heads of traditional matrilineal families, who would not allow their wards enough means even for a decent education.

When E.M.S. began college, Travancore and Cochin were coming alive to the national freedom movement. He abandoned his degree course to join the Independence movement. Even as a schoolboy, Namboodiripad went to Madras to attend the All India Congress Committee (AICC) conference. Later, he attended the Payyannur conference of the AICC, which was inaugurated by Jawaharlal Nehru whose socialist leanings within the Indian National Congress had attracted E.M.S.' admiration.

After 1932, E.M.S. devoted his energy to fighting British imperialism and this was a period when he was either incarcerated or forced into hiding. The experience gave E.M.S. the opportunity to meet freedom-fighters from different parts of the country. While in jail at Kannur and Vellore, he established links with socialist leaders within the Congress. In 1934, he joined the Congress Socialist Party. E.M.S. retained links with the Pradesh Congress Committee and attracted national attention when he was elected PCC secretary. A majority of the newly elected PCC members supported the Left-socialist viewpoint, unlike the PCCs in other parts of the country.

Academic Movement

E.M.S. steered the progressive literary and intellectual movement in Kerala and made his mark also as the first Marxist historian in the State. The progressive literary movement evoked a social response and achieved a sincerity of approach to people's problems. It encouraged the creation of outstanding works in all areas of Malayalam literature.

These years were also spent shaping the party newspaper, Desabhimani. In April 1997, soon after the daily launched its fifth edition, E.M.S. told Frontline: "When Desabhimani was started...the Communists were a small but committed group in Kerala, pursuing a political line (against the British war efforts) that isolated them from the people. The original objective of the paper was therefore to give publicity to the party's line and to answer criticism against it." For a long time it was a party paper meant only for party members, but Desabhimani, which grew under the constant guidance of Namboodiripad, is today the fourth largest circulated Malayalam daily.

The last important phase in E.M.S.' life was his evolution as Marxist thinker and theoretician, especially after the Communist Party of India (CPI) split in 1964. Even as his closest associates faded away into history, E.M.S. guided the movement through the thick and thin of Indian politics. He was elected to the CPI Central Committee in 1941 and to the party Polit Bureau in 1950. In 1962, he was elected general-secretary of the undivided CPI. In 1964, after the party split, he was elected a Polit Bureau member of the Communist Party of India (Marxist), a post that he held until the very end. He was the CPI(M) general-secretary from 1977 to 1992, when he returned to Kerala on account of failing health.

Even after his return to Thiruvananthapuram, he continued his hectic schedule as party ideologue and writer. The handsome income that he generated through his writings went to the party, which in turn looked after his spartan personal needs.

In the last one year, E.M.S. often expressed his concerns about the development crisis in Kerala and said that the acclaimed Kerala model was insufficient to address urgent developmental needs. He prescribed decentralisation of power and involving people from all walks of life irrespective of political affiliations for the all-round development of the State. The State Government incorporated his suggestions in the People's Campaign for the Ninth Plan. E.M.S., who was the chairman of the high-level guidance committee formed to implement the campaign, is known to have complained at the committee's last meeting in September 1997 about the slow implementation of the programme.

Until his last day, E.M.S. remained active. A few hours before his death, he dictated two articles to his personal assistant, Venu.

One was on the need for a joint effort to fight the forces that threaten secularism in the country - coincidentally on the day the Bharatiya Janata Party ascended to power at the Centre - and the other on "Desabhimani's responsibility today", to mark the anniversary of the newspaper's Kottayam edition.

No tribute can do justice to the glorious and multifaceted life led by E.M.S. - anti-imperialist, social reformer, literary critic, Marxist thinker, theoretician and historian, and above all a person loved and held in esteem by millions of people.

Great Revolutionary Figure

E.M.S. Namboodiripad (1909-1998) was, in all probability, the most important revolutionary figure modern India has produced. He was certainly the most accomplished, the most original and creative, and the most enduringly influential on the larger stage. Although their lives, styles and socio-political circumstances could not have presented a more fascinating or educative contrast, Mao Zedong of China alone can rival him in historical importance as an "interpreter of Marxist thought in the less developed world" (as President K.R. Narayanan observed in his warm tribute). E.M.S.' international reputation in Communist and progressive circles rests pre-eminently on his accomplishments as theorist and intellectual pathfinder. His vast body of writings on an awesome range of subjects, which will no doubt be issued in time as his Collected Works, will long be read for the riches they offer to all manner of readers in India and abroad.

As has been pointed out in the assessment by Prakash Karat, a younger colleague, published in this issue, "E.M.S. with his extraordinary intellectual genius was able constantly to stay ahead of his contemporaries in applying Marxism to the specific conditions in Kerala and later the whole of India." His analyses of landlordism and land relations, nationality formation in Kerala and India, the character of the Indian state and society, evolving Indian politics, the opportunities and limits of parliamentary democracy, Communist participation in State governments, the planning process, the caste system and the tricky class-caste equation, the ideology of Mahatma Gandhi and Jawaharlal Nehru, and various aspects of history and culture are contributions of unsurpassed originality, brilliance and influence in the Indian Left.

But E.M.S. was great not just for the creativity and brilliance of his contributions to Marxist theory and thought over more than half a century. Anti-imperialist and patriot, social reformer, Chief Minister of India's first elected Communist Government, architect of India's first serious land reform experiment, leader with a radical educational vision, underground party organiser, great communicator, ex-Congress leader who became general secretary of both the undivided CPI and the CPI(M), he was a Master of practice.

Tolerant, respectful of differences and fair-minded, E.M.S. was known to take his time to arrive at a position (most famously, during a crucial period when the Communist Party of India was in a process of fierce inner-party struggle and splitting). But he never hesitated to take sides once his mind was made up. A believer in democratic dialogue and tireless discussion of issues that matter, he was also a fierce polemicist and controversialist, a mass agitator whom governments and opponents learnt to fear. Free from ego problems and hangups, he felt free to lay out his differences and criticisms straightforwardly and without inhibition and to accept criticism without rancour or subjectivism.

In personal as well as in larger socio-political terms, the life story of E.M.S. can be read as a story of recurrent challenge and creative, obstacle-clearing response. His initiation into public life came with an adolescent struggle to overcome his high-caste, feudal landlord origins through progressive humanism and personal morality of a high order. His first significant success came in the social realm: it was in the youth struggle within the community to "make the Namboodiri a human being". E.M.S.' passion against high caste oppression, untouchability and unseeability was able to move mountains.

E.M.S. made a unique contribution to the development of a theory and practice of participation by a Communist Party in elected State governments without losing sight of the priority of developing mass movements and struggles by the working people. At times, he faced vicious attacks from the ultra-Left and the naxalites of the world for his 'revisionism' and 'right-reformist' practice. But E.M.S.' two terms as Chief Minister of Kerala are unparalleled for leadership vision, the focus brought to two critical issues - land reform and education - and communicating a sense of revolutionary priorities and sheer quality. Nor did he show himself enamoured of office. In fact, after 1969 he showed little interest in becoming Chief Minister again. As Prakash Karat points out, during his last days he was "deeply concerned with the corrosive effects of parliamentarism which subordinates the interests of the mass movements and the demands of class struggle."

Likewise, the man who more than any other helped shape the social, political and economic development of modern Kerala - and its enviable social indicators - was far from complacent about what had been achieved through a combination of struggles and constructive efforts over many decades. He took fierce issue with any scholarly attempt to 'romanticise' the Kerala developmental 'model', insisting towards the end of his life on highlighting the downside of the experience.

E.M.S. the revolutionary showed fortitude, resilience and equanimity of a rare order. Dismissal and destabilisation of Left-led State governments, setbacks to the movement, the collapse of the Soviet Union and the East European socialist systems, ideological and political reversals, repression as well as the dangling of illusions - these were powerless against the strength of his Communist conviction and the sunniness of his disposition.

This is, in effect, a special issue condoling the passing of E.M.S. but also celebrating his manysided gifts. His contribution as a towering genius of the Indian revolution is assessed by longtime comrade and associate, Harkishan Singh Surjeet, who succeeded him as general secretary of the Communist Party of India (Marxist), and also by a colleague belonging to a much younger generation, Prakash Karat. E.M.S.' lifelong engagement with history, and in particular the history of Kerala and of the Indian freedom struggle, is evaluated by a distinguished professional historian, K.N. Panikkar. The quality, power and subtlety of E.M.S.' internationalist vision is analysed by distinguished economist Prabhat Patnaik. E.M.S.' outstanding importance in the social, economic and political development of modern Kerala, indeed in raising the developmental level of a region and millions of working people in particular, is profiled by Frontline Deputy Editor and economist V.K. Ramachandran. There are other interesting contributions providing insights into E.M.S. the man of letters and man of culture, E.M.S. the Chief Minister, E.M.S. the family man and so on (some of which will be published in the next issue of Frontline).

A genius of many sides and gifts, this diminutive, amiable and somewhat shy man with a stammer strode the Kerala and national stage as a colossus. More than any other person on the Indian Left, he succeeded in bridging the gap between theory and practice, conceptualisation and action, movement and organisation, high-soaring individual genius and disciplined collective functioning. E.M.S.' greatest achievement as a revolutionary was the integration of all these sides. This was achieved in a lifelong practice of transparently simple living and high thinking, integrity that remains beyond question, morality and humanism of the highest order that is profound, class-based and partisan in a progressive sense.

Mass Leader

No other single individual has made as immense a contribution as E.M.S. has in the shaping of the destiny of both Kerala and the Communist movement in this country.

IT is with a very heavy heart that I am writing this piece. I am yet to grasp the meaning of the reality of my Comrade E.M.S. Namboodiripad being no more. I write in grief with no certain idea of how much justice I will be able to do to his memory.

Comrade E.M.S. was to me what he was to millions of others in Kerala and outside, a dear and near one. He was one of my closest friends and colleagues. To millions of ordinary people in Kerala, E.M.S., as he was popularly known, was an icon. No other single individual has made as immense a contribution as E.M.S. has in the shaping of the destiny of both Kerala and the Communist movement in this country. The millions who rushed to Thiruvananthapuram on hearing of his death with tear-filled eyes bear test... y to the love and affection they had for Comrade

E.M.S. The serpentine queues that waited for hours to have a last glimpse of the mortal remains of their beloved leader; the virtual stampede in the Durbar hall where the body was placed for public viewing; the lakhs who turned up on both sides of the road that led to the crematorium: all these tell their own tale.

E.M.S. was loved, respected, adored. To the ordinary people of Kerala, a mere sight of their dear leader was a life's desire accomplished. He was an affectionate comrade, caring and enquiring about the well-being of his comrades; he was a leader par excellence who combined theoretical understanding with practical work; he deeply felt for the poor and underprivileged, who in turn cared deeply for him; he was a colleague who respected the views of others even if he had reservations and differences; he was like a saint to many; he was one who lent an ear to anyone who approached him. These are the qualities that set Comrade E.M.S. apart from the broad spectrum of political leadership in the country. He was one of the tallest personalities the 20th century has produced.

Comrade E.M.S. was initiated into politics at a very young age. He began his work by trying to initiate reforms in his own Namboodiri community through the Namboodiri Yogakshema Sabha. Comrade E.M.S. came from a wealthy upper-caste family. Yet he gave up his college education midstream to pursue his goal of being in the service of the people. There was no turning back from this path. In 1931, he was drawn into the Congress movement, and jailed for participating in the Civil Disobedience struggle. Disillusioned with the Congress, he became one of the founders of the Congress Socialist Party in Kerala with a view to linking the struggle for national freedom with the struggle for social revolution.

Leaders pay their last respects. (Clockwise from left) E.K. Nayanar, Harkishan Singh Surjeet, A.B. Bardhan, L.K. Advani, Prakash Karat, P. Ramachandran, Sitaram Yechury and S. Ramachandran Pillai.

In this the October Socialist Revolution was a big inspiration. Comrade E.M.S.' everlasting thirst for knowledge led him to study the theory of scientific socialism. In 1938, he along with P. Krishan Pillai, A.K. Gopalan and others formed the illegal Communist

Party in Kerala. At that time, Kerala was part of Madras Province, which comprised parts of the present Andhra Pradesh, Tamil Nadu and Kerala, excepting those parts of these States which were under princely rule. All Communists were working together inside the Congress Socialist Party and the Congress at that time. Comrade E.M.S. took the final decision to join the Communist Party after he came in touch with Comrade P. Sundarayya who was tirelessly working for developing the Communist Party in the South. While joining the Party formally in 1938, E.M.S. was discharging his responsibilities as the General Secretary of the Kerala Pradesh Congress Committee and the General Secretary of the Congress Socialist Party in Kerala. His organising capabilities and leadership were illustrated when he carried the entire Kerala unit of the Congress Socialist Party to the Communist Party along with him. By now, E.M.S. had won the hearts of thousands in Kerala who, while struggling for freedom, also dreamed of social revolution. After Nehru became Congress president in 1936, the ideas of socialism became widespread in India.

E.M.S. was also one of founders of the All India Kisan Sabha in 1936. When he was elected to the Madras Provincial Legislature Assembly in 1939, he marked himself out as a legislature of a new genre. He was a revolutionary parliamentarian who linked up the issues and demands of the people, particularly the peasantry, with the freedom struggle.

In the first Congress of the Communist Party of India held in 1943, E.M.S. was elected to the Central Committee of the party. From then, the cause of the party remained foremost in his mind. He gave all he had for the cause of the party. As I noted earlier, E.M.S. belonged to a wealthy landlord family. He had inherited a substantial part from the ancestral property. He donated the entire proceeds of the sale of this property, Rs. 1.8 lakhs, an astronomical sum at that time, to the party funds.

He was an untiring worker. I recall that when he used to work from the All India Centre at 14, Ashoka Road in New Delhi, E.M.S. used to reach the office at 8.00 a.m. sharp, well before the others arrived. Before arriving at the office, he would have already glanced through the daily papers at his residence. He would begin his day at the office by dictating letters, notes and articles. By the time all of us reached the office for our daily morning meeting, he would have finished all these tasks. Except for a half-hour nap in the afternoon, he used to remain in the office till the evening. This was the routine until a few months before the Madras Congress of the CPI(M), when he left the Centre owing to ill health. His personal life was spartan, and his requirements were restricted to the bare minimum.

E.M.S. was a prolific writer who wielded a lucid pen. His language was straight and simple. He spoke from the heart. An orator par excellence, E.M.S. had his audience mesmerised. People turned out in large numbers for his meetings, wherever they were held or at whatever time, and heard him with rapt attention. His audience did not consist of party comrades alone. His political opponents, despite their disagreements, would come to hear E.M.S. speak. That was the level of respectability and acceptability he commanded throughout the country.

I still treasure the memory of my first meeting with E.M.S. It was at the Tripura session of the Congress Party in 1939. Subhash Chandra Bose was elected Congress president at this congress, defeating P. Sitaramaiah, Mahatma Gandhi's candidate. Bose was elected with the support of the Left inside the Congress. A faction meeting of the illegal Communist Party was held at that time. An unassuming man in a white dhoti and shirt was speaking at the meeting. It was E.M.S. The second occasion I met him was in 1946. This was *en route* to Nethrakona, which is now in Bangladesh, to attend the All India Kisan Conference. At the station, I observed him lending a helping hand to other delegates to get down from the train; he also helped them board the ferry. Since January 1954, when both of us were elected to the Polit Bureau at the third Congress of the Communist Party, I have had the privilege of working closely with him.

In the history of the Indian Communist movement, the period after the Third Party Congress was one of crisis. Although the Communist Party of the Soviet Union (CPSU) tried to help, the programme and policy statement that was adopted at the special conference in 1951 and endorsed at the Third Party Congress failed to stand the test of time. India, which had been submitting to US imperialism, had started taking a stand against imperialism in support of national liberation movements. The Bandung Conference marked a significant turning point in India-China relations. With this started a debate inside the Communist Party.

This debate, which began in 1954-55, led ultimately to a split in the Communist Party in 1964. As opposed to the three trends that were emerging in the Party, E.M.S. always tried to take a stand which he thought would help unify the party. At Palghat, the line of class collaboration was being advocated. One-third of the delegates, however, opposed this line. Comrade E.M.S. stood with those who wanted to fight the line of class collaboration.

E.M.S., Dada Amir Haidar Khan and M. Basavapunnaiah. Khan was an early organiser of the Communist Party in South India and was responsible for the induction into the party of P. Sundarayya, who in turn brought E.M.S. into the Communist movement.

It was during this tense and uncertain period that the relationship between E.M.S. and me grew closer. He frankly exchanged views with me. Till the end of his life, the healthy practice of placing one's views forthrightly was a trait observed in E.M.S. Whenever he disagreed, he used to note down his views and submit them in writing. Over the last year, E.M.S. stopped attending meetings, owing to the worsening of his arthritis and on the advice of his doctors. But this did not prevent him from sending his notes to the Polit Bureau and Central Committee meetings. When a divergent view was expressed, he was always ready to listen to others and willing to accept the other view and correct his own when he was convinced. He learnt from the criticisms made against him. No streak of ego or the airs that affect other leaders ever touched him.

Para 11.2 of the CPI(M) programme, which envisages participation in government in the States, was an original contribution from E.M.S. Initially when the programme was drafted, this clause did not find a place. E.M.S. initiated the discussion on this point and it was made part of the programme.

Comrade E.M.S. never hankered after power or position. When we required his services at the party centre and asked him if he was willing to move to Delhi, he readily agreed. Many times E.M.S. expressed his desire to retire from active public life owing to failing health. But we always were able to persuade him to continue to be part of the team that worked together for decades.

He was an internationalist in the true sense of the term. During the India-China war in 1962, braving the chauvinist onslaught, E.M.S. campaigned throughout the country advocating a peaceful settlement of the border dispute. Similarly, during the India-Pakistan war, he advocated a peaceful settlement of the dispute. As a true Communist, he always thought the Indian Communist movement to be a part and parcel of the world revolutionary process. In all solidarity campaigns in support of the national liberation movements, in defence of peace and socialism, he was always in the forefront. He left an imprint on leaders of Communist parties the world over. Whenever I go abroad, enquiries are made about the health of Comrade E.M.S.

E.M.S. was more than an inspiration. His life and work are a guide for future generations. Simple living, dedication to the cause, spirit of self-sacrifice, always at the service of the people, combining theory and practice - Comrade E.M.S. stood wide apart from the broad spectrum of politicians in the country. He will continue to be adored and loved. There can be no better way of paying homage than pursuing the path followed by him. One should be sure thousands of people in Kerala and elsewhere, while mourning his death, will have already resolved to do so.

Vision about World Order

What is remarkable about the vision of E.M.S. is not only its appeal, which arises because of its essential correctness, but also its quality of being fresh and forward-looking.

Like many of his youthful contemporaries, E.M.S. Namboodiripad was drawn towards socialism by the experience of the Great Depression of the 1930s. The fact that even as the capitalist world was reeling under the impact of massive unemployment and unutilised resources, the Soviet Union, untouched by the crisis, was taking gigantic strides towards developing its productive forces, opened his mind to the stark contrast between the two systems. It won him to the socialist cause; it also left him with two of his abiding intellectual interests: planning and social laws.

E.M.S.' interest in planning was enthusiastic in the extreme. He wrote a book Indian Planning in Crisis (Chintha 1974) which was in fact his presentation to a conference of the Indian School of Social Sciences held in Bombay that year. In more recent times when very few people took much notice of the national Plan documents, E.M.S. was a notable exception, and could put one in an embarrassing situation by engaging one in a discussion of the latest essay of the Planning Commission. Linked to this was his interest in social formations and the laws governing them, on which again he wrote extensively. Notable in this connection is his paper presented at another Indian School of Social Sciences seminar on "Lenin and Imperialism" held in Delhi in 1981. The proceedings of the seminar are published as Lenin and Imperialism (edited by this writer, Orient Longman, Delhi, 1986).

The two Marxist ideas, namely that capitalism is a system governed by spontaneous economic laws which are objective and independent of human will, which manifest themselves *inter alia* in periodic crises, and whose operation can only be somewhat modified through intervention but never nullified without undermining the system's functioning, and that, by contrast, socialism is a system which allows conscious intervention through a plan, must have appealed to him greatly in the midst of the Depression. But the intervention and planning that socialism provides the scope for, do not mean that "anything goes". They have to be "correct", have also got to follow certain laws. In overcoming the spontaneity of capitalism, socialism too has to follow certain rules, or laws, of intervention.

It follows that both capitalism and socialism are law-governed systems, but there is a fundamental difference in the nature of the laws governing the two systems: the laws of capitalism are an ensemble of spontaneous tendencies; the laws of socialism are essentially rules of action.

This basic idea underlay E.M.S.' thinking all his life. It enabled him not only to recognise the fact of social and economic crisis in the socialist countries, but even to explain it, pithily and brilliantly, within his socialist theoretical perspective: the crisis in capitalism is because of the operation of its laws, the crisis in socialism is because of the violation of its laws. When the laws regarding correct relationship between the Party and the State, or regarding inner-Party democracy, are violated, socialism runs into crisis, even though in principle it is crisis-free. The purpose of conscious praxis in a socialist society, of which planning is a part, should be to ensure that these laws are not violated systematically.

An interesting offshoot of this idea of E.M.S. needs to be noted. Since the Communist parties, even in bourgeois societies, represent in a sense the early embryonic stage of the socialist praxis, they too have to follow certain laws of intervention, not only in their organisation and overall functioning, but also in the kind of planning which they undertake in the regions administered by them within the constraints of a bourgeois society. It is this perception which prompted E.M.S. (at the International Conference on Kerala Studies organised under his leadership) to be somewhat critical of the "Kerala Model" which the whole world was lauding, on the grounds that there was an imbalance underlying it: the development of the productive forces had lagged behind; this had to be rectified.

Capitalism and socialism have their own laws. But what happens when they coexist? This is the question which E.M.S. is concerned with in his paper at the "Lenin and Imperialism" seminar, after having given, explicitly or implicitly, the perspective on social laws and crises outlined above.

Clearly, the socialist forces have to resist the operation of capitalism's spontaneous tendencies, for the sake of their own survival, by following correct strategy and tactics. The thwarting of such operation disrupts capitalism; the thwarting in some sphere aggravates capitalism's contradiction in some other sphere. It follows then that such resistance can be successful, and that it is simultaneously a part of the process of struggle for the transcendence of capitalism. The specific context in which E.M.S. discussed this issue related to imperialism.

After arguing that the contradictions of the imperialist era highlighted by Lenin have been further intensified since his writing, that inter-imperialist contradictions are no less fierce than they were at his time, and that there is the overarching contradiction between the imperialist world and the socialist world, E.M.S. asks the question whether these contradictions would propel the world towards yet another global war. Lenin had argued that war was inherent in imperialism. Is another global war then inevitable?

"The answer is by no means simple" since there are two contradictory tendencies: on the one hand there is "the powerful military-industrial complex propped up by multinational firms having their grip on the entire capitalist world and seeking to use the armaments industry for making maximum profits", whose operations promote the prospects of war, and on the other hand there is the growing camp of peace, consisting of the socialist countries, the newly-liberated countries of the Third World, and the working class movement, together with the anti-monopoly, anti-war element in other sections of society, in the advanced capitalist countries. A "running battle" between these two trends is the main feature of the political situation and forms the background against which the contradictions noted by Lenin are operating.

Lenin's call "Transform the imperialist war into civil war", cannot be applied in that form in the contemporary context. What is necessary is an integration of the activities of the "forces of proletarian and national revolution" with those of others who are trying to prevent the imperialist war from breaking out. "Though the final and complete elimination of war requires the end of the imperialist system, the outbreak of a new world war is no more inevitable." In fact, the social revolution in particular countries is "inseparably connected with the global struggle against the most aggressive ruling circles of imperialist countries".

Having thus underscored the need for socialist intervention for thwarting the tendency of capitalism to perpetrate war, E.M.S. turns to the question of why socialist praxis may go wrong. Given the complexity of this praxis, two kinds of difficulties may come in the way of correct strategy and tactics: first, unity with the bourgeoisie in the Third World countries against imperialism and its warmongering has to be combined with a struggle against the anti-people policies of this very same bourgeoisie, and an underestimation of either task can lead to distorted praxis. The possibility of such distortion is strengthened by the second difficulty, namely, the fact that the foreign policy interests of the socialist countries have to be combined with the basic commitment to proletarian internationalism.

The incorrect handling of these difficulties can give rise to Right Opportunist or Left Sectarian errors. To underplay the struggle against domestic bourgeois governments because of their opposition to imperialism is the hallmark of Right Opportunism which also derives sustenance from the support of ruling Communist Parties to such bourgeois governments as part of their foreign policy. On the other hand, to run down the anti-imperialist role of the domestic bourgeois governments amounts to underestimating imperialism and the need for a struggle against its warmongering, which constitutes a Left Sectarian error. This error too, in a situation where the fight against Right Opportunism in the world Communist movement has already given rise to the opposite extreme of Left Sectarianism among another section of ruling Communists, derives support from the latter and gets strengthened. E.M.S. refers to the Indian experience and underscores the need for a correct praxis avoiding both types of distortion.

At a Car Factory in the Soviet Union in 1987: E.M.S.' analysis, covering the entire expanse from Marx's notion of laws to the crisis of socialism, unifying his discussion of Lenin's theory of imperialism with his perception of the divisions in the Indian Communist movement, affirming his basic commitment to the Leninist perspective even while clearly delineating the changes since Lenin's days, is in the best traditions of Communist literature. Today, of course, the specific context is different. One is naturally tempted to ask: if E.M.S. were writing another article of the same breadth today, how would he have brought his analysis up to date? One can only speculate on the basis of some brief offerings he left behind (for example, Frontline, April 3, 1998).

The distortions that led to the overthrow of socialism in Eastern Europe were such that their rectification would have to take the form a "rebirth"; there is no going back to what existed before 1991. Marx, Engels and Lenin had visualised a slow and protracted development of working class state power based on the solid alliance of all exploited and oppressed classes and strata under the leadership of the working class. This dictatorship is to be directed against a small stratum of the former ruling classes. In short, the alliance underlying state power has to be broad-based and inclusive. Correspondingly, the target of this alliance has to be a narrow stratum; it follows that private property, other than monopoly private property, has a place in "reformed Communism". The distortions of erstwhile Communism then consisted in the fact that the dictatorship of the proletariat it sought to establish was too exclusive, too sweeping in its attack on all forms of private property, and too narrowly-based in terms of social support to survive being transformed into a dictatorship of the party which in the course of time turned into the "cult of personality".

Implicit in this conception is the possibility of a multiplicity of forms in which the working people would use state power, that is, a multiplicity of "models". And such a process of "rebirth" of Communism would simultaneously be a process of putting imperialism once again on the defensive.

What is remarkable about this construction of E.M.S.' vision is not only its appeal which arises because of its essential correctness, but above all its quality of being fresh and forward-looking, free both of despondency and of any desire to put the clock back. There can be no greater testimony to the strength of E.M.S.' intellect.

E.M.S, As Columnist of 'Frontline'

In the words of a staffer between December 1991 and March 1998, octogenarian E.M.S. Namboodiripad wrote 128 columns for Frontline on an impressive - indeed awesome - range of subjects. For these seven years and more, his was simply the most dependable contribution from the standpoint of the editorial desk. The E.M.S. column always arrived early, invariably on time, and never strayed beyond a self-judged readability limit. No full-time professional journalist could hold a candle to E.M.S. when it came to showing deadline discipline or responding to breaking news or accommodating a special theme-related publishing request. He was a Master at handling history on the wing.

Between December 1991 and April 1994, E.M.S. wrote one column a month for Frontline. Then he proposed in a letter that he had decided to write for every issue, an offer that was gratefully and immediately accepted.

"Perspective", the E.M.S. column, ranged over politics, philosophy, economics, education, social movements, literature, cultural affairs, religion and books. He wrote about Marxism and revolutionary socialism, Mao Zedong and Deng Xiaoping, Gandhism, Jawaharlal Nehru, Subhash Chandra Bose, the Indian freedom struggle, other liberation movements and their leaders (especially Nelson Mandela), the ruling classes, planning, secularism, the Rig Veda, Advaita, Hindutva, Centre-State contradictions, budgets, new economic policies, self-reliance, foreign policy, liberation theology, religious fundamentalism, corruption, the politician-criminal nexus, Congress affairs, Sitaram Kesri, Sonia Gandhi, the United Front, coalitions, panchayati raj, decentralisation, nuclear policy, working class struggles, empowering women, and handling river water disputes. His last column, posthumously carried in this remembrance issue, is titled "Centre, States and river waters"; it is sharply critical of the AIADMK's demand that the Centre should take over the States' rights over river waters.

How the E.M.S. column began, may be of interest to readers. E.M.S. has always valued serious journalism and been contemptuous of trivialising, entertainment-led tendencies masquerading as journalism. When he was in Chennai for the 1991 Party Congress of the Communist Party of India (Marxist), he conveyed to Frontline's Editor appreciation of what the magazine offered (revealing that he read it from cover to cover) and contrasted this with the vast amounts of "trash" put out in print. When a request was made that he write a regular column, it was accepted and, in typical E.M.S. style, immediately acted upon.

Within a couple of days after the first cheque by way of payment for the column reached E.M.S., it was returned with a courteous signed letter. E.M.S. noted that for quite some time he had not been accepting any payment for his articles, royalties and so forth. He was therefore returning the cheque. However, if Frontline wished, any payment for his contributions could be sent to the AKG Centre in Thiruvananthapuram (to which he had assigned all his royalties and so forth). The party's receipt on account of royalties and payments for articles due to E.M.S. had been very substantial.

Father, Friend, Philosopher and Guide

In the words of his son, Malathi Damodaran: My first distinct memory concerning my father goes back to when I was eight years old. One day in January 1947, when I woke up in the morning, I found a number of policemen standing outside my house. I was told that they had come to arrest my father. Meanwhile, someone came and told me that my baby brother had been born the previous night. My father was suffering from chickenpox at that time. He was arrested and subsequently moved to hospital.

In the next four to five years, I met my father only twice, while he was underground. When I joined Queen Mary's College in Madras, he used to visit me often and take me out to the movies and to have ice-cream. When I joined the Christian Medical College, Vellore in 1957, he was the Chief Minister of Kerala and my fellow students were quite curious to know how a Chief Minister's family lived - in particular, how many servants we had and how many cars we owned. They were surprised to learn that we did not own a car and that my mother had only one person to help her. During his first visit to CMC to see me, he addressed a meeting of staff and students and started his speech by stating that this was his first visit to Vellore as a free man - he had been in Vellore on several occasions, as a detainee in the Central Jail. This shocked those gathered there.

Following the severe colitis that he suffered in 1969, he came under the supervision of doctors for a variety of ailments. He could be called a doctor's delight for his complete faith in them and his complete compliance with their advice. He was on a strict, bland diet since 1969 and followed it faithfully. What he loved to eat was sweet dishes, which he was allowed to eat. All of us made it a point to make something sweet for him whenever possible.

He took great pleasure in spending time with his grandchildren whenever he could, right from playing with them when they were little to taking a great deal of interest in whatever they were doing as they grew up and became adults. He also lived to see his great-granddaughter, who was born last year. He was looking forward a great deal to seeing her again this summer.

In the words of his son in law, A. D. Damodaran: I got married to E.M.S.' daughter Malathi in September 1965. Our marriage was conducted without any traditional rituals, something highly unusual in those days. After our marriage, when we were to leave for my home, E.M.S. gave me a copy of his celebrated book Keralam, Malayaalikalude Maathrubhoomi with an autographed inscription: "Vivaahithayaayi makal thante bharthrugruhathil pokumbol oru pithaavinundaakaavunna vikaaravichaarangal prashastha kaviyaaya Kaalidaasan thante viswotharakrithi Shaakunthalathil savistharam prathipaadichittundu. Aa vikaaravichaarangalku ee aatom yugathilum prasakthiyundennu innu enikku thonnunnu." (The great poet Kalidasa has, in his Shakuntalam, described the emotions and feelings of a father whose daughter is departing for her husband's home after marriage. I consider that even in this atomic age, these feelings are relevant.)

Those were the days when E.M.S. was under strict police vigil and as one working in the Department of Atomic Energy I also came under scrutiny, in the process going through great mental tension, something I had never experienced before. Subsequently, when we settled down in Bombay (and later moved over to Hyderabad), he used to visit us often and stay with us, even when he was the Chief Minister. I cannot even begin to recount what a profound influence he has had in shaping my professional and personal life. Having great faith in science and technology, he was quite interested in my research and S&T activities, be it in the Department of Atomic Energy, the Council of Scientific and Industrial Research or the Government of Kerala. He used proudly to recall always his visit to the Bhabha Atomic Research Centre. I can recall his delight in going around the Nuclear Fuel Complex at Hyderabad and appreciate its great strategic-technological significance. He abhorred mediocrity and was very much concerned over the growing "amateurishness" in different walks of life including the ranks and, as was emphasised by one and all, he used his pen as a great weapon. The three books which have attracted me the most are:

(a) Economics and Politics of India's Socialist Pattern, describing the evolution of the Indian bourgeoisie. (b) Kerala Yesterday Today and Tomorrow with his Jaathi-Janmi-Naaduvazhi formulation of the Kerala feudal system, and (c) A History of the Indian Freedom Struggle, published originally through the columns of Desabhimani daily during the Emergency period.

He considered the completion of his recently published Marx Engels Lenin Vicharaprapancham, Oru Mukhavura as a major accomplishment. We happened to visit him on the day this work was completed and his face glowed when he said this to us.

Remembering E.M.S. Namboodiripad on his Hundredth Birth Centenary

More than eleven years have passed since E.M.S. Namboodiripad breathed his last in Thiruvananthapuram on March 19, 1998. Yet it seems as if it was only the other day that one walked into his room in the party office in the Capital for a refreshing conversation as one used to have with him and two of his party colleagues occupying leading positions in the CPI (M) as Polit Bureau members, B.T. Ranadive and M. Basavapunnaiah. They were the three stalwarts of the Indian communist movement, all of them renowned Marxist theoreticians whose lifelong passion had been realisation of the 'Indian revolution'. With their demise a whole age—an age which had produced, besides the aforementioned stalwarts, such eminent Communist revolutionaries as Muzaffar Ahmad, S.A. Dange, P.C. Joshi, P. Sundarayya, Ajoy Ghosh, S.V. Ghate, Dr. G. Adhikari, Bhowani Sen, Somnath Lahiri, Abdul Halim, Bankim Mukherjee, A.K. Gopalan, S.G. Sardesai, C. Rajeswara Rao, Bhupesh Gupta, C. Achutha Menon, C.K. Nayanar, P.K. Vasudevan Nair—came to an end. Thereafter two other dedicated and selfless Communists, Benoy Chowdhury and Indrajit Gupta, passed away and only recently we lost Harkishan Singh Surjeet, the person who succeeded E.M.S. as the CPI (M) General Secretary. The only Communist leader of eminence of those days still with us is Jyoti Basu. They gave up everything for the cause of the party and the goal of building a socialist society, a goal which remains unfulfilled to this day.

E.M.S. was all that and more. He was undoubtedly the tallest figure in the Indian communist movement by dint of being a combination of an ideologue and a mass leader—an uncommon combination indeed, something absent in his contemporaries with the exception of S.A. Dange, P.C. Joshi and P. Sundarayya. But Namboodiripad was different and perhaps that is precisely why he came closest to being regarded as a national leader from among the frontranking Communists in the country.

E.M.S. shot into international prominence when he headed the first Communist Government to come to power through the ballot in an Indian State (Kerala) in 1957. One is reminded of those days when he was warmly received at Palam Airport on his first visit to Delhi as the Kerala Chief Minister, and this writer—then a schoolboy of 12—had pinned on E.M.S.'s shirt a badge (he had prepared the previous night) bearing the hammer and sickle and the words: "Long Live the Communist Government in Kerala", only to receive an affectionate hug from the person who would live to be respected as the patriarch of the Indian communist movement.

The country and the world have undergone stupendous changes in these 52 years. E.M.S. himself had traversed a long distance since those heady days of 1957. The current situation is vastly different even from what prevailed in the seventies and eighties when one was privileged to have frequent meetings with BTR, MB and E.M.S. at the CPI (M) headquarters in New Delhi. And yet it is the memory of that crisp morning at Palam Airport that remains indelible in one's mind—in spite of the fact that five decades separate the present from that day. Why? Because in E.M.S.' smiling eyes one had seen at that time the first rays of the future, a future of hope and optimism for the continually suppressed and yet intensely resilient toiling people of our varied and diverse landmass.

Even today it is that future which beckons us to surmount the phenomenal difficulties attempting to block our collective advance and thereby smother our dreams of a new India.

E.M.S. had throughout the post-independence period tried to give shape to Left politics in India. Twenty-one years ago in 1988, he sought to draw a line demarcating the Left stand from the position of the BJP. Even though there was some blurring of that dividing line in the aftermath of the 1989 Lok Sabha poll when both the Left and the BJP extended support from outside to the V.P. Singh-led National Front Government at the Centre, that policy of E.M.S. has stood the test of time as the latest developments conclusively prove.

That policy was succinctly spelt out in an article he had exclusively written for Mainstream Annual 1988. One would like to conclude this humble tribute to the grand old man of Indian communism with the following words of E.M.S. from that article, words that retain their significance and validity even after twenty years:

"The differences between the Centrists and a party like the BJP may for the time being be papered over in the interests of the electoral unity of the Opposition. They would, however, come up prominently during the election campaign and particularly after the campaign ends in success. The question will then come: what policies will be pursued by the new Government? The Left will press for policies based on the principles of secularism and radical democracy. The BJP for its part will fight for its own approaches and policies. Will this not result in the same type of conflict in and come to the same end as the Janata Government of 1977-79?

> "Political developments of the period that began with the fall of the Indira Gandhi Government in 1977 have made it clear that those who oppose and fight the Congress are of different categories—Left and Right, secular and communal, those who stand for and oppose national unity on the basis of State autonomy, etc. It is idle for anybody to hope that all these can be brought under one omnibus united front, or that a Centrist force can pursue a policy of 'equidistance' with these forces."

On the occasion of E.M.S. Namboodiripad's birth centenary (he was born on June 13, 1909) we remember him by reproducing that article "Indian Left Today". We also carry tributes to E.M.S. from Ashok Mitra, Kuldip Nayar and Prabhat Patnaik that appeared in The Kaumudi (E.M.S. Namboodiripad Global Edition in English—October-December 2008) from where those are being reproduced with due acknowledgement.

4

Builder of Modern Kerala

EMS and Modern Kerala

To trace the political and intellectual career of E.M.S. Namboodiripad is to trace, in substantial measure, the history of the social, economic and political development of modern Kerala. No person has played as important a part in the socio-political and cultural life of a region of India for as long a period in the 20th century as has E.M.S. in Kerala.

As is now well known, Kerala's progress in crucial spheres of social and economic development has been substantial, and significantly better than other States of India. Consider some statistics that are often used by social scientists as indicators of social development, and from these, some of the changes that E.M.S. saw in a lifetime. In 1911-20, the years of E.M.S.'s childhood, the expectation of life at birth in the areas that make up modern Kerala was 25 years for men and 27 years for women. In 1990-92, men could expect to live 69 years and women 74 years (the corresponding figures for India in 1990-92 were 59 years and 59.4 years). The death rate in Kerala was 37 per 1,000 in 1911-1920 and 6.1 per 1,000 in 1990-92 (the All India figure in 1990-92 was 9.8). The infant mortality rate in Kerala, 242 per 1,000 live births in 1911-20, was 17 per 1,000 in 1992 (All India, 1992: 79). The birth rate in Kerala, 40 per 1,000 in 1931-40, was 18.5 per 1,000 in 1990-92 (All India, 1990-92: 29.5 per 1,000).

The people of 20th-century Kerala have altered radically a system of agrarian relations that was among the most complex, burdensome and exploitative in India, and have won important victories against some of the country's most monstrous forms of caste oppression. Public action in recent decades has narrowed the gap in health and educational facilities and achievements between the districts of the north and the districts of the south, a gap that widened during the period of colonial rule.

Modern Kerala and the Communist Movement

E.M.S. Namboodiripad straddled the history of 20th century Kerala and the Indian Communist movement in a manner which invokes awe. The word "history" is what recurs in the Malayalam media while paying tributes to him. History maker, history's man, epochal figure: these are some of the terms which underline the recognition that E.M.S. was something bigger than a successful political leader.

E.M.S. began his public activities in 1930, when as a student he participated in the Namboodiri social reform movement. The quest to "make the Namboodiri a human being" by breaking the shackles of hidebound uppercaste conservatism began the remarkable journey to the making of a proletarian revolutionary who strove to liberate the whole of humanity.

E.M.S., like many other potential Communist leaders, was a product of the major social and political movements of the early decades of the 20th century. As an activist in the social reform movement, he focused on the inhuman system which kept Namboodiri women in gilded bondage. Anti-caste revolt was the first spark. Next came the broader canvas of the anti-imperialist movement. He became a young leader of the Malabar Congress and one of the key organisers of the Congress Socialist Party.

The next big step in the background of the rising peasant struggles against landlordism was the introduction to Marxism and becoming a lifelong adherent to the cause of Communism. This trajectory of political development is mirrored in hundreds of militant young men and women who joined the Left movement in the 1930s.

Two things set E.M.S. apart from all of them and made him unique. First, E.M.S. with his extraordinary intellectual genius was able constantly to stay ahead of his contemporaries in applying Marxism to the specific conditions in Kerala and later the whole of India. He was a pathfinder. In 1939, even when his study of Marxism was elementary, he wrote a brilliant note of dissent on the Malabar Tenancy Reforms in the committee set up by the Madras Legislature, of which he was a member. The trenchant analysis of the jenmi (landlord) system and the advocacy of radical land reforms presaged his later pioneering role in initiating land reform measures as the first Chief Minister of Kerala in 1957.

This is only one example; there are many others. His The National Question in Kerala published in 1952 was the first creative application of the Marxist-Leninist approach to the nationality question to a specific nationality in India. This work brought him international attention in Marxist circles. He provided the historical basis for the development of the linguistic nationality of Malayalees, which translated into the foundation of Aikya Keralam, the unified linguistic State which was formed out of Travancore-Cochin and Malabar in 1954.

It is this quality in E.M.S. - of grasping the theoretical essence of the Marxist approach and translating it into political movements and practical solutions - which made him stand above most others. E.M.S. was not only a theoretician; he was a master of practice. The Kerala Communist movement was fortunate in having P. Krishna Pillai, the founder and master-organiser; A.K. Gopalan, the mass leader; and E.M.S. In the annals of the movement, history will record the pre-eminent position of E.M.S. in this brilliant trio who fused his immense theoretical abilities with unerring practical politics.

E.M.S. was also the most innovative in expounding the role of parliamentary democracy in India and relating Marxist strategy and tactics to developing the working-class movement in such conditions. From 1957 onwards, E.M.S. was the pacesetter in clarifying and developing the role of a Communist Party which participates in governments where it has popular mandates, while continuing to keep the major focus on developing mass movements and the struggles of the working people. Not for him the sterile sectarianism of abjuring the mass politics of parliamentary democracy or the crass parliamentary opportunism which many people comfortably slipped into. During his last days, E.M.S. was deeply concerned with the corrosive effects of parliamentarism, which subordinates the interests of the mass movements and the demands of class struggle.

The second outstanding quality which E.M.S. possessed and which made him a phenomenon rarely seen in India is his role in shaping society and politics by unleashing the democratic impulses of the people. Whether it was implementing land reforms to transform feudal Kerala, or creating the climate for an alternative vision within a parliamentary democratic system in a bourgeois state, or an ideological struggle against the dominant ideology of the ruling classes, E.M.S. was unparalleled in communicating to the people the necessity to organise and act. His was a life of democratic dialogue and polemical debates. It was a daily engagement with the people of Kerala and its politicians through the print media and his public meetings. What E.M.S. stated became part of the political discourse instantly. This, along with his personal example of intellectual commitment, integrity and simplicity, made him the most beloved thinker Kerala has produced. A.K. Antony, the Congress leader, expressed the feelings of all Malayalees when he said: "Kerala will not be the same again without E.M.S."

Kerala changed for the better in the 20th century due to the mass democratic endeavours of its working people. To an enormous extent, the credit for this goes to E.M.S. Namboodiripad.

Architect of Unified Kerala

Elankulam Manakkal Sankaran Namboodiripad aka E.M.S. as he was popularly known, was one of the architects of unified Kerala. He was renowned as a brave and committed socialist, historian and a marxian theorist. E.M.S. was born on June 13 1909 in Perinthalmanna taluk of the present Malappuram district.

In his early years itself, he was associated with V.T. Bhattathiripad, M.B. Bhattathiripad and many others to fight casteism and reactionary conservatism which existed in the Namboodiri community. He became one of the office bearers of Valluvanadu Yogakshema Sabha, an organisation of progressive Namboodiri youth. During his college days, he was deeply associated with the Indian National Congress and Indian Independence Struggle. In 1934, he joined the Congress Socialist Party, a socialist wing within Indian National Congress. Later he was elected as the Kerala State Congress secretary. His commitment to socialist ideals and compassion towards the downtrodden working class made him join the ranks of the Communists, for which he had to go in hiding for many years.

India achieved its independence in 1947 and the state of Kerala was formed in 1956. In 1957, E.M.S. led the Communists to victory in the first popular election. Soon he introduced the revolutionary Land Reform Ordinance and Education Bill, which caused the dismissal of his government by the central government using the controversial article 356 of the Indian Constitution. However, this had changed the outlook of Kerala society dramatically and laid the foundation for what has become known as the Kerala Model. Even during the later part of his life, he influenced Kerala society by his visions on decentralisation of power and resources (People's Plan) and the Kerala Literacy Movement.

Foremost Leader of the Communist Party

Comrade E.M.S. Namboodiripad was one of the foremost leaders of the Communist movement in India and one of the founding leaders of the Communist Party of India (Marxist).

In his nearly seven decades of public life and revolutionary activities, E.M.S. Namboodiripad left an indelible imprint on the progressive and working class movement of the country. As a young man, he became active in the social reform movement against caste. He left college in 1931 to join the freedom struggle and was jailed in the satyagraha movement. From then onwards, he played an important role in the Congress movement and was one of the founders of the Congress Socialist Party in Kerala. In

1934 he became the all India joint secretary of the Congress Socialist Party. It is in this period that E.M.S. while leading the Congress Party as General Secretary of the Kerala Pradesh Congress Party became acquainted with Marxism. He was one of the five members who formed the founding group of the Communist Party in Kerala in 1936. E.M.S. Namboodiripad represented the coming together of the two streams, the anti-imperialist and the anti-feudal struggles, which laid the foundations for the development of a powerful communist movement in Kerala. He was one of the key proponents of Aikya Kerala which led to the formation of Kerala as a unified linguistic state.

E.M.S. Namboodiripad was first elected to the Madras Provincial Legislative Assembly in 1939. As an important leader of the fledgling Communist Party he donated the proceeds of his landed property to the Party. He went underground building the Party in crucial periods between 1939-42 and 1948-50. He was elected to the Central Committee of the Communist Party of India in 1941. He became a member of the Polit Bureau of the CPI in December 1950 and later its Secretariat. He became General Secretary of the united CPI in 1962.

In 1957, after the state of Kerala was formed in the first elections in 1957, the Communist Party won a majority and E.M.S. Namboodiripad became Chief Minister of the first elected Communist ministry in India. It was the E.M.S. ministry which initiated the path breaking land reform legislation and other democratic measures, till the ministry was dismissed undemocratically in 1959. E.M.S. Namboodiripad became Chief Minister of Kerala again in 1967 heading a United Front ministry till 1969.

E.M.S. joined the leading group from the united Party who formed the CPI(M) and was elected to the Central Committee and the Polit Bureau of the Party at the Seventh Congress of the Party in 1964 and he continued to serve in these positions till his death.

E.M.S. Namboodiripad was elected the General Secretary of Central Committee of the Communist Party of India (Marxist) in 1977 and he led the Party in this capacity till the 14th Congress in 1992 when he stepped down due to ill-health. His leadership in rallying all the Left, democratic and secular forces was invaluable.

E.M.S. was a brilliant Marxist theoretician. He made outstanding contributions to the application of Marxism-Leninism to Indian society and in working out the strategy and tactics of the Indian revolution. His vast body of writings bear the mark of an original and creative mind which mastered the dialectics of Marxist theory. His writings on land relations, Kerala, society and politics and his writings on Marxist philosophy, literature and history — mark him out to be one of the most influential communist thinkers of the country and the world.

E.M.S. Namboodiripad was a rare example of a Communist leader who hailing from a traditional landlord family graduated to become the foremost leader of the proletarian revolutionary movement. He spent three years in jail and six years underground. His was a life of sacrifice and simplicity. He set an example which has inspired tens of thousands of communists all over the country. In Kerala he was a legend in his lifetime who was adored and respected by all sections of the people. Till the last day of his life, despite failing health, E.M.S kept to his daily routine of writing articles and providing guidance to the Party.

In S. Ramachandran Pillai's Words

The formation of the Communist government in Kerala headed by E.M.S. Namboodiripad on April 5, 1957 was hailed in India and across the world by the Left and progressive forces. The Communists had no previous experience of running a state government in India; neither were there any comparable precedence around the world where a Communist Party came to power by winning democratic elections.

The state government was of course constrained to work within the framework of the Constitution of India and the policies pursued by an antagonistic Central government, coupled with strident opposition from the Congress Party allied with various vested interests and caste and religious organisations. Despite this, the Communist government under the leadership of E.M.S. Namboodiripad took many pioneering steps to further people's interests through its policies in agriculture, industry, education, public health, public distribution system, social security measures, decentralisation of power, police policy, administrative reform, etc. People's active participation in the evolution and execution of these policies became the role model for subsequent state governments led by the Left parties in West Bengal, Kerala and Tripura. The experience of this Communist government contributed greatly to the evolution of the understanding of the Communist Party of India (Marxist) about the Party's participation in state governments.

Demarcating from the approach of Congress governments of relying upon landlords and other richer sections, the Communist government tried to unleash the creative energies and productive capacities of the common people. The people were encouraged to intervene in the evolution of policies and their execution. While making attempts to improve the functioning of the bureaucracy for better administration, the Communist government's thrust was on people's participation, even in the field of administration.

The Communist government was guided by the understanding that the correctness and efficacy of policies can only be ensured through people's active intervention in policy formulation and implementation. The policies of the Communist government combined with the intervention of the Communist party and mass organisations and the participation of the people, unleashed a process that brought about a shift in the balance of class forces in the state in favour of vast sections of the poor. It is this shift that has eventually enabled Kerala to achieve high levels of social development despite comparatively low levels of material production.

Industrialisation

The effort to develop industries in Kerala was a very difficult task due to various reasons. The Central government refused to locate any major public sector industries in Kerala. The state government did not have adequate financial resources to start public sector undertakings. The only alternative, therefore, was to encourage private industrialists to start new industries. There were difficulties in attracting entrepreneurs from outside the state, as there was incessant propaganda that with a Communist government in Kerala the employer-employee relations would not be congenial for establishing industries. The Communist government had to take determined steps to come out of these difficulties. It made public pronouncements that assistance would be provided for setting up new industries with healthy employer-employee relations. According to E.M.S., *"Settling disputes through negotiations, arriving at agreements and making sincere and serious efforts to implement agreements were the major planks of the government labour policy. The policies helped start several small and medium sized industrial units and two major ones."*

One of the large units to be started was under the ownership and management of G. D. Birla. The large-scale industrial unit of Gwalior Rayons was set-up on the basis of an agreement between the government and G. D. Birla after protracted negotiations. The unit provided employment to nearly 15,000 people together with trade and other subsidiary occupations.

Though the Central Committee of the Party subsequently noted some defects in the terms of agreement with G. D. Birla, it approved of the agreement as a whole since it would help find a partial solution to an immediate problem of the people. Industrialisation through the private sector was one of the means by which the backward economy of a resource starved state could be taken forward. Some other private industries proposed that the government should purchase certain number of shares if they set up industries in Kerala.

The positive response from the government helped in setting up several enterprises. If the government had been able to continue its work of industrialisation and other policies for the economic development of the state unhindered, Kerala and the people would have made much progress in the production of material values.

Agrarian Reforms

The most important contribution of the Communist government was in the sphere of agrarian reforms. The approach of the government was guided by the understanding of the Communist Party that the peasant question stood as a foremost national question. The government passed many legislations to help the peasantry solve their problems as well as redress different problems in agriculture, the Kerala Agrarian Relations Bill being the most decisive step.

The Statement of Policy announced by E.M.S. Namboodiripad on April 5, 1957 after taking oath as Chief Minister of Kerala explained the immediate aims of the Communist government on the agrarian question:

> It is acknowledged by all that the agrarian question in our State is rather complicated. This question will, therefore, require consultations with the various sections of the people concerned for working out the details of agrarian reforms. Certain broad lines of policy have already been worked out which can provide the basis for such discussion. These are the lines of policy laid down by the Land Reforms Panel of the Planning Commission. They have secured the support of such All India parties as the Congress, the Communist Party and the PSP as well as of several organisations representing the peasantry. Therefore, the above-mentioned consultations need not take a long time, but can be finished relatively quickly. Within a short and definitely-fixed time-limit, we expect to prepare one or more bills fixing fair rent, giving fixity of tenure to the tenant, fixing a ceiling on landholdings in keeping with the peculiar conditions of Kerala, distributing surplus land above the ceiling fixed, giving such safeguards as are legitimate for those small landholders who stand to lose by the above-mentioned reforms, etc. Since the peasants require some immediate relief while the above-mentioned reforms are being worked out, it will be necessary to bring in emergency legislation staying all evictions.

As promised in the Policy Statement, the government issued an ordinance on April 11 (just six days after forming the government) prohibiting all evictions of tenants, subtenants and occupants of homestead land on any ground including failure to pay rent. Furthermore, all court proceedings initiated by landlords against tenants, subtenants or occupants of homestead were stayed. The ordinance was issued as a prelude to the Agrarian Relations

Bill that the government intended to pass. The ordinance was necessary in view of past experiences with the Congress government wherein the period between the announcement of agrarian legislation and the date of actual enactment of the law would be used by landlords and vested interests to evict tenants in large numbers and to execute transfer deeds to evade the provisions of the law.

The ordinance was promulgated to prevent landlords and vested interests from resorting to those illegal practices. The prohibition of evictions shook land relations in Kerala. The Kisan Sabha and Agricultural Workers Union came to the forefront and actively intervened to stop all evictions, and wherever these organisations were weak, they gained strength and came forward to stop evictions. The law passed by the government and the active intervention by mass organisations, together protected the interests of tenants and occupants of homesteads.

Contrary to the land reform measures undertaken by the Congress state governments, the Agrarian Relations Act passed by the Kerala Legislative Assembly contained many important provisions to protect the genuine interests of tenants and occupants of homesteads. Other legislations defined the term 'tenant' so narrowly that large numbers of intended beneficiaries were excluded. But the new legislation introduced by the Communist government defined 'tenant' to include not only tenants but subtenants and every authorised or unauthorised occupant of a piece of land or a small patch of land on which a hut had been built. All such tenants were given fixity of tenure and they were not liable to be evicted for any reason whatsoever.

The land that was illegally evicted from certain tenants was also restored to them. The rent to be paid by the tenants was substantially reduced and they needed only to pay the fair rent fixed as per the provisions of the legislation. The tenant could purchase the proprietary rights of the land they cultivated by paying a comparatively lesser amount calculated on the basis of fair rent. Considering the density of population and the shortage of land, the Agrarian Relations Act provided for a low ceiling of land and made provisions for distribution of ceiling surplus land to the landless and poor peasants through the involvement of popular committees. The rights of the occupants of homesteads were protected. All transfers of land made to avoid the provisions of the law (after the publication of the Act on December 18, 1957) were made null and void. Protection was given to small owners and trusts without adversely affecting the genuine interest of tenants and agricultural workers.

The other important provision of the law was that elected people's representatives would be involved in the proper implementation of the provisions of the law. Committees of the Communist Party, Kisan Sabha and Agricultural Workers Union at all levels from the state to the village level were engaged in the process of consultation, conflict resolution and reconciliation for framing the provisions of the law.

It was the outcome of a genuinely collective and participative effort.

E.M.S. explained this process in his book, *The Communist Party in Kerala – Six Decades of Struggle and Advance* as follows:

> The process of land legislation was a complicated one because different kinds of tenures existed in each of the three regions of Malabar, Cochin and Travancore. The minister who presided over the work of drafting the Bill spent sleepless nights and discussed the law with a very wide variety of persons who presented their points of view to the government for its consideration. The state committee of the Party, the Party legislature group and committees of the Kisan Sabha at all levels from state to the village were all engaged in the near interminable process of consultation, conflict and attempts at reconciliation. The process was so time consuming that it took place nearly two years between the introduction of the Bill and its final adoption in the Assembly.

The Ordinance, which prohibited evictions and the final Bill adopted in June 1959 marked a new stage in the economic and sociocultural life of the people of Kerala. E.M.S. Namboodiripad gave great importance to the Ordinance and the passing of Agrarian Relations Bill:

> It ended the economic oppression and the sociocultural domination by a small minority of the upper castes on the mass of the rural poor. The sociocultural movements of over half a century that were directed against caste domination, outmoded systems of family organisation and obscurantist beliefs and practices culminated in the release of the rural masses from every kind of exploitation and oppression. Even if it had to its credit only the enactment of the Agrarian Relations Bill, the 28 month existence of the Communist government would find a place in the history of modern democratic Kerala. (Emphasis added) (The Communist Party in Kerala – Six Decades of Struggle and Advance)

The Agrarian Relations Bill was opposed by the landlords, Nair Service Society, certain Christian organisations, Indian National Congress, Praja Socialist Party and Indian Union Muslim League. Within hours of the closure of the Assembly session during which the Bill was passed, these sections unleashed what they called a "liberation struggle" to bring down the Communist government in Kerala. The government was dismissed by the Congress Central government on July 31, 1959.

The President did not give assent to the Bill but it was returned with a directive to regularise all transfer of land made by landowners in between December 18, 1957 when the Bill was published and on July 27, 1960 when the Bill was returned by the President to the Kerala Legislative Assembly. The Congress-led state government was formed after the Communist government brought an amendment to that effect.

It is to be noted here that the number of transfers executed during this period was more than one million. Many lakhs of landless people and agricultural workers lost many benefits including land they would have got had the original provisions remained. That was the price that vested interests extracted for sabotaging the agrarian relations legislation and by dismissal of the Communist government.

The Congress-led government which came into power after the dismissal of the Communist government could not give up the agenda of land reforms altogether and was forced to pass a land reform legislation with dilutions in many provisions of the original Agrarian Relations Act. The people's upsurge unleashed by the introduction of Agrarian Relations Bill could not be ignored by the Congress-led government that came into office after the Communist government was dismissed.

The debt relief legislation passed by the Communist government also gave great relief to indebted peasants and agricultural workers. The government also passed a legislation to regulate private money lending. The maximum interest rate was fixed at 9 per cent. The passage of the Kerala Compensation for Tenants Improvement Act 1958 ensured adequate compensation for lessee, sub-lessee, mortgagee and sub-mortgagee of land.

Government land was distributed to the landless and agricultural workers with the involvement of popular committees comprising of representatives from all political parties. This ensured transparency and equity in land distribution.

Minimum wages were fixed for agricultural workers. The government also took certain steps to ensure fair prices for agricultural produces. A State Trading Corporation and many marketing societies were organised to help the peasantry.

New Orientation towards Development and Production of Material Values

The Communist government gave a new orientation to the concept of development by giving importance to the production of material goods while preserving and making efforts for expansion of areas such as education, public health, social security measures, communication, etc. E.M.S. had consistently stressed the importance of increasing the production of material values:

> The idea was to be hammered home to our people that none of their problems for example, the food crisis or unemployment (in respect of both, all these problems Kerala was worse of than the rest of the country) could be solved unless there was an orientation towards the production of material values.

(The Communist Party in Kerala – Six Decades of Struggle and Advance)

Major steps were taken in that direction. A vigorous drive was launched for increasing agricultural production. The drive to start a large number of small irrigation works with the cooperation of the people and the drive for large-scale use of green manure were very significant steps in that direction. Various forms of cooperative societies were organised for strengthening small and cottage industries. Efforts were made to start large-scale industries in the private sector with or without State participation.

5

A Literary and Cultural Icon

When we ponder over the contribution made by E.M.S. Namboodiripad (1909-1998) to the literary, artistic and cultural life of Kerala, and the intermittent interventions he made in the intellectual and literary controversies in Malayalam during the last seven decades or so, we are reminded of Frederick Engels' evaluation of the renaissance personalities of Europe: In his celebrated but unfinished work Dialectics of Nature, Engels spoke of them as the "giants in power of thought, passion and character, in universality and learning". After listing and describing a few of them he continues:

> "The heroes of that time were not yet in thrall to the division of labour, the restricting effects of which, with its production of onesideness, we often notice in their successors. But what is especially characteristic of them is that they almost all live and pursue their activities in the midst of contemporary movements, in the practical struggle; they take sides and join in the fight, one by speaking and writing another with sword, many with both. Hence, the fullness and force of character that makes them complete men".

If we resort to our ancient Indian usage E.M.S. was a rare combination of the "Gnana Yogin" and "Karma Yogin". Besides being a working class revolutionary, Marxist-Leninist theoretician of eminence, a party-builder he could easily switch over from underground to over-ground, from prison to street demonstration, from editorial desk to legislature, from opposition to treasury benches and prove his versatility as an administrator par excellence. It is with all these heavy claims on his routine and energy, that E.M.S. made himself a vibrant and seminal force in Malayalam literary life as a critic, historian and cultural activist.

But his cultural and literary activism and prodigious number of articles, tracts, pamphlets, full-scale books, reviews, columns, and addresses resulting from them were in no way a diversion from his main concerns. Like all revolutionaries in general, and socialist revolutionaries in particular, E.M.S. was convinced, in his early social reformer stage by instinct and later political stage by deep study and experience, that culture was of decisive significance in human affairs, both for the cementing of power structure and for altering it.

With this deep understanding of the role of culture in society and social transformation, E.M.S. was pleasantly surprised and inspired when he discovered the epoch-making Prison Notebooks of Antonio Gramsci. Though E.M.S. knew of Antonio Gramsci, the great Italian anti-fascist martyr and Marxist for a long time, somehow he had missed reading him thoroughly till very late in his life. So when in the early nineties, he came across Gramsci's Prison Notebooks, he was almost overwhelmed by his range and depth of thought and the significance and relevance of Gramscian thought to contemporary Marxism and revolutionary practice. True to his character E.M.S. called for his other works and after reading them, straightaway set out to write a book on Gramsci. This writer was asked to collaborate and the result is one of his last significant books Gramscian Revolution in Thought, (1996) in Malayalam (Gramscian Vichara Viplavam).

The reason why Gramsci so overwhelmed him is easily explained. For long decades E.M.S. through deep study, wide experience and practice was actually groping towards the ideas and theories brilliantly worked out by Gramsci with help of his innovative concepts like civil society, political society, ideology, culture, hegemony — or to be more accurate, with the new dimensions of meaning he invested them with. Instead of limiting the role of culture and ideology as a derivative superstructure, Gramsci seemed to confirm E.M.S.'s view of culture as a positive catalytic agent in social transformation. Though the idea of the superstructure positively acting on the basis is not alien to classical Marxism, it was Gramsci who worked out and enriched the idea in a more scientific and thorough manner, drawing from the rich experience of countries with bourgeois parliamentary systems. So E.M.S. considered Gramscian insights particularly relevant to the Indian working class movement. This also shows how E.M.S.'s mind was alert and open to new ideas even in his mature age.

Years of Formation

This long process of the evolution of E.M.S.'s thought on art, literature and culture, which may be said to have rounded up with the discovery and interpretation of Gramsci, began in the twenties of this century when he was a student activist in the social reform movement in his Namboodiri Brahmin community. "Yoga Kshema Sabha", formed just a year before the birth of E.M.S., was the main organisation of the Namboodiris for social reform. It was in the hands of moderate conservatives when E.M.S. and a band of young radicals like V.T. Bhattathiripad, M.R. Bhattathiripad, M.P. Bhattathiripad and others began to be active in the Sabha. Women's education, right of widows to remarriage, abolition of polygamy, etc., were on the militant agenda of the youngsters. Thrissur was the centre of the young Namboodiri activists.

E.M.S. joined St. Thomas College in 1929 for his intermediate course and immediately found himself in the whirlwind of action. In the same year Unninamboodiri, the monthly organ of the Sabha, began to appear as a weekly and it was almost taken over by the young group. Though some older people were in charge, 20-year old E.M.S. became its *de facto* editor and main contributor. Even before he turned 20, E.M.S. was noted as a contributor to the magazine and so they were all very confident that this young man could fulfil the task credibility - and he did. Articles, columns, reports on activities, book reviews and literary dissertations flowed in succession from E.M.S.'s pen. E.M.S. wrote in his autobiography that the Unninamboodiri was the workshop where he had his apprenticeship in writing and editing including literary criticism. He also said that his apprenticeship in public life was complete in the three years (1929-32) that he spent in college.

Though he was a very brilliant and hard working student, winning admiration of both his teachers and classmates, he was unable to resist the call of the civil disobedience movement raging all over India under the leadership of Mahatma Gandhi and left the college before taking the degree. He went to Kozhikkode and offered Satyagraha which landed him in prison.

The Gandhi-Irwin pact of 1932 which brought the movement to an abrupt end deeply disappointed E.M.S. alongwith the radical and young elements in the Congress all over India. E.M.S. and his close colleagues like P. Krishna Pillai, A.K. Gopalan and others came out of prison very disillusioned with Gandhi and the right-wing leadership of the Congress. In Kannur central prison these young radical Congressmen had opportunities to meet a number of militant revolutionaries from Bengal, dubbed "terrorists" and a new world of Left-wing and radical thought was opened up before them.

Coming out of prison E.M.S. found himself a famous man, distinguished much more than his age and experience would warrant. Moothiringot Bhavathrathan Namboodiripad, a well-known man of letters and very senior to E.M.S. in age and experience invited E.M.S. to write an introduction to his landmark novel "Uncle's Daughter" (Aphante Makal, 1933). The novel depicts the plight of younger brothers in Brahmin families due to the system of primogeniture and the emotional and legal contradictions resulting from its system of inheritance. Though E.M.S. was not yet a Marxist, his introductory essay shows very well how he was groping towards Marxist concepts of social and literary criticism.

It is during these formative years that E.M.S. and his young colleagues began to explore the potential of the performing arts in social and political struggle. In the same year E.M.S. joined the college (i.e., 1929) his senior colleague in the Yogakshema Sabha, V.T. Bhattathiripad wrote a play named "From Kitchen to the Arena (Adukkalayil Ninnu Arangathekku). It vividly portrayed the inequities and oppression suffered by Namboodiri women and the revolt against them. Though E.M.S. did not venture into creative writing after some adolescent exercises in poetry, he was a live-wire organiser of drama troupes and performances. V.T.'s play was a tremendous success on stage and its successive performances created quite a stir in the community. It was followed by some others like "The Great Hell in Face-covering Umbrella" (Marakkudakkullile Mahanarakam) and the "Pubescent Girl" (Ritumathi) and others. The climax of these series of resurgent plays was K. Damodaran's "Arrears of Rent" (Pattabakki) (1937).

Jeevat Sahitya Movement

Unlike the earlier ones which dealt with social and family problems, Damodaran's pioneering play directly took up the issue of class struggle between landlords and tenants. It was preceded by the first narrative poem on the same theme by the young rebel poet Changampuzha Krishna Pillai, "The Bunch of Bananas" (Vazhakkula). This progress from VT's social classic to Damodaran's saga of class struggle coincided with the metamorphosis of the social and political climate of Kerala. The decade from 1929 to 1939 marked a crucial turning point in the history of Kerala — we may even say that the contours of modern Kerala were drawn during this decade. In this decade of flux and ferment, the year 1937 may be characterised as the fulcrum. In 1937 the northern part of Kerala which was directly under the British rule in Madras Presidency (unlike the native princely states Kochi and Travancore in the south) had a foretaste of democracy — Rajagopalachari formed the Congress Ministry in the Presidency under the Government of India Act of 1935. The year witnessed the formation of the first unit of the Communist Party of India with P. Krishna Pillai (Secretary), E.M.S. Namboodiripad, N.C. Shekhar and K. Damodaran. A year before, all the Hindu temples in Travancore state were thrown open to the so-called untouchable castes and next year witnessed massive struggle of Travancore for representative government.

To crown all these historic events, Kerala Jeevat Sahitya Sanghom (Association for Kerala's living literature), the initial form of the Purogamana Sahitya Sanghom (Progressive Writers

Association, PWA) was established in 1937. The inspiration for this came from the founding conference of the Indian Progressive Writers Association under the chairmanship of the famous Hindi writer Prem Chand at Lucknow in 1936. The initiative was taken by a group of young Left-wing Congressmen including E.M.S., K. Damodaran, A. Madhavan, K.P.G. Namboodiri and K.A. Damodara Menon. E.M.S. was the ideological head of the group which met at Thrissur. He published an article in the Mathrubhumi weekly (19 July 1937) titled "Jeevat Sahithyavum Soundarya Bodhavum" (Living Literature and Sense of Beauty) which served as the initial manifesto of the movement. In this article E.M.S. replied to the criticism that progressive literature denied or at least downgraded the role of beauty. This was perhaps the first serious attempt to apply social, historical and Marxist criteria in the evaluation of art and literature in Malayalam. Both the founding of the PWA and E.M.S.'s article in 1937 were epoch-making events which served as the launching pads for the great takeoff movement in Malayalam literature and arts during the next 60 years.

In his introduction to a collection of his early articles in 1974 E.M.S. evaluates these events and the development that followed thus:

"When the Jeevat Sahitya movement took shape in 1937, the central controversial issue between its founders and traditional writers was this": "Whether art is for art's sake or for the sake of social progress?" The protagonists of Jeevat Sahitya argued that the aim of literature should not be just social progress in general. The central thrust of social progress should be politics of anti-imperialism, anti-feudalism and socialism, they asserted. The other side opposed this.

"Those who took initiative to form the Jeevat Sahitya Movement were actively associated with Left-wing politics and peasant and working class movements including those who participated in the civil disobedience movement of 1930-32. Later by about 1943-44 many writers of established fame joined the movement and accepted the policy of "writing for social progress" with "definite social ideals". With this changed scenario an expanded Progressive Writers Movement was formed in which both the Left-wing political activists and those who were not so active participated. (In 1944, at the instance of E.M.S. the name of the organisation also was changed to Purogamana Sahitya Sanghom — Progressive Writers Association — in tune with the All India practice — PG)

"By this time it may be said that the controversy around the slogan "Art for Art's sake" almost subsided. But differences again arose on the question of what constitutes social progress. These differences became still more acute after the British left the Indian shores and the regime fell into the hands of Congress". (Marxism and Malayalam Literature, 1974)

Political Dimensions

These differences developed into a furious public controversy, which took overt political dimensions. The literary and philosophical attacks on Communists coincided with the reign of terror unleashed by the Congress governments against the Communists and the mass movements led by them. From underground shelters and under pseudonyms, Communists hit back at their detractors. The bloody clashes which took place in various centres in Kerala like Kavumbai, Munayankunnu, Padikunnu, Pariyaram, Onchiam and the heroic tales of the Telangana struggle gave a particularly sharp edge to the spirited response of the Communists.

The political line of the CPI adopted at the 2nd Congress at Calcutta which was later to be given up as sectarian, rendered a self-righteous tone to the Communists repartees. All these led to a split in the PWA in 1949 and some of the highly respected supporters and leaders of the movement such as critics M.P. Paul and Joseph Mundassery, creative writers like Thakazhi Shiva Sankara Pillai and P. Kesavadev crossed over the fence to the other side and Communists and their close associates were isolated. E.M.S. alongwith a band of highly talented Marxists like M.S. Devadas, C. Unniraja, K.K. Warrier and others put up a stiff fight on behalf of the Marxists. Though the Communists' position was flawed on a number of points the controversy was not a futile exercise. That is why even while accepting the mistakes of those days E.M.S. ventured to republish those articles without any correction. Though E.M.S. was very frank and unreserved in owning up the mistakes he and his comrades committed in those traumatic years, he was totally opposed to those among the friends and foes who could see only the negative aspects and no positive elements at all.

In politics as in cultural thought and practice the Communist even when they occasionally deviated, were basically driving towards the chosen ideal. A judicious balance sheet of those years as well as perhaps the later years, could never show the debit out-balancing the credit. E.M.S. says:

"In the period 1947-52, we were participating in literary debates without fully understanding the current developments in Marxist-Leninist theory of literature. Besides, as was admitted earlier, there were serious deviations in the political practice followed by the Communist Party. These two factors contributed to the mistakes in the first four articles of this collection.

"Considering all these circumstances it might seem surprising that more mistakes and deviations did not enter these writings. There is reason for that. The reason is that Communists had a basic class approach which could not be neutralised by just a few ideological lapses and practical deviations.

The socio-political outlook they held on firmly to was one based on the toiling sections of the people in general and the working class in particular. The mistakes and deviations occurred in the course of practical activities based on this outlook. Communists ought to have realised these mistakes and tried to strengthen this outlook overcoming those drawbacks. But instead of doing that there was a revisionist attempt to give up the class outlook altogether. It was this which led to the split in the Communist Party.

> "This tendency became wide spread in the literary and cultural field, as it did in the practical politics. The trend of totally condemning the ideological struggle carried on by the Communists against non-Communists went to the extent of even rejecting the basic Marxist positions altogether". *(Ibid)*

Literary Issues

Apart from the overt political controversies between the Communists and non-Communists, there emerged two contentious issues which were more of a literary character than political. The first of these, as we saw earlier was around the slogan of "Art for Art's sake". Though the controversy subsided to a large extent by 1943-44, when the PWA was reorganised with the widest possible participation of writers of different political and ideological persuasions, some points still remained unresolved.

The post-independence period, and especially 1950s brought in a number of Marxist classics and writing on Marxist aesthetics by authors like Christopher Caudwell, Ralf Fox, Georg Lukacs, Franz Mehring and others. All these helped E.M.S. and other Marxist critics to deepen their understanding of literary issues. Armed with these new insights and enriched by the experience of literary activism of about a decade and half, E.M.S. introduced some new ideas in Malayalam literary criticism. These may be summarised in his own following words:

> "That literary production should have a social ideal to realise, that the writer should write with the objective of social progress — all these are incontrovertible. But the problem is not resolved by asserting this alone. Because, there are great men and women of letters in world literature, who were not conscious of the ideals which emerge out of their creations. But the creations of many of them directly serve the cause of social progress. But when they were composing their works they may not have been conscious of any such ideals. On the contrary, there are instances of writers who were subjectively holding views opposing social progress but wrote works which went against their subjective predilections".

To prove this argument, E.M.S. relied on what Marx and Engels wrote on the great French novelist Honore de Balzac and Lenin on Leo Tolstoy. Though Balzac was a royalist and feudal loyalist, his great realistic novels depicted the degeneration of feudalism and the vibrance of the new classes of bourgeoisie and the proletariat.

The possibility of the subjectivity of a writer coming into conflict with the objectivity of his text opens up wider vistas of literary and artistic evaluation. E.M.S. cited the examples of the outstanding Malayalam novelist Chandu Menon and the great innovator of Malayalam poetry in the 20th century, Mahakavi Kumaran Asan to prove his contention.

The 19th century novelist Chandu Menon was subjectively a supporter of the joint family system and matrilineal inheritance. But his great novel Indulekha happens to be a sharp critique of these outdated and harmful practices. Kumaran Asan who revolutionised 20th century Malayalam poetry was a great fighter against the caste system, himself belonging to an "untouchable" caste. He distrusted the upper caste leaders of the national movement and gave the impression of being a supporter of the alien rulers, receiving presents and titles from them. But Vallathol, a contemporary of Asan was an ardent nationalist both in his life and poetry. It was conventional wisdom of the literary critics to extol Asan for his anti-casteism, but condemn his alleged anti-national stand. E.M.S. did not agree with this. He pointed out that the freedom movement was a multifaceted and multi-stream phenomenon and the anti-caste struggle was an important strand which strengthened the movement for national liberation. To underestimate the role of the struggle of the Dalits in the freedom movement is like underestimating the role of workers' and peasants' class struggle in the fight for freedom. In fact, Gandhi and the right-wing leaders opposed such class struggles alleging that such antagonisms will alienate the bourgeoisie and landlords who could be mobilised against the British.

This Marxist position advocated and applied by E.M.S. helped to give a new dimension to literary criticism in Malayalam and more thorough and analytical attention to the text proper. This also paved the way for broadening the base of the united movement of writers and artists and to heal the wounds inflicted by sectarian infighting.

Form and Content

The second important issue which in the late forties and early fifties led to furious controversies was about the relative primacy of form and content. The Left-wingers in the movement with E.M.S. at its head argued for the primacy of content over form. Though in his landmark article in 1937 E.M.S. took a judicious and balanced position with regard to the question of form and content, his articles from underground with the pseudonym "P.S.", tended to take an extreme position on the decisive role of content in a work of art. The opponents under the able captainship of Prof. Joseph Mundassery who was later to be the Education Minister in the first E.M.S. Ministry, and a powerful supporter of PWA, and the Communist movement, took an equally extreme position on "form". He coined the phrase "Roopa Bhadrata" as against "Bhava Bhadrata", "perfect form" and "perfect content" respectively. The controversy, quoting "chapter and verse" by both sides raged on for months and years.

The new political climate of the 1950s, celebrated by some historians as the "Red Decade" of Kerala, took all these controversies in its stride and it is hard to pinpoint when these controversies concluded. Actually issues did not die out and were to raise their heads again and again during the next decades.

E.M.S. watered down his extreme position on content and went back to his original stand of 1937 in the early fifties itself. But a final solution to the problem of form and content and the whole controversy with Mundassery and others had to wait for few more decades.

In a series of lectures (1975) at Chennai E.M.S. made a sharp correction of his view on the primacy of form. He borrowed the ideas in Engels' letters to Minna Kautsky (1885) and Margaret Harkness (1888) to adduce support for the correction. But it was in 1995 in course of a lecture in Perinthalmanna that he made a full assessment of the whole controversy. In it he turned upside down the very terms of the controversy as it was carried on in the late forties and early fifties. He resurrected the classic philosophical stand of Marxism and asserted the unity and complementarity of form and content and rejected as un-Marxian the dichotomy of form and content. Form is the mode of existence of content and content is what is contained in the form. Though it is quite legitimate for us to consider form and content apart for the purposes of analysis and study, it would be absurd and unscientific to tear one from the other as irreconcilable categories. Therefore, not only the "Bhava Bhadras" like himself but also "Roopa Bhadras" like Mundassery were in the wrong, E.M.S. said. To quote him in detail:

"When we own up our mistakes some people interpret as if we alone were in the wrong. The fact is that just as we did, they also committed mistakes. If in the debate on Roopa Bhadrata we erred, people like Mundassery also erred equally.

"It is the fact of life that a truth emerges out of a conflict between two wrongs. The development of society is through contradictions. Thus the Roopa Bhadrata argument which arose out of our conflict was wrong, in another sense it was correct too. Evaluating the worth of literature we should never confine ourselves to content alone. Mundassery was correct in insisting that form too is to be evaluated. In his own words it is not enough to have perfect content, it must also have perfect form. That is Roopa Bhadrata. Is that not correct? Yes, it is. We accept that we were wrong on that count. Those of us who founded the Jeevat Sahitya Sanghom were political workers. We looked at literature too through political eyes. So we did not pay sufficient attention to the artistic structure of literature. That was our mistake.

> "But when people like Mundassery tried to correct us, they viewed form and content as two separate categories and argued for perfection in both. That was their theory. In fact the form and content are not so separate of conflicting categories. For progressive content there must be progressive form. The progressive form is the same as perfect form. Those like Mundassery did not realise the relation between the two."
>
> *(Literary Debate — Sahitya Samvadam, 1996)*

This argument is not hairsplitting or pettifogging. The dichotomy of form and content and evaluation of each separately is based on an unstated assumption that in order to make literary and artistic creation perfect there are some hoary rules of composition and styles of presentation and any deviation from them would be unsuitable. Such assumptions do not accept as legitimate the continuous process of change in artistic and literary forms, to suit the changing ethos and values of society, and the resulting changes in people's taste.

Perfect Form, Perfect Content

Not only did E.M.S. theoretically accept the concept of perfect form for perfect content. He applied these criteria in evaluating progressive literature and arts and sharply criticised works of progressive art when their form failed to do justice to the progressive content. For example, his criticism of the Communist hero in the famous play "You made me a Communist" is well-known. "You made me a Communist" was the first significant production of the Kerala Peoples Art Club (KPAC) organised by the CPI in the 1950s.

It was a tremendous success on stage and people went to the extent of claiming that the victory of the Communists at the hustings in 1957 was due to the whirlwind campaign that this play conducted. The Congress government of the erstwhile Travancore-Cochin state was stupid enough to ban this play and lifted the ban when a furore of popular protest shook it to its roots.

The play was written by a well-known Communist playwright Thoppil Bhasi. His is a name to contend within the annals of Kerala's performing arts. In spite of all these points in favour of this play E.M.S. with his keen eye could detect a major flaw in the characterisation of the Communist hero. E.M.S. summarises his criticism as follows:

"A brief reference may be appropriate here to a particular flaw in the progressive plays staged in Kerala. A large number of these plays are acknowledged even by non-Communist critics to be of high artistic value. They are openly tendentious, conveying the message of working class or peasant struggles.

"You Made Me A Communist, for instance, took the people of Kerala by storm. All sections of the people, from the illiterate agricultural labourers to the most sophisticated intellectual, paid enthusiastic tribute to the author, producer, actors and to other artists connected with its staging. There was, however, one major defect in this particular play as well as in most other plays produced and staged by the revolutionary progressive writers and artistes in order to convey the message of the struggle of the toilers.

> "In contrast to those characters in the play through whom the author succeeded in portraying realistically the various manifestations of social conflicts, the characters who present the cadres of the Communist Party are invariably lifeless. The landlords or capitalists at one end; and the oppressed agricultural labourers, tenant cultivators, industrial workers and other toiling people at the other, with their families and surroundings — these are all portrayed true to life. The class and social struggles through which they live are realistically portrayed. But when it comes to portraying a live, active cadre of the Communist Party the author fails, making the `comrade' talk and behave in such a way that we are led to exclaim: "If the leading Communists are so boring, how did this Party take roots among the People?".

"In other words, the thoughts and emotions of characters typical of ordinary men and women engaged in class and social conflicts in general are expressed in live images but the characters representing the cadres of the Communist Party are created not from life but out of the author's preconceived notions. The thoughts and emotions of the author regarding the Party are conveyed abstractly, not in live images.

> "Communist writers and critics must apply themselves as much to the study of the laws according to which man's capacity to imagine develops as to the study of the laws guiding the development of man's thinking capacity".

(Marxism and Literature, Chennai, 1975)

A Theoretical Issue

Another important theoretical issue E.M.S. had to clarify in defence of Marxism was the relation between basis and superstructure. From a superficial reading of Marx's class description of basis and superstructure in his preface to A Contribution to the Critique of

Political Economy (1859) a section of Marx's followers as well as opponents have come to the conclusion that the superstructure of ideology is only a derivation of the economic basis, it was no more than a lifeless mirror reflection. Such an understanding tend to deny art, literature and culture any positive role in social life or transformation. This oversimplification reduces dialectical materialism to mechanical materialism and distorts historical materialism to a deterministic dogma or a teleological construct.

Quoting Engels' letter to J. Bloch in 1890, E.M.S. refuted this simplistic understanding for the benefit of both friends and foes. Engels clarified in this famous letter:

> "According to the materialist conception of history the ultimately determining element in history is the production and reproduction of real life. More than this neither Marx nor I have ever asserted. Hence, if somebody twists this into saying that the economic element is the only determining one, he transforms that proposition into a meaningless, abstract senseless phrase".

E.M.S. frankly admits that among those who misread Marx in this fashion were himself and other comrades in the early years. He says:

> "It would be a grievous error — and this was precisely the error committed by us in our polemics against our non-Communist colleagues — to think that aesthetic production is more or less an exact copy of class struggle in its economic or political forms."
> (Marxism and Literature)

Then he goes on to explain the intricate and sometimes elusive relation between class struggle and social realities on the one hand and aesthetic production on the other. He says:

> "Class struggle is, of course, relevant and crucial to aesthetic production and appreciation, as it is to every other form of social activity. This is a truth worth repeating and emphasising, since it is denied by non-Communists. It should be clearly borne in mind,

however, that the class struggle manifests itself in the field of aesthetic production in a way different from other fields, and that aesthetic production and appreciation have their own laws independent of, though related to, laws in other fields". *(Ibid)*

Besides silencing the detractors, this clarification of E.M.S. has helped young Marxist writers and critics to steer themselves clear of the pitfalls of crudity and easy sloganising.

Literary and Cultural Movement

All these explorations, discoveries and clarifications in theory and practice of Marxism was possible for E.M.S. and his comrades not by delving deeper into the classics alone but also from the experience of building the literary and cultural movement of Kerala.The PWA was born as Jeevat Sahitya Sanghom in 1937 and registered phenomenal growth in the next decade and then split into Communist and non-Communists pieces towards the close of the forties. The reason for the split was partly the faulty line pursued by Communists and partly the inevitable new alignments of forces after the transfer of power, mainly the split in the anti-imperialist front of pre-independence era. We have also dealt briefly with the process of introspection of self-criticism undertaken by E.M.S. and other comrades and the series of steps taken by them in the following decades to enrich the Marxist and progressive understanding and practice of literature and arts.

But as an organisation the PWA did not survive long after the split in 1948-49. Outstanding leaders of All India PWA like Mulk Raj Anand, Harindranath Chattopadhyay, Kishan Chander, K.A. Abbas, and Balraj Sahni visited the state several times and spoke to young audiences. E.M.S. with the able assistance of M.S. Devadas, Unni Raja, Damodaran, Achutha Kurup and others with the blessings of the patriarchal figure Mahakavi Vallathol carried on their ideological and practical literary campaign. All these gave a great fillip to the movement and salvaged very much the damages inflicted by the split. A new generation of young writers, poets and playwrights like Vayalar Ramavarma, ONV Kurup, Thoppil Bhasi, P.J. Antony, K.T. Muhammed emerged on the scene. Old pioneers of the PWA like Thakazhi, Basheer, Varkey,

Cherukat, Pottakkad and others who were only short-story writers blossomed into powerful novelists. A number of highly talented poets like Vyloppilly Sreedhara Menon and Edassery Govindan Nair, who were younger to the famed trio of 20th century Malayalam poetry, viz, Asan, Ulloor, and Vallathol but senior to Vayalar and ONV like Vyloppilly and Edassery significantly contributed to revolutionising the Malayalam poetic life of the latter half of the century. A new set of innovative writers like M.T. Vasudevan Nair, Madhavikutty (Kamala Das), T. Padmanabhan entered the arena of story telling. They were not associated with PWA, and were not content with the old realism of pioneers, but their innovations enriched the corpus of progressive writing.

Performing arts like theatre and visual arts like film and plastic arts like painting and sculpture also showed new signs of awakening in 1950s. We have already mentioned KPAC among the performing arts groups. Others which made a mark in this field in the 1950s were the Pratibha Arts Club of P.J. Antony, (Bharat Award winner for acting in Cinema) Kendra Kala Samity of K.T. Muhammed and others and Sakti group of Cherukat. In all these and the slowly growing Malayalam cinema the most influential creators and performers were all under the influence of the PWA. To crown all these developments in literary and art fields the political scene in Kerala was assuming a deep red hue.

In 1956 the united Kerala state was formed as part of the All India state reorganisation and in the general elections which took place in 1957 Communists came to power in the state with E.M.S. Namboodiripad, the most articulate theoretician of and campaigner for the unification of Kerala, as the Chief Minister. No wonder some authors dubbed the fifties as the Red Decade of Kerala. With all these all-round advances in literature, arts and politics it may seem strange, but is true that, the PWA as an organisation did not take any roots. But the movement flourished and progressive literary and artistic production increased unprecedently.

Dawn and Sunset

The red dawn of the 1950s began to fade by the 1960s before reaching its apoqee and the literary sky was overcast by dark clouds. This decline started from the rise and temporary victory of the anti-Communist front in getting the duly elected government of E.M.S. undemocratically dismissed. The political anti-Communist front comprising Congress, social democrats, communalists and casteists with the support of the church and mullas, spread out to literary and cultural fields. Ex-Communist forums and anti-Communist writers associations, some with the support of the CIA-financed Congress for cultural freedom made their entry into the state for the first time.

The India-China border conflict, in 1962, the split in the Communist movement, and the consequential developments threw the Left movement into temporary disarray. Some weak-kneed Leftists and opportunists found it safe and advantageous to cross over to the right. Some Communist writers like Thoppil Bhasi and Vayalar Rama Varma found greener pastures in commercial films.

Some talented writers like O.V. Vijayan, M. Mukundan, Kakkanadan, M.P. Narayana Pillai, and Kakkad who were known for their Left-wing association adopted the so-called modernist garb and virtually adopted the leadership of hidebound anti-Communists like M. Govindan and C.J. Thomas. The split in the Communist party and the incarceration of thousands of CPI(M) leaders and cadres were a further blow.

Though E.M.S. was still occasionally writing on literary and cultural issues, the major share of his time and energy was claimed by other pressing duties. A large section of the Communist writers like Damodaran, Induchoodan and Devadas found themselves in the revisionist camp and were given to the intellectual pusillanimity of which E.M.S. warned us in the name of self criticism they were even giving up the basic class positions. They sought to put all the blame for the split and decline of the progressive literary movement on the head of E.M.S. and his followers.

The release of comrades from prison and the general elections which proved the greater mass base of the CPI(M) and the formation of the seven-party United Front government under the Chief Ministership of E.M.S. made a qualitative change in the political as well as literary situation. Despite all his preoccupations, with Party and governmental duties, E.M.S. set himself to pick up the broken threads of PWA and began mending the fences. The first step in this direction was to found an illustrated cultural weekly as a supplement to Deshabhimani daily. With the prospect of a serious split in the anti-Congress front in the offing, and most of the established Left writers having deserted the Marxist fold, it was a tough job to mobilise sufficient number of writers to run a regular weekly.

It is in this gloomy situation that E.M.S. called this writer, then the Chief Editor of daily and weekly and asked to build up a team of writers around the weekly. He asked us not to depend too much upon big and established writers. Once we get on the rails and move on, the big ones would follow suit, one by one. But our anchor must be young and new writers, whom we must teach, train and promote.

Thus was born the Deshabhimani Study Circle with a dozen or so youngsters and two or three seniors like M.N. Kurup, Cherukat, E.K. Nayanar and of course E.M.S.

By 1969, the Congress split into two and some allies including CPI left the seven-party front to join a Congress front. The second E.M.S. Ministry fell and he had much more time to spare for art and literature. In the Republic Day special issue of Deshabhimani weekly in 1971, E.M.S. wrote an important article titled "Progressive Literature and Communist Literature". It was a panoramic review of 34 years of PW movement assessing both the deviations and achievements. He also charted out a path forward to revive the movement.

This article was widely discussed in literary circles, study circle units and debated in the columns of the weekly. As a sort of rounding up of the widespread discussions and debates, an all-Kerala conference of the activists of the circle and some invited guests not associated with the circle was held on May 27-28, 1971 at Elamkulam, the home village of E.M.S. in central Kerala. Besides E.M.S.'s article the veteran Marxist M.S. Devadas also presented a paper. Nayanar presided over the deliberations.

After frank and thorough debates, interspersed with self criticism and some times complacent of self-justifications E.M.S. summed up the findings. Though the study circle was a designed as a loose organisation, with a lot of freedom for participation and dissent, central committee with the famed activist, dramatist, and novelist Cherukat as the President and poet-journalist M.N. Kurup as the General Secretary was elected. Thus the wide road was opened up for the revival and as ward of the defunch PWA.

Study Circle

The onward march of Deshabhimani Study Circle in the turbulent decade of 1970s was spectacular. E.M.S.'s prophesy proved correct. Alongwith a number of young writers, poets and playwrights trained and promoted by the circle a number of established writers gave their weighty support to the circle. The non-sectarian openness which was the hallmark of the circle from the very beginning had its salutory results. Outstanding men and women of letters, who were no longer young and some of whom began their literary career as anti-Communists and critics of PWA, joined the movement and gave it wide spread acceptability. Among them may be mentioned the critic Thayatt Sankaran, M.K. Sanu, M.N. Vijayan, M.S. Menon, Erumeli Parameswaran Pillai, Parappurath Sukumar Azhikkode and many others. Though there are still criticise the movement as a Communist outfit, such critics do not have their former credibility. The role of the study circle during the suffocating oppression of Emergency Declaration (1975-77) was bold and fruitful.

The movement took the next long step forward on 14 August 1981, the seventieth birth day of Mahakavi Vyloppilly Sreedhara Menon, to transform and expand and rename the Study Circle as Purogamana Kala Sahitya Sanghom — Progressive Association for Art and Letters, PAAL for short. Mahakavi Vyloppilly, the greatest 20th century Malayalam poet after Kumaran Asan and Vallathol was elected President. Vyloppilly, besides his poetic brilliance and progressive commitment, earned a special niche in the heart of Malayalees as a forthright opponent of Emergency. There were not many senior writers in Kerala who can claim this title, though there were many younger ones.

As the name indicates the PAAL does not confine itself to literature. Performing arts, plastic arts, music, film, architecture and all other forms of art comes under PAAL's purview. Separate camps, workshops and conferences are being held for different forms of arts. PAAL now is the most powerful and influential organisation fighting communalism and fascism in Kerala. And it is one of the heritages left by E.M.S.

The various comments, self criticisms and the theories from E.M.S. which we quoted were all part of the consistent campaign E.M.S. carried on to resurrect and strengthen the PW movement. Though he was eminently successful in reviving and strengthening the movement, two items on his agenda remained unimplemented. One was to transform PAAL into a still broader body to make it a common organisation of all writers, artists, painters, actors, film-makers, etc., without any sectarian barrier among them. Another, and more important ambition which was close to his heart was to build up an All India forum of Artists and writers.

Let us hope that these unfulfilled items of his agenda will get the attention they deserve from his comrades and admirers.

E.M.S. as a Historian

History had a central place among the intellectual and scholarly interests of E.M.S. Namboodiripad. A substantial part of his voluminous writings - books, pamphlets and articles in both English and Malayalam - deal with history. They mainly cover two areas: the history of Kerala and the history of the national liberation movement. To the study of both he brought an analytical mode to bear that was refreshingly original.

As E.M.S. has often stated, his engagement with history was not academic but an inevitable part of his involvement with politics. Concerned with the transformation of society on democratic and egalitarian lines, he could not but be interested in the way the present was historically constituted. But his scholarship did not remain confined to this political purpose; it scaled heights and reached out to areas which became the envy of many a scholar. His works generated intense debate, within both popular and academic circles.

E.M.S.' ability to deal with historical subjects was evident even during the freedom struggle. His dissent note to the Report of the Tenancy Commission is generally reckoned as an expression of his radical commitment, but it was equally a clear indication of his historical insights. However, his first important work on history, Keralam: Malayalikalude Mathrubhumi (Kerala: The Motherland of Malayalis), was published in 1948. A revised version in English, The National Question in Kerala, was published in 1952. A further expanded and revised edition, entitled Kerala Yesterday Today and Tomorrow, was brought out in 1967.

In his Study

E.M.S. achieved two objectives through these works. First, he outlined the course of social and political transformation from ancient times through feudalism and colonialism towards a united peoples' democratic Kerala. Secondly, he traced the formation of the identity and personality of Kerala as embodied in the democratic struggles of the labouring castes and classes. While doing so, he focused on the material imperatives which made social transformation possible and the role and intervention of different social classes which either facilitated or retarded this process. Understandably, his analytical mode, informed by Marxist method, aroused criticism and debate, more so among scholars in Kerala. He was dubbed by some as a "feudal socialist" and as a Namboodiri who was not able to overcome his caste prejudices. For a person who, even when young was part of a movement which sought to change "Namboodiris into human beings", the accusation must have been more amusing than hurtful.

E.M.S. attracted criticism principally because of his characterisation of pre-Aryan society and his description of the process of caste formation in Kerala. His critics were of the view that E.M.S. did not give due recognition to the achievements of pre-Aryan culture. They held that his sympathies lay with Aryan culture, because of which he tended to lionise it at the expense of the pre-Aryan. They also attributed this to his upbringing and identity as a Namboodiri.

Responding to this criticism, E.M.S. argued that he did not agree with the view either of pre-Aryan inferiority or Aryan superiority. Both, according to him, were untrue and unscientific. He questioned the wisdom of counterposing Aryan against pre-Aryan and suggested that such attempts were part of the process of legitimation of vested interests:

> "This new theory of Dravidian superiority is as unscientific as the theory of Aryan superiority. For, it goes against all the accepted conclusions of historical research, which have conclusively proved the indivisible links between social and family institutions on the one hand and the stage of civilization on the other."

The second issue related to the process of caste formation in Kerala. In contrast to the then existing view that migration was the main cause of caste differentiation, E.M.S. focused on social changes internal to society. Migration and invasion, he held, were only catalysts which facilitated and hastened the process of differentiation. He advanced this opinion more in the nature of a hypothesis, rather than as a conclusion. He thereby suggested a line of further enquiry and validation, which still remains influential in historical scholarship.

A major part of the writings of E.M.S. on Kerala deals with the nature of colonial subjection and the character of popular struggles against it. His main interest was to identify the forces which enabled the realisation of a united Kerala. He saw in this political project the expression of the democratic aspirations of the people, which were expressed in a variety of struggles, oriented around both caste and class. His analyses of the Malabar rebellion of 1921 and the reform movement inspired by Sree Narayana Guru are rooted in this perspective.

E.M.S. was the first to highlight the anti-imperialist and anti-feudal character of the Malabar rebellion, and at the same time to point to the dangers inherent in a rebel consciousness circumscribed by religion. He pointed out that the rebellion was both a call for action and a warning. About its alleged communal character, he stated:

> "It is far from the truth to say that the rebellion was a communal riot, that the objective of the rebels was the destruction of Hindu religion and that the six months of rebellion were six months of anti-Hindu atrocities... All this, however, does not mean that religious fanaticism was totally absent in the rebellion. The numbers of forced conversions which did take

> place cannot by any stretch of imagination be explained by any other motive than religious fanaticism... One can and should, however, state explicitly that the main force behind the rebellion was not fanaticism which was simply a by-product..."

Among the writings of E.M.S. on the national movement, two works deserve special mention: The Mahatma and his Ism and A History of the Indian Freedom Struggle. The first was initially written as a series of articles in 1955-56 offering a review of D.G. Tendulkar's eight-volume biography of Gandhi. The second, originally written in Malayalam in 1977, is a comprehensive account of the history of the freedom struggle. Jointly, these two works represent E.M.S.'s uncanny ability to apply the materialist understanding to historical events and to undertake class analysis without missing the ideological dimensions.

The essays on Gandhi are an attempt to evaluate the character and significance of the Mahatma's ideas and movement. Carefully selecting events from the freedom struggle, E.M.S. located them in the context of the evolving class society under imperialism. Such an approach admitted of a multidimensional analysis which enabled him to comprehend the complexities of the Gandhian movement. Gandhi's tactics, he held, were "perfectly suited to the requirements of a class that was daily growing in Indian society and was increasingly asserting itself in its national-political life."

At the same time, E.M.S. did not characterise Gandhi as the representative of a particular class alone. Unlike many of his contemporaries, said E.M.S., Gandhi "associated himself with the masses, their lives, their problems, sentiments and aspirations." Quite clearly, E.M.S. was sensitive to the contradictions and complexities of the Gandhian movement and was conscious of the need to understand it in a non-mechanical manner:

> "Like several other historical personages, Gandhi had a highly complex personality, his teachings, too, are incapable of oversimplified assessments on the lines of his being 'the inspirer of the national movement who roused the masses to anti-imperialist action', 'the counter-revolutionary who did all he could to

prevent the development of our national movement on revolutionary lines', etc."

E.M.S. had recently suggested the need to explore the areas of identity between Gandhism and Marxism. This was obviously no flash in the pan. A Gandhian during his younger days, E.M.S. was sensitive to the positive dimensions of Gandhism even when he was critical of some of its elements. His analysis of Gandhi and the national movement reflects a creative Marxist mind, an outstanding one of this generation.

E.M.S. was always open to new ideas. It was only at the last stages of his life that he read the Prison Note Books of the Italian Marxist Antonio Gramsci. He was fascinated by Gramsci's ideas, which he thought deserved wider dissemination and discussion. The result was a book that he authored in collaboration with P. Govinda Pillai.

Always ready to learn, ever ready to imbibe, E.M.S. was a Marxist par excellence, both as theoretician and practitioner.

Eminent Writer

The talk in the streets is that violence and non-violence are mutually exclusive. Following this, it is axiomatically held in the political field that the Marxian and Gandhian ideologies cancel each other at least in theory. But keen students have discovered that what stands out between these two philosophies is more their consanguinity than their contradiction. I have found that this view if extended to a relative study of the personalities of Marx and Gandhiji would unravel hitherto unknown affinities between these two world leaders.

Let us study one of these affinities. Both Marx and Gandhiji were tireless writers, their literary output being unusually massive. They did not take to the mission of writing casually, but in a severely professional manner, pressing into service all their innate skills and proficiencies. The stupendous corpus of writing they bequeathed to the world underscores the creative affinity of their selves. When every ten minutes from a quarter hour in one's wakeful life for about six decades is devoted to either speaking or writing, this incredibly corpulent mass of about tens of thousands of printed pages would be the inevitable result.

The hundred royal-size volumes of the collected works of Gandhiji is an instance illuminating the above principles.

The second would be the works of E. M. S. Namboodiripad, which has not yet been collected in their entirety. But if a rough and ready reckoning of the vast physical extent of the works left behind by him could be attempted, the final score would place him as a close runner-up after Gandhiji in this likely contest.

The sturdy foundation for E.M.S.' literary inspirations was laid during his college days. It was none other than the doyen of social reform in Kerala, V. T. Bhattathiripad, who initiated him into the secrets of writing literary and journalistic pieces for his organ Unni Nampoothiri. The first book Nampoodiripad wrote was about Jawaharlal Nehru. All these tentative footsteps in the field of writing were taken in the early part of the 1930s. This ceased only with the final breath of the writer.

The very number count of this body of writing, under various genres and classification, would be a shattering experience. The books authored by E.M.S. in Malayalam come to 75. In English, the number of books would be about 15, including such works as A Short History of the Peasant Movement in Kerala, The Mahatma and his Ism, Marxism and Literature and Selected Writings. A political leader of great intellectual capability that he was, he had always been a vigorous pamphleteer. He had a flair for writing polemics on all the live contemporary political, social and literary issues. The total number of all these could be as high as 200.

Another unchartered area in the writing field covers his articles on a variety of subjects published in various journals, which emerge in an interrupted stream of printed matter. Add to this the introductions he gave to authors, which enhanced the reputations of the works. Then come the columns he contributed for journals such as Chintha, Desabhimani and People's Democracy, besides Frontline.

The bewildering range and variety of these writings is itself a tribute to the ever-alert, computer-like intellect of the author. But the fastidious among the readers would not be carried away by mere proclivity. They would sniff around for quality. Profusion in creation generally tends to take away quality from artistic and intellectual productivity.

This happened neither in the case of Gandhiji, nor in the case of E.M.S. It was Edward Thompson, the British poet and critic, who escorted Gandhiji to the Round Table Conference as his private secretary; he confessed that he failed invariably to pick any error in the statements dictated by Gandhiji.

Namboodiripad would not pardon himself for any stylistic shortcomings in his works. For he was a writer with finicky tastes who would not allow himself to deviate from the King's Malayalam. His concern for purity and quality in Malayalam writing was as profoundly genuine as that of any good Malayalam writer. He, in fact, constituted himself as a one-man army to fight for the cause of good Malayalam. His mastery was heard at all the forums of Malayalam writers and journalists.

The countless writings notwithstanding, his style has unfailingly impressed the reader by its care in avoiding the pitfalls of verbosity, looseness in expression, needless exuberance and long-windedness. In his writings, the celebrated aphorism of Buffon - "Style is the man"- came to life.

Namboodiripad the person led a simple life, was austere in his habits and was lofty in his thinking. His style does not take another way. His style may look dry, but it only means that he has avoided unwanted fat and padding. The inartistic verbal tendencies rearing their heads in modern journalism and literary prose, such as inappropriate exaggeration and subjective excesses in imagination and chaotic rumbling, are hard to find in the written and spoken words of E.M.S. His speech when transcribed could go to print unedited.

To me it seems that E.M.S. was at heart influenced by Gandhiji, though his intellect was dominated by Marx. His style had the qualities of Gandhian simplicity, clarity and lack of artificiality.

E.M.S. wrote as he lived, his writing cannot be separated from his life - an integration few writers could achieve.

6

E.M.S and Marxist Ideology

Historical Materialism

Historical materialism is a methodological approach to the study of society, economics, and history, first articulated by Karl Marx (1818-1883). Marx himself never used the term but referred to his approach as "the materialist conception of history." Historical materialism looks for the causes of developments and changes in human society in the means by which humans collectively produce the necessities of life. The non-economic features of a society (e.g. social classes, political structures, ideologies) are seen as being an outgrowth of its economic activity. The classic brief statement of the theory was made by Marx in the Preface to *A Contribution to the Critique of Political Economy* (1859):

> "My enquiry led me to the conclusion that neither legal relations nor political forms could be comprehended whether by themselves or on the basis of a so-called general development of the human mind, but that on the contrary they originate in the material conditions of life, the totality of which Hegel, following the example of English and French thinkers of the eighteenth century, embraces within the term "civil society"; that the autonomy of this civil society,

however, has to be sought in political economy. The study of this, which I began in Paris, I continued in Brussels, where I moved owing to an expulsion order issued by M. Guizot. The general conclusion at which I arrived and which, once reached, became the guiding principle of my studies can be summarised as follows: In the social production of their existence, men inevitably enter into definite relations, which are independent of their will, namely relations of production appropriate to a given stage in the development of their material forces of production. The totality of these relations of production constitutes the economic structure of society, the real foundation, on which arises a legal and political superstructure, and to which correspond definite forms of consciousness. The mode of production of material life conditions the general process of social, political, and intellectual life. It is not the consciousness of men that determines their existence, but their social existence that determines their consciousness. At a certain stage of development, the material productive forces of society come into conflict with the existing relations of production or — this merely expresses the same thing in legal terms — with the property relations within the framework of which they have operated hitherto. From forms of development, of the productive forces, these relations turn into their fetters. Then begins an era of social revolution. The changes in the economic foundation lead, sooner or later, to the transformation of the whole, immense, superstructure. In studying such transformations, it is always necessary to distinguish between the material transformation of the economic conditions of production, which can be determined with the precision of natural science, and the legal, political, religious, artistic, or philosophic — in short, ideological forms in which men become conscious of this conflict and fight it out. Just as one does not judge an individual

> by what he thinks about himself, so one cannot judge such a period of transformation by its consciousness, but, on the contrary, this consciousness must be explained from the contradictions of material life, from the conflict existing between the social forces of production and the relations of production."

Since Marx's time, the theory has been modified and expanded by thousands of Marxist thinkers. It now has many variants.

History of Historical Materialism

Marx's attachment to materialism arose from his doctoral research on the philosophy of Epicurus, as well as his reading of Adam Smith and other writers in classical political economy. Historical materialism builds upon the idea that became current in philosophy from the sixteenth to eighteenth centuries that the development of human society has moved through a series of stages, from hunting and gathering, through pastoralism and cultivation, to commercial society.

Friedrich Engels wrote: "I use 'historical materialism' to designate the view of the course of history, which seeks the ultimate causes and the great moving power of all important historic events in the economic development of society, in the changes in the modes of production and exchange, with the consequent division of society into distinct classes and the struggles of these classes."

Historical Materialism in Marxist Thought

In 1880, about three years before Marx died, Friedrich Engels indicated that he accepted the usage of the term "historical materialism". Recalling the early days of the new interpretation of history, he stated:

> "We, at that time, were all materialists, or, at least, very advanced free-thinkers, and to us it appeared inconceivable that almost all educated people in England should believe in all sorts of impossible miracles, and that even geologists like Buckland and Mantell should contort the facts of their science so as not to clash too much with the myths of the book of

> Genesis; while, in order to find people who dared to use their own intellectual faculties with regard to religious matters, you had to go amongst the uneducated, the "great unwashed", as they were then called, the working people, especially the Owenite Socialists".
>
> *(Preface to the English edition of his pamphlet Socialism: Utopian and Scientific)*

In a foreword to his essay Ludwig Feuerbach and the End of Classical German Philosophy (1886), three years after Marx's death, Engels claimed confidently that "In the meantime, the Marxist world outlook has found representatives far beyond the boundaries of Germany and Europe and in all the literary languages of the world."

In his old age, Engels speculated about a new cosmology or ontology which would show the principles of dialectics to be universal features of reality. He also drafted an article on The part played by labour in the transition from Ape to Man, apparently a theory of anthropogenesis which would integrate the insights of Marx and Charles Darwin (This is discussed by Charles Woolfson in The Labour Theory of Culture: a Re-examination of Engels Theory of Human Origins).

At the very least, Marxism had now been born, and "historical materialism" had become a distinct philosophical doctrine, subsequently elaborated and systematised by intellectuals like Eduard Bernstein, Karl Kautsky, Georgi Plekhanov and Nikolai Bukharin. Even so, up to the 1930s many of Marx's earlier works were still unknown, and in reality most self-styled Marxists had not read beyond Capital Vol. 1. Isaac Deutscher provides an anecdote about the knowledge of Marx in that era:

> "Capital is a tough nut to crack, opined Ignacy Daszynski, one of the best known socialist "people's tribunes" around the turn of the 20th century, but anyhow he had not read it. But, he said, Karl Kautsky had read it, and written a popular summary of the first volume. He hadn't read this either, but Kazimierz Kelles-Krauz, the party theoretician, had read Kautsky's pamphlet

> and summarised it. He also had not read Kelles-Krauz's text, but the financial expert of the party, Hermann Diamand, had read it and had told him, i.e. Daszynski, everything about it".

After Lenin's death in 1924, Marxism was transformed into Marxism-Leninism and from there to Maoism or Marxism-Leninism-Mao Zedong Thought in China which some regard as the "true doctrine" and others as a "state religion".

In the early years of the 20th century, historical materialism was often treated by socialist writers as interchangeable with dialectical materialism, a formulation never used by Friedrich Engels however. According to many Marxists influenced by Soviet Marxism, historical materialism is a specifically sociological method, while dialectical materialism refers to a more general, abstract, philosophy. The Soviet orthodox Marxist tradition, influential for half a century, based itself on Joseph Stalin's pamphlet Dialectical and Historical Materialism and on textbooks issued by the "Institute of Marxism-Leninism of the Central Committee of the Communist Party of the Soviet Union".

Later Versions of Historical Materialism

Several scholars have argued that historical materialism ought to be revised in the light of modern scientific knowledge. Jürgen Habermas believes historical materialism "needs revision in many respects", especially because it has ignored the significance of communicative action.

Göran Therborn has argued that the method of historical materialism should be applied to historical materialism as intellectual tradition, and to the history of Marxism itself.

In the early 1980s Paul Hirst and Barry Hindess elaborated a structural Marxism interpretation of historical materialism.

Regulation theory, especially in the work of Michel Aglietta draws extensively on historical materialism. Spiral dynamics shows similarities to historical materialism.

Historical Materialism and Future

In his analysis of the movement of history, Marx predicted the breakdown of capitalism (as a result of class struggle and the falling rate of profit), and the establishment in time of a communist society in which class-based human conflict would be overcome. The means of production would be held in the common ownership and used for the common good.

Reality of Human Existence

Historical materialism started from a fundamental underlying reality of human existence: that in order for human beings to survive and continue existence from generation to generation, it is necessary for them to produce and reproduce the material requirements of life. While this may seem obvious it was only with Marx that this was seen as foundation for understanding human society and historical development. Marx then extended this premise by asserting the importance of the fact that, in order to carry out production and exchange, people have to enter into very definite social relations, most fundamentally production relations.

However, production does not get carried out in the abstract, or by entering into arbitrary or random relations chosen at will. Human beings collectively work on nature but do not do the same work; there is a division of labour in which people not only do different jobs, but according to Marxist theory, some people live from the work of others by owning the means of production. How this is accomplished depends on the type of society. Production is carried out through very definite relations between people. And, in turn, these production relations are determined by the level and character of the productive forces that are present at any given time in history. For Marx, productive forces refer to the means of production such as the tools, instruments, technology, land, raw materials, and human knowledge and abilities in terms of using these means of production.

Writers who identify with historical materialism usually postulate that society has moved through a number of types or modes of production. That is, the character of the production relations is determined by the character of the productive forces; these could be the simple tools and instruments of early human existence, or the more developed machinery and technology of present age. The main modes of production Marx identified generally include primitive communism or tribal society (a prehistoric stage), ancient society, feudalism and capitalism. In each of these social stages, people interact with nature and produce their living in different ways. Any surplus from that production is allotted in different ways. Ancient society was based on a ruling class of slave owners and a class of slaves; feudalism based on landowners and serfs; and capitalism based on the capitalist class and the working class. The capitalist class privately owns the means of production, distribution and exchange (e.g. factories, mines, shops and banks) while the working class live by exchanging their socialised labour with the capital class for wages.

Marx identified the production relations of society (arising on the basis of given productive forces) as the economic base of society. He also explained that on the foundation of the economic base there arise certain political institutions, laws, customs, culture, etc., and ideas, ways of thinking, morality, etc. These constituted the political ideological superstructure of society. This superstructure not only has its origin in the economic base, but its features also ultimately correspond to the character and development of that economic base, i.e. the way people organise society is determined by the economic base and the relations that arise from its mode of production.

Historical materialism can be seen to rest on the following principles:

- The basis of human society is how humans work on nature to produce the means of subsistence.
- There is a division of labour into social classes (relations of production) based on property ownership where some people live from the labour of others.
- The system of class division is dependent on the mode of production.
- The mode of production is based on the level of the productive forces.
- Society moves from stage to stage when the dominant class is displaced by a new emerging class, by overthrowing the "political shell" that enforces the old relations of production no longer corresponding to the new productive

forces. This takes place in the superstructure of society, the political arena in the form of revolution, whereby the underclass "liberates" the productive forces with new relations of production, and social relations, corresponding to it.

Marx's clearest formulation of his "Materialist Conception of History" was in the 1859 Preface to his book *A contribution to the Critique of Political Economy*, whose relevant passage is reproduced here:

> "In the social production of their existence, men inevitably enter Into definite relations, which are independent of their will, namely relations of production appropriate to a given stage in the development of their material forces of production. The totality of these relations of production constitutes the economic structure of society, the real foundation, on which arises a legal and political superstructure and to which correspond definite forms of consciousness. The mode of production of material life conditions the general process of social, political and intellectual life. It is not the consciousness of men that determines their existence, but their social existence that determines their consciousness. At a certain stage of development, the material productive forces of society come into conflict with the existing relations of production or — this merely expresses the same thing in legal terms — with the property relations within the framework of which they have operated hitherto. From forms of development of the productive forces these relations turn into their fetters. Then begins an era of social revolution. The changes in the economic foundation lead sooner or later to the transformation of the whole immense superstructure. In studying such transformations it is always necessary to distinguish between the material transformation of the economic conditions of production, which can be determined with the precision of natural science, and the legal, political, religious, artistic or philosophic — in short, ideological forms in which men become

> conscious of this conflict and fight it out. Just as one does not judge an individual by what he thinks about himself, so one cannot judge such a period of transformation by its consciousness, but, on the contrary, this consciousness must be explained from the contradictions of material life, from the conflict existing between the social forces of production and the relations of production."

Perhaps the most influential recent defence of this passage, and of relevant Marxian and Marxist assertions is G.A. Cohen's *Karl Marx's Theory of History: A Defence.*

Key Implications in the Study and Understanding of History

Many writers note that historical materialism represented a revolution in human thought, and a break from previous ways of understanding the underlying basis of change within various human societies.

The theory shows what Marx called a "coherence" in human history, because each generation inherits the productive forces developed previously and in turn further develops them before passing them on to the next generation. Further that this coherence increasingly involves more of humanity the more the productive forces develop and expand to bind people together in production and exchange.

This understanding counters the notion that human history is simply a series of accidents, either without any underlying cause or caused by supernatural beings or forces exerting their will on society. This posits that history is made as a result of struggle between different social classes rooted in the underlying economic base.

The Materialism and Marx

While the "historical" part of historical materialism does not cause a comprehension problem (i.e., it means the present is explained by analysing the past), the term materialism is more difficult. Historical materialism uses "materialism" to make two separate points, where the truth or falsehood of one point does not affect the others.

First there is metaphysical or philosophical materialism, in which matter-in-motion is considered primary and thought about matter-in-motion, or thought about abstractions, secondary.

Secondly, there is the notion that economic processes form the material base of society upon which institutions and ideas rest and from which they derive. While the economy is the base structure of society, it does not follow that everything in history is determined by the economy, just as every feature of a house is not determined by its foundations. Thus, there is the idea that in the capitalist mode of production the behaviour of actors in the market economy (means of production, distribution and exchange, the relations of production) plays the major role in configuring society.

Marxist Beliefs about History

> "Society does not consist of individuals, but expresses the sum of interrelations, the relations within which these individuals stand." *Karl Marx, Grundrisse, 1858*

According to Marxist theorists, history develops in accordance with the following observations:

- Social progress is driven by progress in the material, productive forces a society has at its disposal (technology, labour, capital goods, etc.)
- Humans are inevitably involved in production relations (roughly speaking, economic relationships or institutions), which constitute our most decisive social relations.
- Production relations progress, with a degree of inevitability, following and corresponding to the development of the productive forces.
- Relations of production help determine the degree and types of the development of the forces of production. For example, capitalism tends to increase the rate at which the forces develop and stresses the accumulation of capital.
- Both productive forces and production relations progress independently of mankind's strategic intentions or will.
- The superstructure — the cultural and institutional features of a society, its ideological materials—is ultimately an

expression of the mode of production (which combines both the forces and relations of production) on which the society is founded.

- Every type of state is a powerful institution of the ruling class; the state is an instrument which one class uses to secure its rule and enforce its preferred production relations (and its exploitation) onto society.
- State power is usually only transferred from one class to another by social and political upheaval.
- When a given style of production relations no longer supports further progress in the productive forces, either further progress is strangled, or 'revolution' must occur.
- The actual historical process is not predetermined but depends on the class struggle, especially the organisation and consciousness of the working class.

This sketch is abstract - real historical understanding needed for developing political strategy and tactics must involve "concrete analysis of concrete conditions" (V.I. Lenin).

Economic Forces and Political Forces

Hunter-gatherer societies were structured so that the economic forces and the political forces were one and the same. The elements of force and relation operated together, harmoniously. In the feudal society, the political forces of the Kings and nobility had their relations with the economic forces of the villages through serfdom. The serfs, although not free, were tied to both forces and, thus, not completely alienated. Capitalism, Marx argued, completely separates the economic and political forces, leaving them to have relations through a limiting government. He takes the state to be a sign of this separation - it exists to manage the massive conflicts of interest which arise between classes in all those societies based on property relations.

Warnings against Misuse

"One has to "leave philosophy aside" (Wigand, *Die letzten Philosophen*), one has to leap out of it and devote

> oneself like an ordinary man to the study of actuality, for which there exists also an enormous amount of literary material, unknown, of course, to the philosophers... Philosophy and the study of the actual world have the same relation to one another as masturbation and sexual love."
>
> *(Karl Marx and Friedrich Engels, The German Ideology, International Publishers, ed. Chris Arthur)*

Marx himself took care to indicate that he was only proposing a guideline to historical research (*Leitfaden* or *Auffassung*), and was not providing any substantive "theory of history" or "grand philosophy of history", let alone a "master-key to history". Numerous times, he and Engels expressed irritation with dilettante academics who sought to knock up their skimpy historical knowledge as quickly as possible into some grand theoretical system that would explain "everything" about history. To their great annoyance, the materialist outlook was used as an excuse for not studying history.

In the 1872 Preface to the French edition of Das Kapital Vol. 1, Marx also emphasised that "There is no royal road to science, and only those who do not dread the fatiguing climb of its steep paths have a chance of gaining its luminous summits". Reaching a scientific understanding was hard work. Conscientious, painstaking research was required, instead of philosophical speculation and unwarranted, sweeping generalisations.

But having abandoned abstract philosophical speculation in his youth, Marx himself showed great reluctance during the rest of his life about offering any generalities or universal truths about human existence or human history. The first explicit and systematic summary of the materialist interpretation of history published, *Anti-Dühring*, was written by Friedrich Engels.

One of the aims of Engels's polemic *Herr Eugen Dühring's Revolution in Science* (written with Marx's approval) was to ridicule the easy "world schematism" of philosophers, who invented the latest wisdom from behind their writing desks. Towards the end of his life, in 1877, Marx wrote a letter to the editor of the Russian paper *Otetchestvennye Zapisky*, which significantly contained the following disclaimer:

> "If Russia is tending to become a capitalist nation after the example of the Western European countries, and during the last years she has been taking a lot of trouble in this direction - she will not succeed without having first transformed a good part of her peasants into proletarians; and after that, once taken to the bosom of the capitalist regime, she will experience its pitiless laws like other profane peoples. That is all. But that is not enough for my critic. He feels himself obliged to metamorphose my historical sketch of the genesis of capitalism in Western Europe into an historico-philosophic theory of the marche generale imposed by fate upon every people, whatever the historic circumstances in which it finds itself, in order that it may ultimately arrive at the form of economy which will ensure, together with the greatest expansion of the productive powers of social labour, the most complete development of man. But I beg his pardon. (He is both honouring and shaming me too much.)"

Marx goes on to illustrate how the same factors can in different historical contexts produce very different results, so that quick and easy generalisations are not really possible. To indicate how seriously Marx took research, it is interesting to note that when he died, his estate contained several cubic metres of Russian statistical publications (it was, as the old Marx observed, in Russia that his ideas gained most influence).

But what is true is that insofar as Marx and Engels regarded historical processes as law-governed processes, the possible future directions of historical development were to a great extent *limited* and *conditioned* by what happened before. Retrospectively, historical processes could be understood to have happened by *necessity* in certain ways and not others, and to some extent at least, the most likely variants of the future could be specified on the basis of careful study of the known facts.

Towards the end of his life, Engels commented several times about the abuse of historical materialism.

In a letter to Conrad Schmidt dated August 5, 1890, he stated that "And if this man (i.e., Paul Barth) has not yet discovered that while the material mode of existence is the *primum agens* this does not preclude the ideological spheres from reacting upon it in their turn, though with a secondary effect, he cannot possibly have understood the subject he is writing about. (...) The materialist conception of history has a lot of [dangerous friends] nowadays, to whom it serves as an excuse for not studying history. Just as Marx used to say, commenting on the French "Marxists" of the late 70s: "All I know is that I am not a Marxist." (...) In general, the word "materialistic" serves many of the younger writers in Germany as a mere phrase with which anything and everything is labelled without further study, that is, they stick on this label and then consider the question disposed of.

But our conception of history is above all a guide to study, not a lever for construction after the manner of the Hegelian. All history must be studied afresh, the conditions of existence of the different formations of society must be examined individually before the attempt is made to deduce them from the political, civil law, aesthetic, philosophic, religious, etc., views corresponding to them. Up to now but little has been done here because only a few people have got down to it seriously.

In this field we can utilise heaps of help, it is immensely big, anyone who will work seriously can achieve much and distinguish himself. But instead of this too many of the younger Germans simply make use of the phrase historical materialism (and everything can be turned into a phrase) only in order to get their own relatively scanty historical knowledge — for economic history is still in its swaddling clothes! — constructed into a neat system as quickly as possible, and they then deem themselves something very tremendous. And after that a Barth can come along and attack the thing itself, which in his circle has indeed been degraded to a mere phrase."

Finally, in a letter to Franz Mehring, Frederick Engels dated 14 July 1893, Engels stated:

> "...there is only one other point lacking, which, however, Marx and I always failed to stress enough in our

> writings and in regard to which we are all equally guilty. That is to say, we all laid, and were bound to lay, the main emphasis, in the first place, on the derivation of political, juridical and other ideological notions, and of actions arising through the medium of these notions, from basic economic facts. But in so doing we neglected the formal side — the ways and means by which these notions, etc., come about — for the sake of the content. This has given our adversaries a welcome opportunity for misunderstandings, of which Paul Barth is a striking example."

The Review

Philosopher of science Karl Popper, in his Conjectures and Refutations, critiqued such claims of the explanatory power or valid application of historical materialism by arguing that it could explain or explain away any fact brought before it, making it unfalsifiable.

Underlying the dispute among historians are the different assumptions made about the definition or concept of "history" and "historiography". Different historians take a different view of what it is all about, and what the possibilities of historical and social scientific knowledge are.

Broadly, the importance of the study of history lies in the ability of history to explain the present. According to its adherents, Historical Materialism is important in explaining history from a scientific perspective, by following the scientific method, as opposed to belief-system theories like Creationism and Intelligent Design which explain the present from a belief-system point of view.

7

Namboodiripad's Legacy

Many commentaries have been published on the life and work of E.M.S. Namboodiripad after his death on March 19, 1998. The more one reads about his multifaceted contributions, the more one's respect and administration grows. He was an outstanding Marxist, who dedicated his whole life to the Communist movement. All his life and energies were spent in the cause of national independence and socialism. This issue of The Marxist is dedicated to his memory.

E.M.S. penned thousands of pages on a host of subjects. They dealt mainly with the rise and the development of the national movement, the impact of socialist ideas in our country and on various aspects of Marxist philosophy, political economy and the social sciences. All these were intended to help and guide the revolutionary movement of the working class; to enable it to make a concrete analysis and chart out the correct course.

E.M.S. Namboodiripad was born into a uppercaste, landlord family of Namboodiri Brahmins. At a very young age he began reacting to the environment in which he lived — the caste-ridden Kerala society and began advocating social reforms. Very soon he was drawn into the national liberation struggle as a young student. He was able to see that the oppressive social order was being protected by the British imperialists and their stooges the local princes. This was the period when Gandhi had already emerged on the national scene. A big upsurge had begun after the adoption of the Lahore resolution in 1930 calling for complete independence. This slogan was able to draw the peasants, workers, students and youth into the national movement. E.M.S. also plunged into the movement.

It was a time when Shaheed Bhagat Singh and his colleagues were on their way to martyrdom in 1931. In his final testament, Bhagat Singh renounced terrorism and expressed the belief that the socialist revolution was the only path for the liberation of mankind. This announcement had a big impact all over the country. Two years later, the withdrawal of the civil disobedience movement caused great disillusionment among the people, particularly the young. Congressmen who were influenced by socialist ideas decided to form the Congress Socialist Party in 1934.

E.M.S. was one of the organisers at that time alongwith Jayaprakash Narayan, Acharya Narendra Dev and others. E.M.S. headed the Kerala unit. The Meerut prisoners were released by that time and the Central Committee of the Communist Party had started functioning openly. E.M.S. came in contact with the Communists working in the Congress Socialist Party and began studying Marxist classics. By this time the All India Kisan Sabha was also set up. In this move too, E.M.S. was one of the initiators.

The Seventh Congress of the Communist International made corrections to the approach to be adopted by the Communist Parties towards the bourgeois-led national liberation movements. The Sixth Congress had taken a sectarian approach and the Communists as an organised forced remained outside the national liberation movements led by the bourgeoisie and was critical of them. In India, however, in the absence of an organised Communist centre, at many places, communists were active inside the Congress. In 1935 there was a total change in the orientation of the Communists. They started working inside the Congress Party, while side by side developing mass and class organisations of workers, peasants, students, youth, etc. Though Nehru had agreed for the direct affiliation of these organisations to the Congress, Vallabhbhai Patel and others seriously objected and finally this could not come about.

Madras was a composite state at that time and comprised the bulk of the present Tamil Nadu, parts of the present Andhra Pradesh and the Malabar area of Kerala. Units of the Communist Party had been formed in some places in Madras province at the initiative of P. Sundarayya. Amir Haider, a dock worker from Western Punjab (who died a few years ago in Pakistan) took the initiative to develop contacts with Communist workers. He was in touch with Ghate and P. Sundarayya. Com. E.M.S. working alongwith the Communists inside the Congress and the All India Kisan Sabha became one of the organisers of the Communist Party in Kerala. In the beginning four comrades joined the illegal party in 1937. They were P. Krishna Pillai, N.C. Shekhar, K. Damodaran and E.M.S.

This was a turning point in the life of E.M.S. He had by his own experience and study come to be influenced by the October Revolution and had begun to study Marxist books, which were not readily available in those days. His study of historical materialism inspired him to undertake an in-depth study of the history of Kerala society. This study further convinced him of the necessity for a socialist revolution. It is this deep conviction which helped him to take the whole Kerala unit of the CSP alongwith him to join the illegal Communist Party. When the ban on the Communist Party was withdrawn in 1942 and the first Congress of the CPI held in 1943, Com. E.M.S. was elected to its Central Committee. He made a big contribution during this period, paying particular attention to the study of the agrarian question and formulating the policies of the Party in this respect.

The post-war period, was a bad time for the Party, due to certain political mistakes committed by it. However, in Kerala, the Party was able to win over more and more sections of the people and emerge as a political force. The Left-sectarian approach damaged the Party a lot. The functioning of the mass organisations also became difficult in this period.

The Kerala unit of the Party led by E.M.S. constantly emphasised on the need to build the unity of the working class and the peasantry to carry forward the agrarian revolution to success. During the anti-imperialist struggle, this linkage was never overlooked. As a result, the Kerala Communists concentrated on developing the peasant movement and later in post-independent India on organising the agricultural labour. The agricultural workers movement is the strongest in Kerala today.

Comrade E.M.S. was one of the pioneers who launched the struggle for the reorganisation on linguistic basis. The Aikya Kerala movement led by him was successful in uniting the Travancore-Cochin Princely states into one whole, Kerala. The Congress party, which had during the course of the freedom struggle promised organisation of states on a linguistic basis and had even formed its provincial committees on this basis, went back on its commitment. The Left took the lead in developing a powerful movement for the linguistic reorganisation of states. This forced the Central Government to set up the States Reorganisation Commission.

It was this tireless work by E.M.S. and his comrades in Kerala that saw the Party emerging victorious in the first ever elections held to the Kerala Legislative Assembly in 1957, soon after the Kerala State was constituted. When E.M.S. became the Chief Minister, he proved himself to be an able administrator. Many measures particularly the land reforms legislation and education bill became a source of inspiration all over the country. The impact that this government had on the people of Kerala and in the rest of the country can be gauged from the fact that the Congress ruling at the Centre undemocratically dismissed his government. When E.M.S. toured the whole country after the dismissal, the mass response was immense with the democratic-minded people in the whole country condemning this action of the Centre.

Comrade E.M.S. was elected to the Polit Bureau in 1953-54 at the third Congress of the CPI. Subsequently, he became editor of the CPI organ New Age and also became General Secretary of the Party after the death of Ajoy Ghosh. In the struggle against revisionism within the CPI which began in 1954 and which culminated in the formation of the CPI(M), E.M.S. while disassociating from the revisionist position, was apprehensive whether the fight against revisionism would take the party on to the sectarian path. Thorough discussions with comrades convinced him that in the interests of the Indian communist movement the split had become inevitable and he decided to take up the fight against the class collaborationist line. After that he played an important role in building and developing the CPI(M) in the country. History has confirmed the line pursued by the CPI(M) to be by and large correct. Today it is the biggest force amongst the Left in the country. E.M.S. was the General Secretary of the Party from 1977 to an important phase in the 34 year old history of the Party.

He was an excellent campaigner and agitator. In 1965, during the Indo-Pakistan war, when most of us were in jail, and the Party advanced the slogan of peaceful solution of the problem, it was E.M.S. who conducted the campaign throughout the country.

When the agitation against the Mandal Commission recommendations was going on, he wrote a booklet on the need for reservations. It dealt in depth about the need for reservations in a caste-ridden society. At the same time he opposed the concept of providing reservations to the "creamy layer" among the backward castes. There was no subject which he did not deal with, whether it be Marxist philosophy, political economy, Indian philosophy, literature or culture. He never underestimated the importance of culture in developing the democratic movement in the country. He was always emphasising on the study of concrete conditions prevailing in each state and formulating policies and slogans on that basis. As General Secretary of the Party he used to pay special emphasis on developing the mass and class organisations and stressed on their democratic functioning and independent role by making them more broad based.

Throughout his life, particularly after he joined the Communist Party, E.M.S. wrote innumerable articles and books on a variety of subjects. Notable among his works are Kerala Society and Politics, The Mahatma and The Ism, History of the Indian Freedom Struggle, Indian Planning in Crisis and Nehru, Ideology and Practice. His selected writings printed in English in two volumes covers the whole gamut of his ideas in the sphere of culture, philosophy, economy and politics. He also wrote an outline history of the Communist Party in Malayalam.

Even during his last days, despite his failing health, he used to contribute regularly to the party dailies, weeklies, theoretical organs and of course to the Polit Bureau and the Central Committee. It was an exceptional capacity that very few possess. His work was ceaseless and he kept a strict schedule.

His simple style of living was a source of inspiration for everyone. His whole life was a life of selfless sacrifice in the cause of the Party and the working class. He gave the entire money from the sale of his ancestral property to the Party. When he was arrested in 1963, his wife had no house to go to. Their residence used to be in the Party headquarters in those days. His life was a model to be emulated by other revolutionaries. All those committed to the cause of the working people, who wish to advance the socialist ideas, will learn and draw sustenance from his life and work. Hopefully, this issue of The Marxist will contribute to that effort.

Parliamentary Democracy

E.M.S. held a unique position as far as communist participation in parliamentary democracy is concerned. Having been the head of the first elected communist ministry in the country in 1957, he had the direct experience of working within a constitutional set up where real State power did not rest with the state governments but with the Centre.

The 28 months of the first communist ministry in Kerala headed by E.M.S. saw policies being implemented which had far-reaching implications. The first act of the government was to issue an ordinance banning evictions of tenants. This was followed by the Agrarian Relations Bill which provided for fix of tenure, lower rents and right to buy ownership for the tenants; for the landless labourers security of tenure on homestead land and distribution of surplus land was proposed.

While the legislation on land reforms and the education bill are well known and became the focus for the landlord and reactionary interests to gang up and topple the government, there was another policy measure which is equally significant. This was the police policy adopted by the E.M.S. ministry. For the first time in post-independent India a government proposed a democratic police policy. The essence of the policy was that the police had no role to play in labour disputes or in disputes between landlords and peasants. The police was not an instrument for capitalists and landlords to break up the struggles of workers and peasants. The police intervention should come into play only if there was a problem of law and order created with any side trying to take the law into their own hands. Explaining this policy, E.M.S. wrote:

> "The crux of that policy is that it is not the job of the police to suppress the trade union, peasant and other mass activities of any mass organisation, or a political struggle waged by any political party; it is the job of the police to track down and punish those who commit ordinary crimes."
>
> *(Twenty-eight months in Kerala, p.134, Selected Writings, Vol. 2)*

This policy which could not be fully put in place by the first E.M.S. government was developed further by the CPI(M) when the United Front governments took office nearly a decade later in the 1967-70 period.

The "Kerala way" advocated by a reformist view of the electoral advance in Kerala was refuted by E.M.S. much before the 1964 split in the Party. He did not believe, having seen the dogged pursuit of the ruling class interests by the Nehru-led Congress, that any parliamentary road to power had opened up. There would be no successive Kerala-type victories leading to power in Delhi. Instead he foresaw increasing electoral success of the Communists resulting in intensification of the class struggle.

The experience of the first Communist ministry was explained by E.M.S. as follows:

> "If the "experiment" in Kerala showed anything, it is this: The struggle in the parliamentary arena, including the formation of state governments when a majority is secured, is one specific form of class struggle in which the struggle on the parliamentary arena would have to be subordinated to, though being integrated with, the extra-parliamentary struggle."
> *(Reminiscences of an Indian communist)*

It is this experience which helped the CPI(M) subsequently in formulating its tactics regarding participation in the state governments within a bourgeois-landlord system. When the 1964 Party programme was formulated, as pointed out by Harkishan

Singh Surjeet, a paragraph defining the participation in state governments was included at the instance of E.M.S. Subsequently, the Central Committee in its document "New Situation and Tasks" (1967) elaborated on the nature of this participation with regard to the formation and functioning of United Front governments headed by the CPI(M) in West Bengal and Kerala in 1967. After becoming the Chief Minister of Kerala again in 1967, E.M.S. was instrumental in formulating the tactics of administration and struggle while being in the state government.

The idea being that participation in the state government should be utilised to initiate and implement policies which will help the development of the mass movements and democratic struggles. At that time this slogan was opposed by the CPI. E.M.S. countered this by defending the concept of using the state government headed by the Left as an instrument of struggle.

It would be wrong however to limit E.M.S.'s understanding on participation in parliamentary forums to just this role. He had a more fundamental understanding of how the Communist Party should work in the parliamentary system clarifying and defining the role of the Party which participates in governments where it has popular mandates while continuing to keep its major focus on developing mass movements and the struggles of the working people. The work of the Party at all levels in elected bodies whether it be legislatures or other institutions in society should be part of the overall strategy and tactics of developing the democratic movement.

Tactics of Fighting Communalism: E.M.S.'s mastery of political tactics was a result of his remarkable ability to grasp the essence of the changes that were taking place both in relation to the immediate situation and long term strategy. There was none to rival him in foreseeing the line of development once a political phenomenon appeared and he was able to analyse it in class terms. This became evident time and again when he formulated the next stage in a tactical line or, initiated a change in the existing tactics. Very often, his colleagues and the Party took time to come abreast with his changing understanding. A good example is how E.M.S. translated the understanding of the growing danger of the communal and divisive forces formulated by the Party in the

Vijayawada Congress to the concrete situation in Kerala. He was in the forefront as the General Secretary of the Party in leading the struggle to break links with communal parties who were till then part of the united front politics practised by the Party.

The break with the AIML (a splinter group of the Muslim League) came about in 1985 as a result of the firm struggle initiated by E.M.S. who understood that any concession to a communal based party in Kerala would compromise the all -India struggle against the forces of majority communalism and other divisive forces. The 1987 assembly elections saw E.M.S. conducting an intensive campaign, posing the basic question before the people of Kerala that caste and communal politics should become an anachronism and should find no place in modern democratic Kerala society. The victory of Left and Democratic Front and the Party line in these elections was one of the finest moments in E.M.S.'s political career.

On the question of communalism, E.M.S. made another important contribution. At the national level when he was the General Secretary of the Party, the danger of majority communalism grew rapidly in the latter half of the eighties. The rise of the Ramjanmabhoomi movement targeting the Babri Masjid at Ayodhya, the spate of communal riots organised by the RSS and its allied outfits and the growing aggressiveness of the Hindutva forces alerted E.M.S. to the new threat to secular democracy. Well before many of his contemporaries in the secular camp, E.M.S. traced the growing assertiveness of the BJP to the backing of the RSS and the Hindutva ideology which ran counter to the whole orientation and traditions of the anti-imperialist freedom struggle.

The communal threat which existed before independence and its revival again in post-independent India in a big way after four decades was related by E.M.S. to the class nature of the bourgeois-landlord system which compromised with the very forces which sustain such ideology. Therefore, E.M.S. saw the BJP-RSS combine not as a communal force alone but also in class terms as representatives of right reaction in India.

It is this clear understanding which enabled E.M.S. to provide the firm leadership to the Party Central Committee and Polit

Bureau to pursue a two track policy. Firstly, to target the BJP-RSS-VHP combine as a threat to the secular democratic fabric of the country and to work for its isolation; secondly, together with the Left to unitedly strive to gather all the secular opposition forces so that the wider unity of the Left and secular opposition could be forged to fight the Rajiv Gandhi government at that time and also to demarcate from and isolate the BJP which was seeking to intervene and join the anti-Congress struggle.

E.M.S. firmly led the struggle of the Party to foil all efforts to build an "all-in opposition unity" inclusive of the BJP to head the rising mass discontent against the Congress. When the National Front was being formed, initially some of the bourgeois parties wanted to include the BJP. Efforts were made to unite with the BJP on specific issues like support to Giani Zail Singh against Rajiv Gandhi. In all these questions the political stand and intervention of the Party expressed through E.M.S. played a major role in demarcating the National Front from the BJP and laying the foundations for cooperation between the National Front and the Left.

Unified State of Kerala

In contrast to the one nation single culture model put out by the dominant bourgeois leadership of the national movement, it is the communists who pioneered studies on the linguistic—nationality question in India. E.M.S. undertook the job of tracing the development of the linguistic-nationality of the Malayalam-speaking people and provided the theoretical basis for the creation of a unified state of Kerala. His publication in Malayalam titled "One and a Quarter crore Malayalees" in 1945 was subsequently revised and developed into a full-fledged study published in English in 1952 as "The National Question in Kerala.

This was the first concrete application of the Marxist-Leninist approach to the nationality question to a specific nationality in India. His advocacy of "Aikya Kerala" was similar to the works which appeared on the formation of Vishalandhra by P. Sundarayya and Natun Bangla by Bhowani Sen, but the significance of E.M.S.'s work lay in the deep historical insight into how the socio-economic formation in Kerala developed at different stages upto colonialism. This provided the basis both for championing the formation of

Kerala as a linguistic state merging Travancore, Cochin and Malabar, and also getting rid of antiquated socio-economic relations and fetters on production necessary for the emancipation of the people from feudalism and imperialism.

Marxism in Practice

E.M.S. Namboodiripad is a striking illustration of how an individual's life and work acquires a tremendous impact when harnessed to the theory and practice of Marxism. When the individual is a person of E.M.S.'s exceptional intellectual ability and depth of vision, veritably, theory becomes a powerful force and in the hands of a creative practitioner like E.M.S., it produces the impulses for a powerful movement.

The creative thought and practice of E.M.S. moved the people and changed the history of Kerala in the twentieth century as no other individual has done. What made E.M.S. a pre-eminent leader was his ability to stay ahead of his contemporaries in applying Marxism to the specific conditions of Kerala and India. The second unmatched capacity was his natural skill in communicating his ideas and that of his party to the people in a manner which moved them into collective political action.

In the sphere of theorising and putting into practice the policies of the Party of the working class, E.M.S. made an unparalleled contribution. The flowering of E.M.S.'s talents in analysis of contemporary society is evident from the point when he became acquainted with Marxist theory in a rudimentary fashion. After being profoundly influenced by the socialist politics of Jayaprakash Narayan whose book "Why Socialism" opened the window to socialist ideas for the young radical Congressmen of Malabar in 1934, E.M.S. and his contemporaries like P. Krishna Pillai, A.K. Gopalan, K. Damodaran and others, joined the Congress Socialist Party.

Contacts with the Communist Party through the CSP and the formation of the first Communist group in Kerala in 1937 made available some books on Marxism to E.M.S. From here began the efforts to study theory, apply it to the conditions of Kerala society and then extend it to the development of the revolutionary movement. In the early years upto 1945 we see the promising beginnings. The analysis of Malabar agrarian society, the historical development of Kerala society and the linguistic-nationality question of the Malayalees are all utilised to shape the left movement.

The creative vitality of E.M.S.'s political thought stemmed from the method he began applying early in life. He would study the concrete socio-economic conditions and their impact on the various classes in society and out of this analysis he would draw his theoretical conclusions which would be the guide for action.

Experiment of Agrarian Revolution

This was the method he first adopted in dealing with agrarian relations in Malabar. The result was his minute of dissent to the report of the Malabar Tenancy Enquiry Committee set up by the Madras Legislative Assembly in 1939. This document nearly six decades later still retains the brilliance of its insights into the nature of the Jenmi-landlord system in Malabar and its pernicious effects on the peasantry and society. Building on this analysis E.M.S. provided practical guidance to the developing peasant movement against landlordism in the Malabar province.

The militant anti-feudal struggles which carried on till the post-independence period made Malabar one of the strongest units of the Kisan Sabha in the country. It is based on the experience of this powerful movement, which became the spearhead of the anti-imperialist struggle in Kerala, that E.M.S. made his contribution to the All India Kisan Sabha of which he became the Joint Secretary. When he joined the Party Centre at Delhi in end 1953, one of the responsibilities assigned to him was looking after the Kisan Front. The CC resolution of 1954 on "Our Tasks among the Peasant Masses" provided a broadly correct orientation for work on this front; E.M.S. played an important role in drafting this document.

Caste Question

The same approach can be seen in the manner in which E.M.S. tackled the caste question in India. After studying the role of caste historically in ancient Kerala society upto the time the British colonised India, E.M.S. concluded that the feudal system in Kerala consisted of a jati-janmi-naduvazhi medhavitwam (landlord-upper caste-chieftain-domination). Having been an active participant in the anti-caste and social reform movement and then moving forward to the building of class based movements and the Communist Party, E.M.S. with his intellectual abilities was able to synthesise this early experience and formulate the correct position on class-caste relations.

The basis on which he advocated tackling the question of caste by the working class movement has an abiding relevance in the contemporary period where caste divisions are acute in society.

E.M.S. spelt out the basis of the Marxist approach to caste and class. He wanted the working class movement to identify and channelise the aspirations of the most oppressed castes particularly the dalits, in their struggles for social emancipation and an end to caste oppression. Studying Kerala society, in the forties he had shown the close correlation between caste, class and property relations and underlined the vital importance of harnessing the anti-caste revolts to the democratic and agrarian revolution.

While doing so, he resolutely worked for the building of the class organisations and the unity of the oppressed sections of all castes and communities. While being supportive of the struggles of the lower caste organisations against upper caste domination, the Communists in Kerala gave priority to the united movements and organisations of the working people.

E.M.S. talked of the two-front struggle that had to be waged:

> "We had then and still have to fight a two-front battle. Ranged against us on the one hand are those who denounce us for our alleged "departure from the principles of nationalism and socialism," since we are championing "sectarian" causes like those of the oppressed castes and religious minorities. On the other hand are those who, in the name of defending the oppressed caste masses, in fact, isolate them from the mainstream of the united struggle of the working people irrespective of castes, communities and so on."
>
> *(Once Again on Castes and Classes, p.184, Selected Writings, Vol. 1)*

Throughout E.M.S. maintained:

> "Our Party and myself as one of its activists have thus been basing ourselves on the Marxist theory of class struggle and subordinating the problem of caste oppression to the needs of uniting the exploited against the exploiting classes, irrespective of the caste to which each belongs." *(Ibid, p.190)*

He noted that with the development of capitalism and the breakdown of the old order, sections of the upper castes who were property owners had become pauperised and joined the ranks of the urban and rural proletariat. At a later stage, he pointed out that sections of the backward castes (or Other Backward Classes) had also benefited from the socio-economic changes and gone up the ladder either through access to education, jobs or improved economic conditions. It is this understanding which E.M.S. first put forward in the report of the Administrative Reforms Committee that he headed when he was Chief Minister of Kerala in 1957. In this report it was recommended that reservation continue for other backward classes and that the elite sections from these classes be excluded from the benefit of reservation.

Much before the "creamy layer" issue became a controversy, three decades before that, E.M.S. had already formulated such an approach. The stand on reservation which E.M.S. elaborated after the Mandal Commission Report was implemented in 1989 was based on the above class understanding which stressed the importance of the unity of all sections of the working people. But within this mass of the working people, Marxists should recognise that there are some sections who are historically and socially disadvantaged and oppressed by the caste system.

This oppression has not been eliminated even after decades of capitalist development and political independence. It is in order to draw these masses into the common movement and to eventually break down caste barriers that reservation is supported by the Marxists as a concept for a period of time with limited aims. E.M.S. firmly took on upper caste chauvinists who oppose reservations and also warned the Party of the working class not to *"allow itself to be turned into a tailist hanger on of the bourgeois-landlord elements growing with the 'backward' communities."*

Women's Movement

E.M.S. made an original contribution to the development of a correct perspective for the democratic women's movement. In his first public activity against the hidebound orthodoxy of the Namboodiri community, a major issue was the status of Namboodiri women. The young E.M.S. who participated in the social reform movement focused on the oppression of Namboodiri women who were even deprived of the right to marriage and had to observe a form of purdah. The emancipation of Namboodiri women from gender oppression in a feudal set-up was the theme of the early writings and the plays prepared by E.M.S. and his colleagues in the Yogakshema Sabha.

Later in the development of the anti-imperialist and anti-feudal struggles in Malabar, E.M.S. paid particular attention to the increasing participation of women in the democratic movement. Writing in 1942 about this aspect, he noted that rights were accorded to women in most communities in traditional Kerala society unknown in other areas. He hoped this tradition would be renewed in the modern contest which would enable them to play an equal role with men in the social transformation of society.

When he was first working at the Party Centre in the period 1954-56, E.M.S. was responsible for guiding the work on the women's front. At that time, he set out the broad outlines of the nature of the women's organisation. It should encompass all sections of women belonging to different classes as they all suffer from a common gender oppression, at the same time, women coming from the working class and the peasantry would constitute the bulk of the membership as they suffer from the double oppression, both class and social.

Later, in the leadership of the CPI(M), drawing from experience, he set out the basis for the building of a powerful democratic women's movement. He pointed out three aspects that have to be taken into account. Firstly, of women as women who irrespective of their class status suffer from gender oppression in a bourgeois and semi-feudal society; secondly, women as workers who suffer from the class exploitation given their position as agricultural or industrial workers and thirdly, women as citizens who have to struggle alongwith men for democratic rights, democracy and a just society. It is these three aspects combined together, which provides the correct orientation to draw in all sections of women in the struggle for women's equality and against class and gender exploitation.

Left, a Distinct Force

Another sphere in which E.M.S. made a distinctive contribution was in articulating the role of the Left as a distinct force in Indian politics, tracing its roots from the anti-imperialist struggle. Having been an active Congressman in his early political career, then a leading Congress Socialist Party worker and eventually a Communist leader, E.M.S. sought to put the whole experience of the anti-imperialist movement in a systematic manner in which the role of the Left could be delineated at every stage of the development of the anti-imperialist movement.

The struggle within the Congress between the Right and the Left, from the Lucknow session when Nehru became president in 1935 to the Tripuri session when Subhash Chandra Bose won the elections; the role of the fledgling Communist Party; the impact of the October revolution and later the anti-fascist struggle; the formation of the AITUC and other class and mass organisations — these events were put together to provide a coherent narrative of how the proletarian. Left stream developed in the freedom struggle vis a vis the bourgeois dominated movement.

Here again there was no mechanical analysis or simplification. While characterising the leadership of Mahatma Gandhi as essentially bourgeois in class terms, E.M.S. made sophisticated and insightful analysis of the role played by Gandhi in the national movement. The Mahatma And The Ism first published in 1958 was a product of a number of articles written in the New Age monthly in the period 1955-56. It was the first serious attempt by a Marxist leader to analyse the crucial role played by Gandhi in developing the Congress-led mass movement for freedom. Gandhi's positive role and its serious limitations were seen not in individual terms but put within the framework of the overall interests of the national bourgeoisie. The unique tactics adopted by Gandhi such as individual satyagraha and civil disobedience were understood in this context. While acknowledging the greatness of Gandhi and his contribution, the book also sets out the divergent approaches to the anti-imperialist and anti-feudal tasks which the Communists and the bourgeois leadership of the Congress had.

From this seminal work, which E.M.S. himself recognised as one of his major works, the idea of the two streams, bourgeois and proletarian, within the freedom struggle, complementary to the overall aim of fight against imperialism but divergent in its class interests was worked out. Thus, began the quest for constructing the proletarian challenge to the hegemony of the bourgeois political forces. Tracing the heritage of the Left in the anti-imperialist struggles and demarcating from the bourgeois and petit bourgeois trends of the Congress leadership, E.M.S. subsequently paid a great deal of attention to the whole question of countering the ideological hegemony of the ruling classes.

Not by economic struggles and political slogans alone can the ruling classes domination be countered. E.M.S. right from the beginning of his revolutionary career recognised the importance of the role of the media, culture and intellectual work to project an alternative Left perspective. His lifelong and fruitful association with media and cultural activities was nurtured by this comprehensive understanding of a proletarian movement.

Global Socialism

It is not necessary to dwell at length on the internationalist outlook of E.M.S. which he shared with the collective leadership of the CPI(M). A characteristic feature of this outlook, as distinct from the CPI stream, was the adherence to proletarian internationalism which was not circumscribed by loyalty to any particular communist party in working out the international understanding and application of Marxism-Leninism. While defending socialism from the onslaughts of imperialism whether it be in the case of the Soviet Union or China, the CPI(M) leadership, of which E.M.S. was an integral part, firmly stood for an internationalism which was partisan towards socialism and unremittingly hostile to imperialism. However, it also refused to accept any direction or guidance on how the communists should work out their strategy and tactics in India. To E.M.S. fell the difficult task of putting out the principled communist position in 1962 during the Indo-China border conflict and in 1965 during the Indo-Pakistan war when most of his colleagues were in jail. He became the spokesman for the Party for a line which opposed national chauvinism and which stressed peaceful solution of disputes with both the neighbours.

His understanding of the socialist countries and the international working class movement had two distinctive trends in the later period — after the splits in the international communist movement and in the post-Soviet Union era. In the first instance, while opposing revisionist and sectarian manifestations in the communist movement, he firmly maintained that each country and the revolutionary party there will have to find its own path to socialism and this cannot be strait-jacketed into any single model of revolution in the name of Marxism-Leninism or proletarian internationalism. Thus, he could appreciate the immense contribution of the Chinese revolution and urge a more serious study of Mao Zedong's contribution to the theory and practice of Marxism, while at the same time, resolutely opposing any move to mechanically transpose them to Indian conditions. It is this consistent approach which led to the naxalite movement and Maoist ideologues in India targeting him for attack in the late sixties and early seventies.

After the collapse of the Soviet Union, he began the process of looking back at the whole experience of building of the Soviet Union in order to come to some deeper understanding of this first experiment of a socialist society. In a number of articles he stressed the necessity of going back to the period of Lenin and the New Economic Policy (NEP) and to then trace the roots of dogmatism and revisionism in the Soviet model. He was in this context sympathetic to the Chinese efforts to reform the economy so as to avoid the mistakes made in the Soviet Union. He did not agree with the view that the reforms initiated by Deng Xiaoping were primarily a negative development for the future of socialism in China.

E.M.S. in his last years urged the Party to undertake a thorough reappraisal of the experience of the building of socialism in the Soviet Union and the causes for its downfall and integrate it with a contemporary and comprehensive approach to the development of the international working class movement and the struggle for socialism. He felt the Party had not been able to move forward on these lines after the important beginning made in the form of the ideological resolution adopted by the Fourteenth Congress in 1992. This is a major task which needs to be undertaken by the Party in the spirit of E.M.S.'s quest for a renewal of the worldwide socialist project and its concomitant ideological work within India.

Communicator of Ideas

Unmatched by any other Communist leader, E.M.S. was the most successful communicator of ideas giving practical guidance to the mass of the people. This was a unique phenomenon basically confined to Kerala where E.M.S. could use the mass media of the Party as the vehicle for his dialogue with the masses and for polemics with rival political circles. Even when he was based in Delhi he would intervene in the political debates raging in Kerala through the medium of his columns and articles. The prodigious output which he sustained till the end of his life through daily articles, weekly columns, editorials, review of books and cultural events constitutes a chapter in the public life of Kerala which will be unique in the annals of the Indian communist movement. No other political thinker in post-independent India could acquire this stature and access to the people which E.M.S. had. This was possible because his was a political thought and practice which exemplified the best Marxist synthesis of theory and practice.

8

Namboodiripad's Select Writings and Speech

The 34th and 35th volumes of the *Complete Works of E. M. S. Namboodiripad* contain some important documents of the period 1962-66 which have a bearing on the India-China war and the split in the Communist Party of India (CPI). The Left-wing Communists were under attack at the time for alleged pro-Beijing leanings. E.M.S. responded by charging the other side with adopting an anti-Beijing position.

While calling for resolution of the border conflict between the two countries through talks, he laid stress on the reality that Aksai Chin was in China's possession and "Azad" Kashmir in Pakistan's hands. He also makes out a strong case for India and China to learn from each other's experience.

The writings on the ideological split in the Communist movement are characterised by polemical attacks on the "revisionists". The CPI comes in for severe criticism for its willingness to help the Congress against the Jana Sangh and the Swatantra Party.

A document of immense interest to students of the Communist movement is a 100-page note on the CPI programme, which was prepared by E.M.S. at the height of the ideological conflict. It was submitted to the party's national council, but not taken up for discussion.

The Left-wing circulated it shortly before the seventh party congress, where the split finally took shape. In this document, E.M.S. describes Indian society as an unusual mixture of caste, communal and tribal institutions and monopoly capitalism.

He argues that it is the duty of the proletariat and its party to bring together all the revolutionary and progressive forces to destroy the pre-capitalist elements and check the growth of monopoly capitalism.

In an article, E.M.S. discusses the issue of national integration from the Marxist standpoint. In another he provides a detailed analysis of Kerala's unusual election experience in 1965. The poll had thrown up an assembly that was too fractured to permit the emergence of a government.

Congress Socialist Party and the Communists

It is full 50 years since the formation of the Congress Socialist Party whose beginning can be traced to a preliminary consultation held at Patna in May 1934, where an organising committee was formed with Jayaprakash Narayan as convener.

This was followed by the regular All India conference held in Bombay in October where the Constitution of the party was adopted and the first national elected.

Being one of those who participated in the two conferences, I can take legitimate pride in the role played by that organisation in radicalising the then congressmen and developing a powerful anti-imperialist united front in the 1930s. I was therefore extremely happy when I was informed by one of those who have been in the socialist movement for the last half a century that the jubilee of those two conferences is being observed.

I was asked to associate myself in some way with this project. I shall certainly cherish the sweet and bitter memories of the struggle inside that party which took me from the Gandhi-Nehru ideology to Marxism.

I however, cannot endorse the view of the friends who proposes to observe the year 1984 as the "golden jubilee of the birth of India's socialist movement." For, though a very important stage, the formation of the Congress Socialist Party did not signify "the birth" of India's socialist movement. The socialist movement was in existence much earlier.

Pioneers of the Movement

The beginning of the propagation of socialist ideas in India should be traced to the year 1912 when, within a few months of each other, a Hindi and a Malayalam biography of Karl Marx were published. The former was written by the well-known revolutionary, Lala Hardayal, and the latter by Ramakrishna Pillai.

Four years earlier, in 1908, the first political strike of the working class in the India had taken place-the strike of the Bombay workers in protest against the arrest and conviction of the militant nationalist leader from Maharashtra, Lok Manya Tilak. The two prerequisites for an organised socialist movement-the emergence of a politically conscious working class and the propagation of Marxism-had thus been present in India at least two decades before the CSP was formed.

The big revolutionary upsurge of the years immediately following the end of the First World War took the militant national movement several steps forward. For the first time in the history of India's freedom movement, the working class, the peasants and the fighting middle classes rallied behind the non-cooperation-Khilafat movement led by Mahatma Gandhi. Industrial strikes, citywide hartals, huge demonstrations and rallies of all sections of the working people-those became common features of our political life.

This led to the emergence of that typical form of militant proletarian action, the strike, and the corresponding organisation, i.e., the trade unions strike committees, etc. Along with these started the more systematic propaganda of the teachings of Marx, Engels and Lenin.

Communist – Socialist ideas came to India, as to the rest of Asia, through the reports (distorted though they were) about the epoch-making events, which led to the mergence of Bolshevik Russia. To paraphrase Mao Se Dong, "it was the salvoes fired in revolutionary Russia that brought the message of communism" to India.

Stirred by the stories of the revolutionary upturning of society in Bolshevik Russia and frustrated at the compromising policies of the Congress leadership, rank and file Congressmen turned to two alternative paths: either the doctrine of individual terror against the British rulers and their Indian agents, or communism.

It may be noted that the well-know revolutionary leader, Bhagat Singh, in his last days moved towards communism and that many of his colleagues subsequently joined the CPI.

Several other who were thrilled by the world shaking revolution in Russia undertook their "pilgrimage" to the land revolution, braving the ordeals of the Himalayan shows and the difficult terrain which they had to negotiate. Thus, were the seeds of socialism/communism sown on Indian soil.

Emergence of Communist Groups

The birth of India's socialist movement should, in other words, be properly traced to the early 1920s when two parallel developments took place – the birth of the All – India Trade Union congress and the mergence of the early communist groups. These latter, like pioneers in any country, had to cross many hurdles, which their successors cannot even imagine. No socialist of later days can forget the grim conditions under which the first generation of communists had to fight and pave the way for the subsequent formation of the organised socialist movement.

Those who propose to celebrate 1984 as the completion of half a century after "the birth of India's socialist movement" are therefore less than fair to those pioneers whose self-sacrificing work of propagating socialism preceded the formation of the Congress Socialist Party.

To state all this is not to deny the positive contribution made by the Congress Socialist Party in carrying forward the work that had earlier been done by the pioneers. Nor is it to claim for the pioneers that they did not suffer from various weakness and shortcomings, which prevented them from developing an All India party with branches in the major states. Despite these weakness and shortcomings, however, the communist groups, which operated for over a decade before the birth of the CSP were the real pioneers of India's socialist the pioneers of India's communist movement were persecuted at every step by the British rulers who launched three conspiracy cases- Peshawar, Kanpur and Meerut- in the course of less than a decade in a planned drive to prevent the growth of communism on Indian soil. Hundreds of militant trade unionists and radical Congressmen were hunted as communists, while those who were members of any communist group in any part of the country had to undergo various kinds of persecution.

Politically, too the communists whose job it was to master and apply the theoretical principles of Marxism-Leninism had to face such a powerful adversary as the Indian bourgeoisie, the most nature and cleverest of that class rowing in any colonial, semi-colonial or dependent country, the ideological – political difficulties arising out of this could have been overcome to a large extent, and mistakes speedily corrected if only the various communist groups functioning in the country could have had the opportunity to hold continuous discussion among themselves and with the leadership of the deliberate policy adopted by the British rulers.

These difficulties, however, did not prevent the small and scattered communist groups from developing a militant trade union movement, popularising the main objectives and slogans of revolutionary socialism among the rapidly growing group of radical Congressmen and shaping, though only in a limited way, the policies of the Indian national Congress itself.

The manifesto issued to the delegates of the Ahmedabad session of the Indian National Congress and various other pronouncements made in the name of the CPI informed the mass of Congress about the existence, of and the revolutionary programme adopted by, the slowly emerging Communist Party. The small band of communist working within the Congress allied themselves with radical Congressmen in popularising the concept of complete independence and pushing forward with the programme of direct mass action.

Above all the communists were more active than anybody else in developing the militant trade union and other mass movement through the popularisation of the advanced ideology of Marxism-Leninism was combined with militant mass action.

With these activities did in a small way influence the thinking and activities of anti-imperialist militants in the Indian National Congress, and while a section of the Congress leaders like Jawaharlal Nehru and Subhash Bose were also influenced by them, the mass of Congressmen were outside the influence of the organised communist movement. They, in fact, were the victims of anti-communist prejudices spread by the British rulers. The main reason for this is that, at the very time when a furious battle was going on between the left and the right in the leadership of the Congress, culminating in the Lahore session of the Congress adopting complete independence as the goal of the Congress and President Jawaharlal Nehru declaring that he was a socialist, all the top and middle-level leaders of the Communist Party and pro-party unionists were going through the Meerut conspiracy case trails.

This all India case and scores of lesser known persecutions shattered the organisation of the Communist Party from top to bottom so that for full four years (1929-33) there was no all- India centre of the Communist Party. It is therefore unfair of the socialist and other critics of the Communist movement in India to argue (as was seriously argued by the leaders of the newly formed congress Socialist Party) that the communists were "completely out of touch with the congress and having no influence on the national movement." (Meerut Thesis adopted at the second All India conference of the Congress Socialist Party in January 1936)

Epoch-Making Developments

The mass of Congressmen and other anti-imperialists in the country were, however influenced by the epoch-making developments in the world. The deepest crisis of the capitalist world economy stood in marked contrast to the epoch-making first five-year plan being successfully implemented in the Soviet Union. No more were the theories of socialism abstract questions of philosophy to be debated by economists, but principles that were being applied in a part of the world and proving its superiority in the face of the crumbling economy of capitalism. India's anti-imperialists saw in the speedy development of socialism in the Soviet Union a picture of their own country's future if only they were able to win freedom throwing the British rulers out. This opened the eyes of rank and file Congressmen who began to rally round the ideas of Marxism-Leninism. This found reflection in the thinking and pronouncements of those All India leaders of the Congress who were moving to the left, Nehru's presidential address at the Lahore session being an example.

Developments in the Country

Development inside the country too made the bulk of militant anti-imperialist have a second look at the strategy and tactics of the struggles against imperialism. Followed as the Salt Satyagraha of 1930 and the second Civil Disobedience Movement of 1932-33 was by the compromising politics of the national leadership represented by Mahatma Gandhi, on the one hand, and the advocates of the parliamentary programme, on the other, radical Congressmen started having serious reservations on the Gandhian ideology, programme and policies. They were disillusioned also of the parliamentary programme advocated by a section of the top leadership of the congress-a programme with which Gandhi said he had reservations but which he "blessed". On the other hand, the efficacy of the weapon of working class strikes and other forms of mass direct action was proved during the 1930-32 satyagraha. This made the mass of anti-imperialist political activists look for ways and means of organising the working class, which drew them towards communism and socialism.

The meeting of the All India Congress committee held in Patna in May 1934 and the following All India session of the Indian National Congress held in Bombay in October 1934, became the seems of a furious between Gandhi, the Parliamentary programme- *wallahs* and other sections of the right leadership on the hand, and the leftist headed by the socialists, on the other. The newly born Congress Socialist Party came out more or less as the "leader of the opposition" to the "ruling group" in the Congress, which consisted of the Gandhians, the parliamentary and other rightists.

As for the communists, they had just come out of the condition into which they had been driven during the years of the Meerut conspiracy case. Although the various communist groups had come together under a centralised leadership just before the formation of the CSP the newly set up all India centre of the CPI had to work underground, since the British government imposed a ban on it. Their contribution to the development of the left at this stage was therefore, minimal.

Genesis of the CSP

The Congress Socialist Party, as is known, was directly born out of the above-mentioned developments inside the Indian National Congress. The first preliminary conference to take steps to form the party was held in Patna a couple of days before the AICC session in May 1934. The first regular All India conference too was held in October the same year in Bombay, just preceding the All India session of the Indian National Congress. The two sessions of the party were thus preparations on the part of the socialist for the battle that was ahead in the AICC and the Congress session. The attempt was thus to clearly define the attitude of the leftists to the problems being placed before the Congress.

Among the voluminous material on the birth and development of the Congress Socialist Party, a prominent place should be given to a book written by Jayaprakash Narayan under the title, *Why Socialism.* That opened the eyes of a large number of young Congressmen and women who were grouping towards a new path since they had become frustrated with the utter futility of the programmes and practices adopted by the rightwing leaders of the Indian National Congress.

Striking a personal note, I may state that J. P.'s *Why Socialism* showed us, the young Congressmen of Kerala, that the path mapped out by socialism was for superior to Gandhism, the parliamentary path as well as individual terrorism-three ideological approaches which were then contending for ascendancy in the Congress. *Why Socialism* therefore became the textbook through which we imbibed the elements of the new ideology. This was true of young

Congressmen and women all over the country who were all yearning for a new ideology.

The crux of J. P.'s book consisted not so much of its advocacy of socialism as the ultimate objective towards which India should move after attaining freedom, as of its assertion that the ideology of socialism enables the radical Congressmen to rally the mass of working people in the struggle for freedom. In other words, socialism was not *desirable as the final objective but also the effective method for the country's attainment of independence.* The programme advanced in the book therefore contained an exposure of the Gandhian programme of khadi and village industries, non-violent resistance, etc.; the parliamentary path advocated by another section of the right-wing Congress leaders with the full blessings of the Mahatma himself and the programme of individual terrorism practised by groups of revolutionaries throughout the country.

As opposed to every one of those methods J. P. advocated mass struggles waged by the industrial and agricultural labourers, the peasants and sections of the working people. The new perspective outlined and the new programme advocated by Mahatma Gandhi, on the other hand, would transform the Congress from a fighting organisation into a combination of non-political Seva Sangh and an efficient machine for waging electoral battles.

Once again striking a personal note, I cannot but recall two incidents, which moulded my political development. The first was J. P.'s visit to Kerala after the preliminary conference held in Patna in May 1934. The visit was in his capacity as the Secretary of the Organising Committee, which was to prepare for the foundation conference of the CSP to be held in October. The speeches he delivered during that visit and the informal discussions he held with us underlined the importance of organising the trade unions and the kisan sabha without which no determined struggle could be waged for independence, or could the compromising policies of the Congress leadership be fought. He sought to generalise the experience of the strikes and hartals which took place during the civil disobedience movement and pointed out how these forms of militant mass action helped in paralysing the administration. Improving on this experience and developing the united strength of the working class, he pointed out, was the only methods through which the mighty British rule could be broken. We saw in this the real alternative to the satyagraha, parliamentary and terroristic methods with which we were so far familiar.

The second incident occurred in February 1935 when a meeting of the first National Executive of the CSP was being held in Nagpur. In between the formal sessions of the executive, J. P. held an informal meeting at which he outlined his idea of developing the CSP in to an effective organisation in the struggle against the British rulers. Pointing out how a bourgeois leader of the Congress, Sardar Patel, created his Bardoli, J. P. asked: "Can we not create our own socialist Bardoli?" This was not meant, he clarified, for merely realising some economic demands but for preparing the peasants to develop their parallel governments. "Seisure of the thana" was the term he used to indicate the direction in which the peasantry should be organised.

The two incidents mentioned here would show that, although using the term socialist and sharing many of the ideas of "democratic socialism" with the leaders of the Socialist International, J. P. was above which would challenge the leading position occupied by the established bourgeois leadership of the freedom movement. The path shown by him was so attractive to the young Congressmen and women that thousands of them plumbed for it in a few months.

J. P. and his comrades, however, were not operating in a vacuum. They had before them the experience gathered by the first generation of Indian socialists who declared themselves to be communists and were working under the leadership of the Communist International. These pioneers could not, as was noted above, consolidate themselves into a well-organised party since imperialism put insuperable obstacles in their way. Furthermore, their ides of how the struggle for socialism should be organised in India came into conflict with those of the new group that was emerging within the Indian National Congress. Questions arose whether the Congress being bourgeoisie, could develop into an instrument of struggle for socialism.

The Meerut Thesis

Serious discussions took place between the spokesmen of the CSP and those of the Communist Party of India, which had in the meantime overcome the split in its ranks and established a united All India organisation. The results of these discussions were spelt out in the document adopted at the second national conference of the CSP held in Meerut in January 1936. That document, popularly known as *The Meerut Thesis*, runs as follows:

> "The Congress Socialist Party grew out of the experiences of the last two national struggles. It was formed at the end of the last C d (civil disobedience) movement by such Congressmen as came to believe that a new orientation of the national movement had become necessary; a redefinition of its objectives and a revision of its methods. The initiative in this direction could be taken only by those had theoretical grasp of the forces of our present society. These naturally were those Congressmen who had cone under the influence of, and had accepted, Marxism socialism. It was natural, therefore, that the organisation that sprang up to meet the needs of the situation took the description: 'socialist'. The word 'Congress' prefixed to 'socialist' only signified the organic relationship – past, present and future- of the organisation with the national movement.
>
> "The socialist forces that were already inexistence in the country were completely out of touch with congress and had no influence on the national movement. Therefore, there did not take place, as otherwise there would have, a fusion of the emerging Congress Socialist Party with the groups previously existing. Giving the adoption of correct and sensible tactics by all the parties concerned, there is every-likelihood of such a fusion-taking place at a later stage.
>
> "The immediate task before us is to *develop the national movement into a real anti-imperialist movement-a movement aiming at freedom from the foreign power and the native system of exploitation. For this it is necessary away its present bourgeois leadership and to bring them under the leadership of revolutionary socialism.* This task

can be accomplished only if there is within the Congress an organised body of Marxian socialists. In other words, our party alone can, in the present conditions, perform this task. The strengthening and clarification of the anti-imperialist forces in the Congress depends largely on the strength and activity of our party. For fulfilling the party's task it will also be necessary to coordinate all other anti-imperialist forces in the country.

"Consistent with its task, *the party should take only an anti-imperialist stand on congress platforms. We should not in this connection make the mistake of placing a full socialist programme before the Congress.* An anti-imperialist programme should be evolved for this purpose suiting the needs of workers, peasants and the lower middle classes.

"It being the task of the party to bring the anti-imperialist elements under its ideological influence, it is necessary for us to be as tactful as possible. We should on no account alienate these elements by intolerance and impatience. *The Congress constructive programme should not be obstructed or interfered with. It should, be scientifically criticised and exposed.*

"In Congress elections, "we should not show keenness to 'capture' committees and offices nor should we form alliances with politically undesirable groups for the purpose.

"This does not mean that the party shall not carry on socialist propaganda from its own platform. It must continue to do so-and do it more systematically and vigorously.

"It follows that the party's own programme must be a Marxist one: otherwise, the party will to fulfil its task and leadership. Marxism alone can guide the anti-imperialist forces to their ultimate destiny. Party members must, therefore, fully understand the technique of revolution, the

theory and practice of the class struggle the nature of the state and the processes leading the socialist society."(Emphasis added)

Conference in Faizpur

A year after The Meerut Thesis was adopted, the third conference of the CSP was held in Faizpur. It developed some of the ideas contained above and said:

> "It is the Congress that we must take as the basis and starting point, and we must attempt to make it an all-embracing united front against imperialism. The Congress has already succeeded to a extent in uniting wide forces in the Indian people for the national struggle and remains today the principal existing mass organisations of diverse elements seeking national liberation.... *While the Congress is a mass organisation, its leadership is predominantly bourgeois. This leadership is unable to develop, while the framework of its conception and interests, the struggle of the masses to a higher level.* At the same time it should be kept in view that the Congress leadership is no longer undivided. *Recently a conscious left has been forming within the Congress and this development is reflecting itself in the leadership also....* Our task within the Congress is not only to wean away the anti-imperialist elements from the bourgeois leadership but also to develop and broaden the Congress so as to transform it into a powerful anti-imperialist front."

Such a transformation of the Congress, the Faizpur Thesis went on is necessary to consolidate the socialist forces. "These forces are unfortunately still divided. *The party from the beginning has stood for unity in the socialist ranks... Apart from unity or agreement among socialist ranks, it is necessary that the forces of the left are also consolidated and an under standing developed* within its leadership." (Socialist Movement in India, Asim Kumar Chaudhari).

CSP-CPI Agreement

It can thus be seem that the leadership of the newly formed CSP was making a bid for bridging the gulf between the earlier groups of socialist-communists and those who rose within the ranks of the Congress in the wake of the international and national development of the early 1930s. Central to this perspective was united action between the reorganised All India leadership of the Communist Party of India and the Congress Socialist Party. A formal agreement was arrived at between the two parties. P. C. Joshi and Jayaprakash Narayan, the General Secretaries of the two parties signed a formal agreement on behalf of the two parties.

That agreement played a big role in the anti-imperialist upsurge of the years immediately preceding the outbreak of the Second World War. It helped in the unification of the trade union movement as well as in the development of the kisan and student movement, both oriented towards the unity of all anti-imperialist forces. At the same time, it helped the radical section of Congressmen, the emergence of a well-organised left in the Congress organisation and a weakening of the hold of the right wing leadership of that party. The electoral defeat of Mahatma Gandhi's candidate for congress president ship, characterised by the Mahatma as his own defeat, was the high watermark of this developing unity of the left.

The agreement between the newly formed Congress Socialist Party and the reorganised All India leadership of the CPI, however united not only these two parties but a large number of anti-imperialist throughout the country, the top leaders of the left in the Congress, like Jawaharlal Nehru and Subhash Chandra Bose, were in broad agreement with them. The pronouncements of Nehru as Congress President for two years and Bose for reflected the views not only for these two individual leaders but of the entire left inside the Congress as well as outside.

Such a broad agreement among all the leftists was possible because of the epoch-making struggle between capitalism and socialism, between war and peace, in world politics. While stirring a large number of Congressmen and drawing them towards socialism, these historic developments helped those who had already organised themselves in the communist, socialist or other leftist parties to extend their activities. The formation of the CSP helped in the crystallisation of process by providing a forum where disillusioned Congressmen could come together, organise united action with the communists and other leftist forces outside the Congress and help in the emergence of a powerful anti-imperialist united front.

The work of developing a powerful anti-imperialist front, however, was not smooth or easy. The struggle was hard, since the differences among the various parties and gropes were wide and sharp. This was particularly true of the difference between the communists on the hand, and other leftists, including the Congress Socialists, and the mass of left Congressmen, on the other.

The Congress socialist Party, as its very name implies was an organisation of Congressmen, with its commitment to socialism being an extension of the congressmen's commitment to the Gandhian, Nehruite and other ideologies of the Congress party. For them and left Congressmen, socialism was a development from the resolution of the Lahore and Karachi sessions of the Congress.

Communist Programme of Action

The communists, on the other hand, tried from the very beginning to apply to the concrete condition of India the proletarian world outlook, strategy and tactics of struggle and organisation. The draft programme of action formulated by the party in 1930 stated, "In this connection, world history and the lesion of class struggle in India prove that only the leadership of the working class can ensure fulfilment of the historic task of emancipating the Indian people, abolishing national slavery, sweeping aside all the fetters which check national development confiscating the land and effecting a far-reaching democratic reconstruction of revolutionary character. The working class of India, organised by the industrial process itself and by the class struggle well, under the leadership of the communist vanguard, perform its historic task of organising the scattered masses of peasantry and town poor for struggle against British domination and landlordism.

"But in order to organise the mass of workers, in order to rally the proletariat as a district class, conscious of its distinct class interests and fighting for the leadership of the national movement for emancipation, in order to bring about the revolutionary alliance of the workers and peasantry in order to liberate the working class, the peasantry and the town poor from the hands of national reformism and direct their revolutionary struggle towards an anti-imperialist, anti-feudal revolution, for all these purposes the working class requires its own proletarian Communist Party."

The latter half of the 1930s witnessed sharp changes in the international situation and, following them, the situation in India changed as well. The 1935-1936 years marked the beginning of the unification of the anti-fascist forces all over the world for which the call was given by the Communist International in August 1935.

In India, too, the bourgeois-led freedom movement saw in the Soviet Union and other socialist-communist forces in the world a reliable and strong ally against British rule. It was this that got reflected in the radical postures adopted by the Congress-not only its left leaders, like Nehru and Bose, but even the right leaders headed by Gandhi.

Even before these developing, the communists were trying to give a proper agrarian orientation to the programme of the Indian National Congress. An amendment along these lines was moved at the 1928 session of the Congress, which, of course was defeated. This struggle enabled the communists in the 1930s, in cooperation with the congress socialist and other radicals to undertake the task of seriously organising the peasantry under the kisan sabha. This was one of the most significant gains of the developing anti-imperialist unity of the latter half of the 1930s in which the CPI-CSP unity played the decisive role.

Battle between Right and Left

However, as the leftists consolidated themselves and grew strong in the wake of the growingly united anti-imperialist front, the right became panicky. They tolerated three years of leftist presidents of the Congress-Nehru and Bose-since it helped the consolidated of the Congress as an organisation capable of winning the electoral struggle in 1937. They however, saw to it that the leftists were in a minority in the Working Committee. Nehru and Bose occupied the post of president ship only because they were allowed to do so and on condition that they should have Working Committee composed predominantly of rightists.

The development of the leftist movement during those three years naturally unnerved the right leadership. While it helped in the mobilisation of the masses behind the congress in its electoral struggle, it stood in the way of the Congress leadership coming to a negotiated settlement with the British rulers. They, therefore, refused to give another year during which the leftist leaders Subhash Bose would occupy the post of Congress President. A fierce would fought between the right and the left for the post of Congress president ship for the fourth year, the respective candidates of the two sides being Subhash Bose for the left and Pattabhi Sitaramayya for the right.

That epic battle, in which the left came out successful, followed by a still more fierce battle in which the right succeeded in manoeuvring the elected Congress President out of office, was the beginning of the break-up of the ant-imperialist front formed three years earlier. If the Lucknow Congress of 1936 marked the beginning of the united anti-imperialist front in which the communists and Congress Socialist cooperated with leftist Congressmen, the Tripuri Congress of 1939 was its end.

This found reflection in the relation between the CSP and the CPI. Although confirmed anti-communists like Masani were in control of the organisational machine, the political leadership of the CSP was provided by Jayaprakash Narayan, who was more convinced than anybody else in the CSP, of the need for communist-socialist unity. He was the author of *Why Socialism*, and the chief architect of the Meerut and Faizpur Theses.

Following as he did, the significant developments in the world indicated the rapid advances of the anti-fascist movement and its betrayal by the bourgeois leaders of the western capitalist countries, he was all for communist-socialist unity on a world scale. In India too, he was for united action leading, if possible to the merger of the communist and socialist parties. He agreed with his anti-communist comrades, like Masani, that cooperation with the two parties would strengthen the communists. He, however, did not mind it because, according to him, the Socialist Party would also grow.

The situation, however, radically changed in the latter half of the 1930s. The Moscow trials against the Trotskyites, including several top officers of the Red Army, made liberal socialist like Jaya Prakash indignant. They began to doubt whether all that Masani and company were saying against the Soviet Union and the communists were as baseless as they had thought earlier. These doubts became enormously strengthened when the Soviet leaders signed the non-aggression treaty with Nazi Germany.

These developments in the world brought J. P. closer to such rabid anti-communists among the leaders of the CSP as Masani, Ashok Mehta Patwardhan and so on. However, a large number of young congressmen and women who had joined and worked in the CSP on the lined laid down in the Meerut and Faizpur theses did not J. P. in moving away from the earlier pro-soviet and anti-fascist to the new anti-communist line. They thought that in the then world situation, the Soviet Union, which was the most dependable bastion of the anti-fascist forces in the world, had to defend itself against enemy agents. They therefore gave wholehearted support to the leadership of the Soviet Union and the communist international.

As for the Soviet-German agreement, it undoubtedly understood, that when imperialism was using every diplomatic and political means to isolate and weaken the Soviet Union, the leaders of the latter were obliged to do everything possible to get out of the isolation into which their country was being forced. Subsequent developments in the world situation-the perfidious Nazi attack on and the heroic resistance put up to it by the Soviet people, culminating in the final defeat of fascism-proved the correctness of the positions adopted by the Soviet leadership.

Break-up of Relations

The months preceding the outbreak of the Second World War and the first years of the war, therefore, led to a break-up of the relations between the CSP and the CPI. Some of the state, district and local units of the CSP (including the entire membership of the CSP in Kerala) transformed themselves in their entirety from the CSP to the CPI. This is ascribed by anti-communist historians of the CSP to the wily machinations of the CPI leaders who are supposed to have made several know communists to "infiltrate into the CSP" and disrupt if from within. Since I happen to be one of those who are thus supposed to have "infiltrated" himself into the CSP, I may state the actual facts. I was elected one of the four Joint Secretaries of the All India congress socialist Party along with Masani, Goray and Gautam at the very first conference in October 1934.

None of the delegates who attended the Bombay Conference from Kerala (including Krishna Pillai, A K Gopalan and myself) had in fact any earlier contacts with the Communist Party at that time. No question therefore arises of "E.M.S., a communist, being permitted to infiltrate into the CSP."

It was a year after the Bombay Conference of the CSP that the late Krishna Pillai and I had the first contact with the Communist Party of India through Sundarayya. It took almost two more years after this first contact 9in 19370 to form the first unit of the Communist party of India in Kerala.

During this whole period, the CSP leaders of Kerala worked as honest and loyal workers in the cause of socialism, to develop the trade unions, kisan sabha and other pass organisations as well as to develop the Congress as a radical anti-imperialist organisation in Kerala. It was this solid work in the urban and rural areas of the state and not the mercy of Masani and Co., that made us leaders of the trade union and the peasant movement, members of the AICC, etc., making me the Secretary of the Kerala Provincial Congress committee and a member of the then Provincial Legislative Assembly of Madras.

Krishna Pillai, AKG and I, in other words were Congress Socialist leaders in our own right and not because J. P. or somebody else "put us in charge" as the anti-communist "historians" want the people to believe. Why, then, did the congress Socialist of Kerala join the Communist Party *en bloc?* Because they were tremendously impressed by the gigantic strides taken by the Soviet Union in its (first) five year plan. They naturally came to the conclusion that the socialist revolution in Russia showed the revolutionaries of India, as the revolutionaries of other countries fighting for freedom, the path forward. They, therefore, joined the very first group of congressmen who declared socialism to be their final objective, the group headed by J. P., Masani, etc.

It may be added here, that, if in fact the founders of the CSP in Kerala had come into contact with the then illegal CPI before the formation of the All India CSP, they might have probably plumed for that party. For, unlike Masani and Co., that did not have the background of the British Labour Party whose 'socialism'; was infected with anti-communist, anti-soviet prejudices.

Naturally, therefore, the moment they got the first opportunity to contact the then illegal CPI, the Congress Socialists of Kerala entered into serious and businesslike discussion with them, and on weighing the merits and demerits of the policies laid down by the leaders of the CPI, on the one hand, Masani and Co., on the other, they found the former more correct. Their change over from congress Socialism to communism was thus as natural as the earlier transition of Gandhite or Nehruite Congressmen into Congress Socialists.

What happened in Kerala, however was no exception. In several other states, the same development took place. It was natural for those who came into the socialist movement through J. P.'s *Why Socialism* and whose convictions were strengthened by the Meerut and Faizpur Theses to refuse to be subjected to the anti-Soviet and anti-communist prejudices which Masani and Co., tried to create in them. If Socialism provided the more effective method of winning independence, as J. P. pointed out in *why Socialism,* the socialists cannot afford to join the chorus of anti-Sovietism and anti-communism. J. P. too, in the first years the CSP refused to too the line of Masani and Co., though subsequently he succumbed to it. May others, including the entire CSP of Kerala and of some other areas in the country, refused to follow J. P. into the anti-communist camp.

Why the Break?

The years preceding and immediately after the outbreak of the war thus saw a clear break between the CPI and CSP his unity in action had helped the consolidation of left forces in the latter years of the thirties. The path traversed by the two parties since then have been so divergent that it would be unimaginable for anybody who does not know the facts that the two parties together had given effective leadership to the left movement at a particular stage in its development. The question arises as to why the break came, the line adopted by which party has been proved more correct.

The stand adopted by the CPI during the latter part of the war, i.e., after Nazi Germany attacked the Soviet Union, did undoubtedly lead to the temporary isolation of the Party from the mainstream of India's patriotic masses. People could not understand how a war waged by the British rulers of India could be "people's war"; as it was characterised by the CPI. The CSP, on the other hand, came to the centre of the stage, played the leading role in organising the popular revolt against British imperialism during the days of the *Quite India struggle*. The socialist leaders therefore hoped that, in the contest between themselves and the communists, they would get the overwhelming support of the people.

It was in fact with this calculation that, following the attainment of independence on August 15, 1947, the then Congress Socialist Party removed the prefix "Congress" and transformed itself into the Socialist Party. Its leaders had the ambition of coming out as the major, if not the only opposition, to the new ruling the Congress. In 1952, when the first general elections under the new Constitution were held, the socialist leaders staked their claim for being the major opposition party in the country as a whole and the ruling party in a few states.

The results of the elections, however, were quite contrary to their expectations. Not only was the Socialist Party humiliated by the massive defeat administered by the electorate, but also the communist Party came out as the major left opposition group. The united front led by the party was in a position to stake its claim for forming the first non - Congress Government in the two southern states of Travancore- Cohin and Madras, while in two other states- West Bengal and Hyderabad-the CPI became the recognised opposition. In the two houses of Parliament, too, the CPI came out as the largest group in the opposition.

These humiliating electoral reverses were followed by intense ideological and political confusion in the ranks of the Socialist Party, which led several anti-communist leaders of the CSP to different paths-J. P. to sarvodaya, Masani to the Congress and then Swatantra, Patwardhan to Sanyas, and so on. The rest followed the tortuous course of the initial merger of the Socialist Party with the Praja Party to form the PSP, the break-up of that party into the PSP and SP; the merger of the two into the SSP; the break-up of the latter; the final merger of all existing socialist groups into the Janta in 1977; the subsequent division into various groups formed out of the old Janta, etc. The path traversed by the Socialist Party since its first electoral defeat in 1952, showed the deep crisis into which in fell.

It is true that the Communist Party too got split into the CPI(M) and CPI. Followed as this was by the rise of the Naxalite groups from the CPI(M) and that of the Dange group from the CPI, it may be superficially compared to the disintegration of the Socialist Party. In fact, there is no comparison between the ideological, political and organisational struggle among the communists and the disintegration of the Socialist Party. For, unlike the socialists the communists fought on question of ideology and politics. It therefore became possible after a time for the two major organisations of communists, the CPI(M) and the CPI, to learn from experience and come together in united actions. The area of unity in action has been steadily expanding, though major ideological issues still remain. No such question of ideology and politics was involved in the mergers and break-ups of the various socialist groups.

The Difference

This difference in the paths traversed by the two parties can be traced to the fact that while the communists with all the weaknesses revealed and mistakes committed on several occasions, stood on the solid ground of the proletarian outlook on international as well as national issues, the CSP has its foot firmly set in bourgeois policies. This was so when the communists joined the CSP in working inside the Congress and tried to develop it into a genuine anti-imperialist organisation. Unlike the CSP, whose membership was confined to those socialists who were primarily Congressmen, the communists joined the Congress as communists. The former had their basic loyalty to the Congress organisation, while the latter's loyalty was basically to their class and party.

During the *Quit India* struggle of August 1942, and in the subsequent years, the CSP was undoubtedly with the anti-imperialist masses but they were only carrying out the decisions of the Congress. When the Congress gave up the path of mass struggle and went in for negotiated settlement with the British rulers, therefore, the CSP could do nothing to prevent it. The CPI, on the other hand, was able rapidly to overcome its wartime isolating from the anti-imperialist masses and come out as the most energetic organiser of such heroic actions a Telangana, Punnapra-Vayalar, Tebhaga, etc.; it plunged fully into such anti-imperialist actions as the demonstrations in support of INA prisoners and the RIN revolt. The role played in these militant mass actions brought the Party one again into the mainstream of the anti-imperialist movement.

Although this was taken to left-sectarian lines after the Second Congress of the CPI (1948), the party was even at this stage not in conflict with the mood of the masses; although overstepping the lines within which the people were giving expression to their discontent against the new Congress regime, the Party was not swimming against the main current, as it was during the days of the Quit *India* struggle. That was why the Party's performance in the 1952 general elections was much better than that of the socialists.

Ideological Struggle

It is now full 32 years after the respective lines of the CPI and the Socialist Party were put to the first test of electoral support. The rich experience gained in this period has taught the CPI(M), the CPI and the various socialist groups into which the original CSP got divided the lesson that they should unite their forces and, together with other democratic forces fighting the ruling party's drive towards authoritarianism and for the preservation of democracy, they should base themselves on the mobilisation of the working people independently of the bourgeoisie.

In this struggle for the unity of left opposition, the ideological difference between the communist and socialist movements should nevertheless be borne in mind.

The communist movement in India arose over six decades ago, as part of the international proletarian movement and withal its ups and downs, stuck to that position; the mistakes and deviations, which no doubt crept in, were overcome, due largely to its basic character, proletarian outlook on international and national questions.

Although to a large extent influenced by the international proletarian movement, the various socialist parties, whose origin should be traced to the formation of the CSP 50 years ago, were, and continue to be, by and large non-proletarian democratic parties.

The two together could make a big contribution in the pre-war years, but drifted apart during the war and after. The unity of action, which has of late been developing is no doubt a positive development, but it should not make anybody blind to the gulf that still separates the two (proletarian and non-proletarian) trends.

Let it be stated in conclusion that the CPI(M) is itself conscious of the need for eternal vigilance and continuous struggle against the non-proletarian trends that may crop up in a mass revolutionary party of the working class. Hence, the emphasis laid in the party documents on continuous ideological struggle against right as well as "left" deviations the use of the method of criticism and self-criticism, without which the party cannot develop itself into a mass revolutionary party of the working class.

Political Ideology

We are proud of our Republican Constitution. We consider its adoption by the Constituent Assembly to be a memorable event in the history of our country. That event put an end to the decades of foreign domination as well as several centuries of caste-ridden, conservative, sociocultural set up; it inscribed on our banner the inspiring slogans of political liberty, parliamentary democracy, an end to all forms of social inequality, and guarantee of all-round progress.

It is therefore understandable that anybody who shows disrespect to, or decries, our Constitution is not popular among our people. Critics of the Constitution are told: if you sec defects and inadequacies in the Constitution, why can you not try to remove them through the methods laid down in the Constitution itself? Why do you decry and show disrespect to that very Constitution which has given you the right to criticise and try to change it? Do you not see that, having adopted a Republican democratic Constitution, our national leadership has gone forward to adopt the programme of establishing a socialist society and to this end evolved the system of planned development of our economy? Is it not therefore the task of those who are interested in further carrying forward the gains secured when the Republican Constitution was adopted by using this very democratic Republican Constitution to make it an instrument of building socialism?

These questions are particularly addressed to those of us who believe in the ideology of Marxism-Leninism. We are supposed to be people who have no faith in the democratic process. Loyalty to the basic tenets of Marxism-Leninism is supposed to be inconsistent with loyalty to the principles and processes of parliamentary democracy. It is therefore with a sense of gratitude that I am taking this opportunity to explain our attitude to the Republican Constitution of India; how we propose to work within its framework in order to bring about these fundamental socio-economic changes that we are striving to bring about.

Let me, at the very outset, make it clear that Marxism-Leninism does not take a rigid or dogmatic stand on the particular mode of bringing about social transformations. No method is excluded, nor is any laid down as the one and only acceptable method. The only criterion on which Marxism-Leninism bases itself when it selects a particular method for bringing about social transformations is whether it will serve the purpose. If there is more than one method out of which a choice can be made, Marxism-Leninism would consider which will yield results more quickly and less painfully. That was why Marx and Engels, who were of the view that State power will have to be seized through the use of force (force is the midwife of the new society), nevertheless thought it necessary to draw attention to the possibility that England with its predominantly working-class population, its growing organisation of the working class and with its system of parliamentary democracy might be able to pass over from capitalism to socialism through peaceful means. Several years after this, Lenin, their loyal disciple who consistently applied theory of revolution pointed out that, while the possibility of peaceful transformation in England did undoubtedly exist in the days of Marx and Engels. It ceased to exist after the transformation of early ("free') capitalism into monopoly-capitalism. I hat was again why the Marxists-Leninists of the world did envisage, in 1957 and 1960, the possibility of relatively peaceful transformations in several countries, since imperialism had got weakened on a world-scale and since indigenous capitalism in individual countries was not so powerful as before. These changes in approach to the possibility or otherwise of peaceful transformations show that the so-called "rigidity" of the Marxists on the question of State power is a segment of imagination of some people. The fact of the matter is that, while Marxism-Leninism will not have that pathetic faith in the efficacy of the bourgeois parliamentary' democratic system which was characteristic of social democracy, they are not allergic 10 the system of parliamentary democracy, as their enemies accused them of.

Let me now come to specific question of the Republican Constitution of India. On a Marxist-Leninist analysis of the circumstances in which that Constitution came to be adopted and the contents of that Constitution the Communist Party of India (Marxist) came to the conclusion that its adoption does certainly indicate an advance for our people. Our programme says: "Universal adult franchise and Parliament and State Legislatures can serve as instruments of the people in their struggle for democracy, for defence of their interests. Although a form of class role of the bourgeoise. India's parliamentary system also embodies an advance for the people. It affords certain opportunities to them to defend their interests, intervene in the affairs of the Stale to a certain extent and mobilise them to carry forward the struggle for peace, democracy and social progress".

Our Party is of the view that, so long as this system continues, it is in the interest of the working class and the working people to so utilise the institutions built up on the basis of this Constitution as to further consolidate and strengthen the struggles of the working people for basic social transformations. That is why the very Seventh Congress of the Party which adopted the fundamental programme of the Party, also adopted a resolution on the (then ensuing) 1965 midterm election in Kerala, which called for such a United Front of the Communists. Socialists and other progressive democratic parties, groups and individuals as "will give the State a stable Government which pursues popular democratic policies". That was again why on the eve of the Fourth General Elections, the Central Committee of the Party in its election manifesto gave the slogans of "removing the Congress monopoly of power in as many States as possible, improving and increasing the strength of the democratic opposition and above all of the CPI (Marxist) in all the States and at the Centre".

While thus considering the adoption of the Republican Constitution as an advance and utilising its provisions for the further strengthening of the working class and democratic movements in the country, the Party has no illusion that the working class and democratic movements will be permitted to use the parliamentary democratic institutions to such an extent and for such a length of time, that fundamental social transformations can be carried out through the much-talked-of "Parliamentary path". The experience of all countries which have so far adopted the system of bourgeois parliamentary democracy (including the experience of the working of our own Republican Constitution) makes it clear that the ruling classes allow the luxury of parliamentary democracy only so long as other rights of the people, the State has been directed to "make effective provision" for "securing the right to work, to education and to public assistance in cases of unemployment, old age, sickness and disablement" (Art. 41): "just and humane conditions of work and for maternity relief" (Art. 42); "a living wage, conditions of work ensuring a decent standard of life and full enjoyment and leisure and social and cultural opportunities" (Art. 43) and so on. These undoubtedly express the hopes and expectations with which our people greeted the new Independent India. Before laying down these Directive Principles of State policy, however, the Constitution-makers make it clear that "the provisions contained in this Part shall not be enforceable by any court" (Art. 37). They have thus been reduced to noble declarations, with no sanction behind them.

As opposed to this is Part III on Fundamental Rights which are enforceable by the Judiciary. Art. 32 lays down the procedure for moving the Supreme Court and the court examining the cases of violation of fundamental rights. It is very significant that the most crucial right embodied in this part of the Constitution is the Right to Property.

It was in relation to this that several cases came before the Supreme Court which gave its judgement against the very moderate social reform measures introduced by the Congress Government. It is again in relation to this that the well-known Subba Rao judgement came to the conclusion that even Parliament has no right to so alter the Fundamental Rights provisions in the Constitution as to take away the Right to Property. It is obvious that, so long as this provision continues to remain in the Constitution, the court will strike down each and every radical legislation. It is also obvious that, so long as the Subba Rao judgement is in force, Parliament will be powerless to make amendments to the Constitution in order to meet this difficult situation.

Right to property, of course, is not the only provision contained in Part III of the Constitution. There are other rights like the right to equality before law, right against discrimination on grounds of religion, race, caste sex or place of birth; right to equality of opportunity in matters of public employment and so on. They are supposed:to be enforceable by courts of law.

But we know very well that, while the Constitution solemnly declares that every citizen of India is equal before another citizen, inequality between the rich and the poor is steadily increasing. This growing inequality cannot be prevented even by the Supreme Court, though this right is (on paper) enforceable by courts of law. As for the right against discrimination on grounds of religion, it is enough to point out how the militant organisations preaching hatred for non-Hindu religious communities, particularly the Muslims, have become a serious threat.

Although the seriousness of this threat is recognised even by the Home Minister of the Union Government, he seems to be powerless to stop the growing attacks on the religious minorities. Here again, minorities who are victims of militant communal organisations of the majority community are helpless; the courts which are supposed to enforce this right are also powerless. Without making a more detailed analysis of other Fundamental Rights, which are sacred and rather important for the common people, it may be pointed out that the most fundamental of the Fundamental Rights—the freedom — has been subjected to the most right to personal serious and shameless violations. The operation of the Defence of India Rules framed in the wake of the border conflict with China has become the subject matter of serious criticism by all sections of the democratic public opinion in the country. The Supreme Court itself, in one of its judgements cast doubts on the legality and constitutionality of certain provisions of the D.I.R. and held back its judgement only on the ground that the very Emergency-declaration made by the President took such measures away from the purview of the Court.

In other words, the very Supreme Court which through a majority judgement banned Parliament from legislating against the Right to Property seemed powerless against the Government's attack on the fundamental right of personal liberty. Would it be unpatriotic on our part under these circumstances to conclude that the net result of the provisions in Part III and Part IV, and the way in which they are interpreted by the Courts and informed by the executive, make it clear that every other Fundamental Right is to be subordinated to the Right to Property, while the essentials of a Welfare State are reduced to mere declarations of pious intentions.

Those who want to bring about radical socio-economic transformations through the "constitutional path" are thus faced with two difficulties. Firstly, if they happen to win a majority in the State Legislature (as has happened in a few cases), the power of the Centre is used against them. The use of this power may go to the extent of dismissal of the elected Ministry (as happened in Kerala in 1959 or in West Bengal in 1967).

It may also happen that, if the elected Ministry is not so crudely dismissed, the radical measures it seeks to pilot through the Legislature are blocked (us happened in Kerala for the agrarian reform and educational bills in 1958-59). Or, it may also take the form of rejecting the legitimate demands of the State Government for food, financial assistance, an adequate share of industrial and other developments, etc. Secondly, if the forces standing for radical socio-economic transformations are able to win a majority in Parliament and to form a radical Government at the Centre, they cannot carry out their programmes of radical changes in property relations unless and until the Constitution itself is amended in important directions.

This will not be easy, but will be a protracted and difficult process. Technically it is difficult since an amendment to the Constitution requires that it is "passed in each House of Parliament by a majority of the total membership of that Home and by a majority of not less than two-thirds of members of that House present and voting" (Art. 368). Politically too, it involves a serious conflict between the champions of those social transformations and their opponents.

The latter, as is well known, are extremely powerful and have under their control all the media of publicity and propaganda through which they can confuse the people. They are also masters of the money purse which they can extensively utilise in order to mobilise considerable sections of the population against the attempted social transformations. It is therefore inevitable that clashes and conflicts take place among the people who are rallied behind the two camps- the champions and opponents of these social transformations. It is unrealistic to think that, in such a situation of growing conflict between the two camps of the people, the Parliamentary democratic system will be preserved intact and not be subverted, as has happened in several other countries.

This, however, is not the only way in which the Constitution may break down. An equally serious threat to the smooth working of the Constitution emanates from the steadily deteriorating relation between the Centre and the States. It is just enough to mention the names of Kashmir, Nagaland. Mizo-land, the Hill peoples of Assam, the Hindi and non-Hindi conflict and the insistent demand of all the States (including Congress-governed States) for greater power and greater share of the economic development of the country. Every one of them is an explosive issue, some of which have, in fact, already reached the stage of veritable explosion. The longer the time taken to find a solution for any of these problems, the more complicated it becomes. On the other hand, every solution that is offered adds a new complexity to the problem which it did not have so far. Those who are trying to find solutions therefore have reached a veritable dead end.

The reason for this, according to our Party, is the totally unrealistic premise on which the Federal State structure has been built into the Constitution—the premise that a "strong and powerful Centre" is necessary for the preservation of the unity of the country. The division of functions between the Federal Centre and the federating units has been so arranged that the essence of State power rests with the Centre, the States being vested with only outside manifestations of power. The entire field of economic development and planning; control over currency, finance, prices and so on: the most clastic and expanding sources of revenue—all these are left to the Centre.

This arms the Centre with adequate power to lay down the economic and financial law for the States. Even in the management of those subjects which have been formally allocated to the States, the Centre is in a position to make the States sub-serve its dictates in the name of All India "coordination"' using for the purpose the absolute financial dependence of the States on the Centre. The Civil Services of the States—the agency through which the State Governments have to carry on the administration—are also controlled by the Centre which has built up a new edition of the old "steel frame" of the British rulers. While the Constitution itself had vested the Federal Centre with extensive powers, the eighteen years of its working has made further inroads into the powers of the States. In the lace of this ever-expanding power of the Centre, the States have been put to the necessity of fighting for greater powers. This conflict between the aspirations of the States and the reality of the central power is leading to as big a conflict as the social conflicts between the rich and poor.

In order to have a proper understanding of this phenomenon, it is necessary to go into the history of how the federal idea got gradually evolved. The birth of the federal idea should be seen against the background of the movement for the formation of linguistic States which had almost half a century of history before the Constituent Assembly started its work of framing the Constitution. As soon as their own class interests are not threatened. A study of what happened in European countries after the First World War, and what our own Central Congress Government did in those cases where the General Election led to the replacing of Congress by another party or coalition of parties, enabling them to form non-Congress Governments in this or that State, exposes the hollowness of the democratic pretensions of the ruling classes. That is why our Party declared in its Programme:

> "The threat to the Parliamentary system and to democracy comes not from the working people and the parties which represent their interests. The threat comes from the exploiting classes. It is they who undermine the parliamentary system both from within and without by making it an instrument to advance their narrow interests and repress the toiling masses. When the people begin to use parliamentary institutions for advancing their cause, and they fall away from the influence of the reactionary bourgeoisie and landlords, these classes do not hesitate to trample underfoot parliamentary democracy as was done in Kerala in 1959. When their interests demand they do not hesitate to replace parliamentary' democracy by military dictatorship. It will be a serious error and a dangerous illusion to imagine that our country is free from all such threats. It is of utmost importance that parliamentary and democratic institutions are defended in the interest of the people against such threats, and that such institutions are skilfully utilised in combination with extra-parliamentary activities".

Let us analyse the structure of power built up as per the provisions of the Constitution. We find that the repository of executive power is the President of India who not only exercises power "either directly or through officers subordinate to him in accordance with this Constitution" (Art 53(1); "The supreme command of the Defence Forces of the Union shall (also) be vested with the President" (Art. 53 (2). The executive power to be exercised by him has, of course, been technically restricted to the field of the 'Union'; the corresponding power in the States is vested in the Governors (Art. 154). In reality, however, the Governor is a nominee of the President and holds office during the pleasure of the President (Art. 155 and 156 (I). The President is also the authority who appoints the Judges of the High Court of every State (Art 217). Another important instrument of administrative power (the Public Service Commission of the State which makes appointments for all the top and middle posts of State Services) is also appointed by the Governor (Art. 316). Such nighty-centralised power vested in the President of the Union and his creatures in the States can very well be so used as to subvert parliamentary democracy behind a facade of "Constitutionalism". This, as is well known, was what happened in several neighbouring countries. That it has not happened in India does not mean that it will not happen here. It only means that the political system in our country has not reached the stage of crisis reached elsewhere.

It is, of course, true that the executive power is to be exercised by the President of the Union and by the Governors of States only in their capacities as Constitutional heads of States. The President of the Union shall exercise his functions only with the aid and advice of the Council of Ministers (Art. 74 (I); the Governors of States also likewise exercise their functions with the aid and advice of his Council of Ministers (Art. 163).

The Union and State Councils of Ministers in their turn do under the established convention of parliamentary democracy, hold office only so long as they have the confidence of the Parliament and the State Legislatures respectively. The Constitution, however, provides that they hold office during the "pleasure of the President and Governor respectively (Articles 75 (2) and 164 (1)." Neither the President nor the Governor is, under normal circumstances, expected to have his "pleasure" in a way different from the fact of the Council of Ministers having the confidence of the Parliament and State Legislature respectively. But in abnormal times, when the political system has reached a stage of crisis, there can very well be a conflict between the "pleasure" of the Constitutional head and the confidence of the Parliament or the State Legislature respectively.

Although vested with extensive despotic powers, it may be said, the President is elected by the electoral college consisting of elected members of both Houses of Parliament and the elected members of the Legislative Assemblies of the Legislative Assemblies of the State (Art. 54). He is also liable under certain conditions to be impeached for violation of the Constitution by either of the Houses of Parliament (Art. 61). This right of the Parliament to punish the President, however, can be negated because, unlike in several other countries having the parliamentary democratic system, our members of Parliament have no immunity from arrest and detention. Whenever there is a political crisis—

and it is only in times when there are crises that the Constitution breaks down—sufficient number of members of Parliament can be put behind the bars.

That this is not a figment of the imagination but can very well become a reality can be seen from two facts. Firstly, several members of Parliament were detained without trial under the Defence of India Rules in 1962-63 and 1964-65. Secondly, 29 members of the State Legislature elected in Kerala in the 1965 midterm election, belonging to the Party that came out as the biggest single party, were detained and this fact was used by the Governor of that State to report to the President that no party is in a position to form a Government; this led to the dissolution of the Legislature even before the elected members took their oath of office. If this could be done to a sufficient number of members of a State Legislature in a time of crisis for this particular State, how can it be assumed that it will not happen at the Centre when the Centre itself is faced with a similar crisis?

Crucial to the discussion of the democratic of the Republican Constitution, the guarantees that it provides for character the peaceful transition from a socio-economic system based on landlord-capitalistic exploitation to a socialist system, is the way in which our political system is enveloped by a growing crisis. That such a crisis is, in fact, developing will not be denied by any one at least after the Fourth General Elections. The crisis had, in reality, started developing as early as in 1952. In three States, the Congress was reduced to a minority in the respective State Legislatures in 1952. The Central Government and the Party that led it, however, used the institutions of the Rajpramukh and the Governor in those States to prevent the formation of non-Congress Governments. That situation was changed slightly in favour of the Congress in subsequent years. But still the Congress could not prevent the formation of a non-Congress Government in Kerala in 1957. Here again, the executive power vested in the President was used in order to dismiss that non-Congress Government. It was only after the third General Elections that the Congress could form its own Government not only at the Centre but in all the States. This, however, was followed by the Fourth General Elections, when there was a veritable landslide against the

Congress. Once again, therefore, the party in power at the Centre used its authority to get as many non-Congress Governments dismissed as possible. The method adopted for this in West Bengal was denounced by such an august body *is* the All India Speakers' conference, presided over by the Speaker of the Lok Sabha.

Seen against this background, the growing crisis of confidence in the leadership of the Central Government, the unconcealed intrigues resorted to by various groups within the ruling party, raise the ominous question: What will happen to the Centre if and when a group of Congress M.Ps defects to the Opposition as happened in Haryana, Uttar Pradesh and Madhya Pradesh in March and April 1967? Again, supposing that in the 5th General Elections the Congress is reduced to a minority in Parliament, is it unimaginable that what was done in 1952, in 1957-59 and 1967-68 in those States where the Congress was reduced to a minority in the Legislature will not be done at the Centre? If that happens to the Centre, will that be very far from a full-fledged military dictatorship?

If we are to have a proper understanding of the essence of the crisis, we should go a little deeper into the socio-economic factors leading to this crisis. For, only a superficial observer of the political scene in our country can look upon these manifestations of the political crisis as passing phenomena. Any objective, truthful study of the situation will reveal that the political crisis is a manifestation of the deep gulf that separates the expectations of the people when the country attained Independence and their experience of what actually happened in the post-independent years. The Preamble to the Constitution which gave expression to the solemn resolve of the Constitution-framers to secure to all Indian citizens "(a) justice, social, economic and political; (b) liberty of thought, expression, belief, faith and worship: (c) equality of status and opportunity" is an expression of the expectations with which the people welcomed the Republican Constitution of India. The Fundamental Rights embodied in Part III and the Directive Principles of State Policy- laid down in Part IV of the Constitution also give expression to these expectations of the people. These are undoubtedly noble declarations. They inspire every Indian citizen with the idea that he or she belongs to a country which is determined to take its place among the most advanced, freedom-loving and democratic countries in the world.

As opposed to this, however, is the living experience of the people. Every one of the fundamental rights inscribed on the banner of the Republic is violated—except of course the right to property. Not the property of the small and medium-size cultivator or artisan who is steadily being pauperised, and thrown into the ranks of the unemployed and employment seeking millions.

It is the right to property of the big landlords and of the growing sections of monopoly capitalists that is protected and in protecting which the Government attacks the mass of the working people. The result is that the people are getting rapidly disillusioned and are therefore losing faith in the Congress and its declaration of building a new India on the foundations of democratic socialism. It is this loss of faith in the Congress that is reflected in the waning prestige and power of the Congress—a process which cannot be reversed, but will, on the other hand, grow from year to year unless the basic policies are changed.

Nobody disputes the wide gulf between the expectations with which the people greeted the attainment of Independence in 1947 and their subsequent experience. It is recognised even by the leaders of the ruling Party who blame it on the fact that the correct policies laid down by them have not been properly implemented. Opposition parties, on the other hand, point out that the policies themselves are wrong. Among the Opposition parties themselves, there are two schools of thought; one, which may be called Left Opposition, is of opinion that the policies are calculated to serve the interests of landlords and capitalists and opposed to the interests of the working people, and the other, which may be called the Right Opposition, thinks that the ruling Party is adopting policies which are too radical, too socialistic and doctrinaire. Both sections of the Opposition, however, plead for a radical change of policies. According to them, change of policies is the only way in which the growing discontent of the people can be removed and the country march along the path of progress.

There are, at the same time, some—our Party is one of them—who hold the view that neither the inadequate implementation of accepted policies (concerned by the ruling party), nor the incorrect policies (pointed out by the Opposition) fully explain the divergence between the people's early expectations and their subsequent experience. According to us, this is inherent in the very State structure built up under the Constitution. Even the most radical reversal of the policies—the adoption of the most progressive, anti-imperialist, anti-feudal and anti-monopoly policies—would not help the solution of the problem unless it is accompanied by a fundamental recasting of the State structure built under the Constitution. As a matter of fact, the very process of laying down and implementing radical progressive policies would be thwarted by the various checks built into the framework of the Constitution.

Recall the fate of the various land reform measures which the Congress Governments had to push through the various Legislatures. These are radical, not to speak of revolutionary, measures. They fall far short of even the measures introduced by the American Occupation Regime in Japan. Yet, within a year of the cowing into force of our Constitution. Parliament had to amend a section of Article 31 in order to give protection to certain land reform legislations (Art. 31 A.). This amendment had to followed by other amendments to the Constitution, all of which were calculated to facilitate the implementation of various agrarian reform legislations.

This process has at last reached a stage when the legality and constitutionality of this process of amending Part III of the Constitution in order to facilitate progressive legislation has been questioned; the well-known majority judgement of the Supreme Court, headed by former Chief Justice Subha Rao rejects the right of Parliament to get such amending legislations pushed through. If this is the fate of legislative measures which can in no way be considered radical or revolutionary, it is obvious that the radical policies advocated by the Parties of the Left Opposition would meet with still more serious obstacles built into the Constitution.

Compare, for instance, Part III and Part IV of the Constitution: The former deals with Fundamental Rights while the latter relates to what are called Directive Principles *of State* policy. It is in the latter that the essentials of what is known as the concept of Welfare State are spilt out. One article included in that Part commits the State to "strive to promote the welfare of the people by securing and protecting as effectively as it may a social order in which justice, social, economic and political, shall inform all the institutions of the national life" (Art. 38). Still another Ankle directs the State to see that "the ownership and control of the material resources of the community are so distributed as best to subserve the common good" (Art. 39 (b): that "the operation of the economic system does not result in the concentration of wealth and means of production to the common detriment" (Art. 39 (c); there is equal pay for equal work for both men and women" (.Art. 39 (d), and so on. Among the anti-imperialist freedom movement came under Mahatma Gandhi's leadership and penetrated into the rural masses, formation of linguistic States became one of the key slogans of freedom fighters.

This was a clear indication of the fact that the "unity of India' for which the freedom movement was renting cannot *be* divorced from the "diversity of the various linguistic cultural groups" that inhabit the country. Neither the military power wielded by the Emperors of Ancient India nor the colonial- engine of oppression perfected by the Rritish, which are supposed to have "United" India, can be used in a free and democratic India. Indian unity today can be maintained only if the leaden of the united India allow full freedom of development to every linguistic-cultural group, reserving for themselves only such minimum powers as are absolutely necessary in the common interest of the entire people. This is the essence of the federal idea.

However, discussion on this question in pre-Independence years assumed a distorted form, since it was mixed up with the problem of Hindu-Muslim relations. The spokesmen of the two major religious communities became the champions of the unitary and federal structures. It was in the course of an attempted agreement between the two communities (the Luck-now Pact of 1916, the All-Party Conference in the years preceding the 1935 Constitution and in the discussions before the 1947 Transfer of Power) that the leaders of National Congress accepted the federal idea. They therefore had serious reservations on it considering their acceptance of the Federal idea as nothing more than a compromise. They therefore took advantage of the first available opportunity—the partition of India which removed the Muslim League from the scene—to bring back as big a part of the unitary concept as they could. This was how, in framing the Constitution, they subscribed to the federal principle in words, but made the federal Centre so powerful that the State structure as a whole is hardly distinguishable from a unitary one.

Light on this is thrown by the manner in which the problem of Kashmir has been dealt with by the Central leaders. In the days of the most acute conflict on the Kashmir issue—in the immediate post-Independence years—, it was agreed that Kashmir would accede to the Indian Union only in relation to Defence, Foreign Affairs and Communications. In relation to every other subject, the State of Jammu and Kashmir was recognised as fully sovereign. Gradually, however, the autonomy of the State was subjected to increasing encroachment leading ultimately to the present situation where the State is almost as much part of India as any other State. This, however, has resulted in the most acute and continuing conflict between the Centre and the State. The series of arrests and releases to which the former Prime Minister of the State, Sheikh Abdulla, has been subjected and the deadlock that has now been reached after his latest release from prison, indicate the depth and seriousness of the crisis of Centre-State relations in so far as it affects this State.

This one example, together with the developing situation in Nagaland. Mizoland and the Assam Hills shows that the unity of India including these areas cannot be preserved except on the basis of the voluntary consent of the people concerned. The use of the overriding powers vested in the Centre will further antagonise the people of these areas. If this continues for some time, it will be impossible to resist their demand for a complete separation from India.

Hindi-non-Hindi controversy and the general demand of all the States for greater powers and greater financial resources have, of course, not reached such an advanced stage of political crisis. There are however, sufficient indications to show that they too will develop along these lines if they are not dealt with in a statesman-like manner and with vision. The essential prerequisite for such a statesman-like approach is the recognition that India is a country inhabited by peoples with different linguistic-cultural affinities. Any effort at forging the 'unity' of the country without taking on account of the "diversity" of its peoples will lead to disintegration and chaos. It is this fact that is underlined by the anti-Hindi explosion of 1965—an explosion which virtually nullified Art 340 of the Constitution on the Official language. Even after 15 years, (the period laid down under Sec. 2 of that Article). English continues to be used for all the official purposes of the Union and it may continue indefinitely. Centre-State conflicts on economic and financial issues too have led to agitations and movements drawing hundreds of thousands of people, sometimes ranging the people of one State against that of another, and sometimes rallying them against the Centre. It is a question of time for all these problems to come up in as acute a form as that of Kashmir, Nagaland, etc. unless, of course, the problem is tackled with sufficient forethought and insight into the real forces working behind these movements.

From this angle too, it is clear, the State structure built as per the provisions of the Constitution requires thorough overhauling. It is not proposed here to spell out in detail how this overhauling is to be done. What is possible and necessary is only to emphasise that the concept of a Federal State with "a strong Centre" having overriding powers on the autonomy of the States has been tried and found wanting. Continuance of such a structure is bound to break the Constitution under the heavy load of tensions which it has heaped on it.

This discussion may now be summed up by restating the attitude of our party to the Republic in Constitution of India.

- We look upon the framing of the Constitution as a historical landmark in the sense that it has given the working people and their political representatives new opportunities for organising themselves and perfecting their weapons of struggle for a new socialist system. The victories gained by them by way of not only reducing the Congress strength in the country as a whole, but also forming non-Congress Governments on occasions in a few States, are a guarantee that the defence of the Parliamentary system is in the interests of the working people.
- It would, however, be a dangerous illusion to think that this system is so perfect that it can be used in order to

transform the present socio-economic system of exploitation into a socialistic system through the mere use of constitutional means. The danger of this system being subverted by the vested interests is very real. Even if that danger is averted and the political representatives of the working people do get a majority in the Central Parliament the Constitution as has been framed and is being worked now should be thoroughly overhauled if it is to be used for bringing about social transformations.

- An equally or more serious danger to the system emanates from the totally incorrect handling of the problems of Centre-State relations which have already led to serious crises in some parts of the country and which may well expand themselves into other parts. The struggle against these incorrect policies of the ruling Party, and for national integration on the basis of the well-known slogan "unity in diversity", is therefore an inseparable part of the struggle for the preservation of the parliamentary democratic system.

  Parliamentary democratic system.

- The threat to the Parliamentary system emanating from the reactionaries can be fought back if and so long as the system continues and the political representatives of the working people use it skilfully. Adult suffrage, declaration of Fundamental Rights and Directive Principles of State policy; legislative forums and the Judiciary—all these can, to a limited extent be used in order to mobilise increasing sections of the people, against the reactionary attempts at the subversion of the Parliamentary system.

It is on the basis of such an approach to the Constitution that our Party has placed before the people a programme of overhauling the State structure from top to bottom. That programme is as follows:

- The sovereignty of the people. The supreme power in the State must be vested entirely in the people's representatives who will be selected by the people on the basis of proportional representation and be subject to recall at any time upon a demand by the majority of the electorate.

- Universal, equal and direct suffrage for all male and female citizens of India who have attained the age of 18 years, in all elections to Parliament, State legislatures and to local Government bodies. Secret ballot, the right of any voter to be elected to any representative institution.
- Widest autonomy for the various States comprising the Indian Federation.
- Completion of the process of reorganisation of States on linguistic basis. All States shall have equal powers.
- There shall be no Governors for the States appointed from above. Nor shall there be the so-called Upper Houses. At the Centre there shall be two Houses, the House of People and the House of States. Both shall have equal powers and equal number of members. The House of States shall have also equal representation from all the States in the Indian Union. The President shall act in accordance with decisions of both the Houses and shall have no other powers.
- The tribal areas or the areas where population is specific in composition and is distinguished by specific social and cultural conditions will have regional autonomy with regional Government within the State concerned and shall receive fall assistance for their development, or have full autonomy.
- In the field of local administration, a wide network of local bodies from the village upward, directly elected by the people, and invested with real powers and responsibility. Adequate finances shall be ensured to the local bodies.
- All administrative services shall be under the direct control of the respective States or local authorities.
- Introduction of democratic changes in the administration of justice. The judiciary will be completely independent of the executive. The appointment of judges will be subject to approval by Parliament, legislatures or appropriate peoples's organs at different levels;
  - — Right of all persons to sue any official in a court of law:

— Free legal aid and advice will be provided for the needy in order to make legal redress easily available for all.

- The people's democratic Government will infuse the members of the armed forces with the spirit of patriotism and democracy. It will ensure them good living-standards and conditions of service, maximum possible opportunities for cultural life, as well as the education and well-being of their children.

- The introduction of graded tax in industry, agriculture and trade; and maximum relief in taxation for workers, peasants and artisans. Profits shall be controlled.

- All our institutions must be infused with the spirit of democracy, of respect for and reliance on the people as well as confidence in their determination to build a democratic society free from bureaucracy and injustice.

  The people's democratic Government will, therefore, extend democratic forms of initiative and control over every aspect of national life. A key role in this will be played by the trade unions, peasant and agricultural labour associations and other organisations of the working people. The Government will take steps to make the legislative and executive machinery of the country continuously responsive to the democratic wishes of the people and will ensure that masses and their organisations are drawn into active participation in the administration and work of the State. Bureaucratisation shall be eliminated. Wide disparities in salaries and incomes are to be abolished.

- Inviolability of person and domicile: no detention without trial, unhampered freedom of conscience, religious belief and worship, speech, press, assembly, strike and combination, freedom of movement and occupation.

- Equal rights for all citizens irrespective of religion, caste, sex, race or nationality, equal pay for equal work irrespective of sex.

- Removal of social disabilities from which women suffer equal rights with men in such matters as inheritance of property, enforcement of marriage and divorce laws, admission to professions and services.

- Abolition of social oppression of one caste by another, untouchability to be punished by law. Special facilities for the scheduled castes, tribes and other backward communities shall be provided in the matter of services and other social and educational amenities.
- Separation of the State from all religions institutions; the secular character of the State will be guaranteed. Interference by religious institutions in the affairs of the State and the political life of the country shall be prohibited;

  Religious minorities shall be given protection against discrimination.
- Right of people to receive instruction in their mother-tongue in educational institutions; the use of the national language of the particular State as the language of administration in all its public and State institutions, as well as its use as the medium of education in the State up to the highest standard; provision for the use of the language of a minority or region where necessary, in addition to the language of the State. Use of Hindi as an All India language will not be obligatory, but will be encouraged as a means of intercourse between the people of different States. Adherence to the principle of replacing English by the regional languages at the State level and Hindi at the Centre as administrative language. Transition from English to Hindi at the Centre should be simultaneous with that from English to the regional languages in the State; the preparation for this transition, which is being made by the Centre with regard to Hindi, should also be made with all necessary Central assistance in States in regard to regional languages. At the same time, for the transition period, the duration of which should be decided with the consent of the non-Hindi-speaking regions. English should be given the status of an associate administrative language. Equality of all national languages in Parliament and Central administration will be recognised. Members of Parliament will have the right to

speak in any national language and simultaneous translation will be provided in all national languages. All acts, Government orders and resolutions will be made available in all national languages. Urdu language and its script will be protected.

Free and compulsory education up to the secondary stage.

- Establishment of a wide network of health, medical and maternity services, free of cost, as well as rest homes and recreation centres for the people.
- The people's democratic State and Government will undertake the important task of unleashing the creative talents of the people for creating and extending the new progressive people's culture which is anti-imperialist, anti-feudal and democratic in character. Necessary measures to foster, encourage and develop such literature, art and culture as will:
  - — help each nationality, including the tribal people, to develop their own distinctive way and in unison with the common aspirations of the democratic masses of the country as a whole;
  - — help the democratic masses in their struggle to improve their living conditions and enrich their life;
  - — help the people to get rid of caste and communal hatred and prejudices and ideas of subservience or superstitions;
  - — help all people to develop feelings of brotherhood with the peace-loving peoples of ail countries and discourage ideas of racial and national hatred.
- The people's democratic Government will take measures to consolidate the unity of India by fostering and promoting mutual cooperation between the constituent States and between the peoples of different States in the economic, political and cultural spheres, it will pay special attention and financial and other assistance to economically backward and weaker States, regions and areas with a view to helping them rapidly overcome their backwardness.

The Beginning of Partition

The Cabinet Mission arrived in India in March 1946. In the next three months there were hectic discussions between the Mission and the representatives of various political parities and groups, particularly with the leaders of the Congress and the League. Though not as part of the Congress leadership. Gandhi also actively participated in the discussions.

The talks were centred round a long-term scheme to frame a Constitution for India as well as a short-term scheme to form an interim governments at the Centre to carry on the administration of the country till the adoption of the Constitution. From 1st to 17th April, 182 discussion sessions were held involving 472 political leaders. This many sessions had to be arranged because separate interviews had to be held with a number of organisations, apart from the Congress and the 1 clinic, claiming to represent different interests, including several small parties without any appreciable popular support and even organisation which remained only on paper.

The members of the Mission left for Kashmir on 17th April to evaluate the different views presented before them during the interviews. Soon after their return on 24th April, Pethick-Lawrence as the leader of the Mission addressed separate letters to the Congress and the League suggesting one more attempt to obtain an agreement between these parties. He also invited the representatives of the Congress and the League for a conference at Shimla with a view to discussing the possibility of agreement upon a scheme based upon the following "fundamental principles".

'The future constitutional structure of the British India to be as follows: A Union Government dealing with the following subjects: the Foreign Affairs, Defence and Communications. There will be two groups of provinces, the one of the predominantly Hindu provinces and the other of the predominantly Muslim provinces, dealing with all other subjects which the provinces in the respective groups desire to be dealt with in common. The provincial governments will deal with all other subjects and they will have all the residuary sovereign rights."

Soon after receiving this letter, the Congress President Azad sent a reply stating that the scheme was acceptable to him and hoped that it would be acceptable to his Party too. However, the members of the Congress Working Committee were unaware of such a reply having been sent by Azad. Consequently, the Working Committee in a resolution stated that it was difficult for the Congress to accept the scheme suggested by the Cabinet Mission. The resolution also specified its objections with regard to the scheme. The Mission thereupon clarified that acceptance of the scheme was not a condition for participation in the proposed conference. On the basis of this clarification, the Working Committee decided to participate in the Conference. The League also decided to participate reserving the "freedom to accept or reject the proposed scheme".

Accordingly, a week-long conference was held at Shimla. The Mission had already introduced certain changes in the light of the earlier discussions to meet the objections raised by the Congress and the Leauge. It was this revised scheme that was presented before the conference. However, even this revised scheme was not acceptable either to the Congress or to the League. It was decided to hold consultations between Nehru and Jinnah to find if it was possible to leave matters on which there was difference of opinion to arbitration and in that case who should be the arbitrator. Since these consultations also failed, the Second Shimla Conference broke down.

The Viceroy and the Mission claimed that they were trying to bring conciliation between the Congress demand of freedom and sovereignty for an undivided India and the League demand of two separate Constitution-making bodies for Pakistan and Hindustan.

It may be recalled that the Communist Party had pointed out that the only practical solution to the problem was to set up a system with wide autonomy to the people speaking different languages by treating them as separate nationalities and a federal government at the Centre to deal with a limited number of subjects like foreign relations, defence, communication, etc. The nationalists at that time accused the party of encouraging "disintegration" of the country. However, when confronted with the problems of framing a Constitution for the country, the Congress was forced to move along the same way. The Congress leaders made it clear that they were not against the Cabinet Mission's proposal for dividing the provinces into groups. But they forcefully opposed the attempt to the forcible merger of a province in either of these groups against its will. They demanded that after the adoption of a Constitution for India, each province should be given the right to join either group of its choice.

The League was totally opposed to it. They wanted a separate Constitution-making body for the Muslim majority provinces of NWFP, Sindh, Baluchistan, Bengal and Assam to frame a Constitution for a federal government of Pakistan.

In other words, the Congress stood for a federal Constitution for India with autonomous provinces and for the right of the Muslim majority provinces within the Indian federation to frame a common group Constitution if they so desired. The League, on the other hand, demanded the formation of Pakistan comprising the Muslim majority provinces with the right to any province to keep away from in only after the adoption of a Constitution for Pakistan. It was due to the irreconcilability of these demands of the Congress and the League that the Second Shimla Conference broke down.

Soon after the conference, the Cabinet Mission announced its own proposals without introducing any basic change in the proposals presented by the Mission before the conference. These proposals included the following:

- There should be a Union of India, embracing both with India and the States, which should deal with the following subjects: Foreign affairs, Defence, and Communications; and should have the powers necessary to raise the finances required for the above subjects.
- The Union should have an Executive and a Legislature constituted from British Indian and State's representatives. Any question raising a major communal issue in the Legislature should require for its decision a majority of the representatives present and voting of each of the two major communities as well as a majority of all the members present and voting.
- All subjects other than the Union subjects and all residual powers should vest in the Provinces.

- The States shall retain all subjects and powers other than those ceded to the Union.
- The Provinces should be free to form groups with Executives and Legislatures and each group could determine the provincial subjects to be taken in common.
- The Constitutions of the Union and of the groups should contain a provision whereby any Province could by a majority vote of its Legislative Assembly, call for a reconsideration of the terms of the Constitution after an initial period of ten years and ten yearly intervals thereafter.

If item 5 above was brought into operation, it was obvious that the NWF Province and Assam which did not accept the leadership of the League could opt out of Pakistan. But there was another provision contrary' to this included in the scheme. It was provided that the Muslim majority provinces of NWFP and Assam would be included in two different "Sections" comprising the Muslim majority provinces in the west and the cast, respectively, "which shall proceed to settle the Provincial Constitutions for the Provinces included in each section, and shall also decide whether any Group Constitution shall be set up for those provinces..." and that the provinces would have the power to opt out of the groups in accordance with the provision that "such a decision shall be taken by the new legislature of the Province after the general election under the new Constitution."

The Congress opposed these provisions and argued that any province should have the right not to participate in the meetings of the sections and that no province should be forcibly brought under a group. The Working Committee pointed out that the scheme prepared by the Cabinet Mission was ridden with contradictions in that in one clause it provided the provinces with the right to opt out of groups while in another it forcibly included them in groups. Therefore the Working Committee gave the interpretation that the provinces had the right not to participate even at the first meeting of the sections. Accordingly, the Committee informed the Cabinet Mission that its scheme was acceptable subject to this interpretation. However, the Cabinet Mission pointed out that this interpretation was wrong and clarified that the provinces were bound to participate in the initial proceedings of their respective sections.

In the light of this clarification, the Working Committee of the League accepted the scheme of the Cabinet Mission on the ground that in the very provision which was criticised by the Congress lay the foundation of Pakistan. As soon as the League declared its acceptance, the Cabinet Mission announced that both the Congress and the League had accepted the scheme. But the Congress had accepted the scheme only subject to its own interpretation of the provision, which was however, rejected by Mission. The General Secretary of the Congress J.B. Kripalani has put it in record that his argument that the Mission's announcement of the acceptance of the scheme by the Congress was contrary to facts was rejected by other members of the Working Committee.

This was, in fact, the beginning of Gandhi and a section of his disciples taking an attitude against the opinion of the majority of the Congress Working Committee. The latter were guided by the fear that unless the long-term scheme was accepted, the short-term scheme would not come into operation. They feared that if the Congress did not participate in the formation of the interim government, the anti-Congress forces including the League would form the government creating apolitical situation which would be most dangerous to the Congress.

Consequently, they were prepared to deviate a bit from their own principled stand with regard to the long-term scheme to avoid this danger. Gandhi's disciple were of the opinion that this amounted to presenting the provinces like the NWFP and Assam and also the entire national Muslims throughout the country who had been resisting the pressures from the British rulers and the League and opposing a demand of Pakistan as a gift to the Muslim League. They were not afraid of the anti-Congress forces forming a government, because they had with them the instrument of satyagraha which could be used in all circumstances. It was with this view that Gandhi proposed to the Cabinet Mission to invite Jinnah to form a government at the Centre.

If Gandhi and his disciples had gone ahead with this stand challenging the majority of the Congress Working Committee and rallied the people against the scheme of the Cabinet Mission, it would have changed the course of Indian politics. For an anti-imperialist people's upsurge which was conducive to this change was taking shape in the country since the end of the War. This upsurge of revolutionary struggles had been steadily gaining in strength while the discussions with the Cabinet Mission were going on large sections of the people including workers, peasants, the intelligentsia, students and the youth, and the people of the princely states were entering in these struggles with great enthusiasm. These broad sections of the people were not affected either by the Congress-League conflicts or the quarrels between the Hindus and Muslims. If Gandhi and his followers were prepared to lead these people, a broad mass upsurge would have developed throughout the country on an unprecedented scale.

But Gandhi and his followers were not prepared for it. As ever before, they were led more by the neglect and opposition on their part to revolutionary struggles than by anti-imperialism. Consequently, they left the majority of the Working Committee alone by merely expressing dissent to the decisions taken by them.

League towards Direct Action

Both the Congress and the League tried equally well during the discussions with the Cabinet Mission to turn the short-term aspect of the scheme (i.e., formation of an interim government) to their advantage, while adhering to their respective stands on the framing of the future Constitution.

The Cabinet Mission declared that the Viceroy would take steps to form an interim government with the participation of the representatives of the Congress and the League with powers of all the subjects including Defence, if these two parties accepted the long-term aspect of the scheme with regard to Constitution-making. That is, acceptance of the long-term aspect of the scheme was an essential condition for the participation in the interim government. That was why the Congress accepted the scheme with their own interpretation and by the League with out any interpretation of their our. Accordingly, the Cabinet Mission and the Viceroy decided that it was time to start discussion on the interim government.

In the third week of June the Viceroy asked the Congress to suggest the names of six Hindus, including a representative of the Scheduled Castes, and the League to suggest the names of five Muslim members to the proposed interim government. He had also informed them that, in addition to these 11 Hindu and Muslim members, there would be three more members in the government representing the Sikh, Christian and Parsi communities. Accordingly, the Congress and the League submitted their lists and the Viceroy accepted the list of the League but struck off the names of Sarat Chandra Bose. Dr. Zakir Hussain and Rajkumari Amrit Kaur from the Congress list. Since the latter two belonged to Muslim and Christian communities, he refused to accept them in the Congress list. The Viceroy insisted that all the representatives of the Congress including the Scheduled Caste representative should be caste-Hindus.

This was objected to by the Congress. It also took objection to the inclusion of Abdur Rab Nistar who had been defeated in the 1916 elections in the League list which was accepted by the Viceroy. The Congress was also opposed to N.F. Engineer, who was the public prosecutor in the INA trial, being included in the list representing the Parsi community.

Gandhi was clearly opposed to Congress participation in such an interim government. In a letter drafted by him on be half of the Congress Working Committee and intended to be sent to the Viceroy, Gandhi placed particular emphasis on the following points.

- Since the League was openly a Muslim organisation, no non-Muslim should be included in the League list of members of the interim government.
- Since the Congress was a national organisation, its list could include Muslims.
- Except in the case of five members alloted to the League, it should not have the right to express opinion on the selection of any one else.
- The interim government should be responsible to the elected members of the Central Assembly.

The Working Committee, however, did not even consider this draft letter. Although the Working Committee was not in agreement with the list prepared by the Viceroy, it was not willing to reject it. The Committee thought it possible to eliminate the ill-effect of the alterations made by the Viceroy in the Congress list.

But the Working Committee bad a firm opinion with regard to the right and status of the interim government. The Congress was not prepared to make compromise on the principle that the interim government should be able to function as a government of a free, sovereign country without interference from the Viceroy. On 30th May. President Azad wrote a letter to the Viceroy to this effect. Azad received a favourable reply from the Viceroy stating that the interim government would be treated with considerations given to a Dominion government. With this, the Working Committee on 18th June took a tentative decision to accept the proposal of the Cabinet Mission with regard to the interim government. It did not, however, communicate this decision to the Viceroy.

The decision to accept the proposal with regard to the interim government, however, widened the difference that had existed within the Congress leadership. For example, Kripalani has stated that Sardar Patel had become angry when he said that, whatever be the decision of the Working Committee, he would resign his position in the Congress if it approved of the scheme to compulsorily merge some of the Muslim majority provinces in Pakistan against their wishes. On 19th June, Gandhi told the members of the Working Committee in clear terms that if the Committee gave approval to a list which did not include a national Muslim and which included N. P. Engineer, he would have nothing to do with it.

In the meantime, an incident took place which was likely to wreck the entire decision of the Congress with regard to the acceptance of the scheme of the Cabinet Mission. The contents of a letter which Jinnah had sent to Wavell appeared in the Statesman. In that letter Jinnah sought from Wavell a number of assurances with regard to the interim government, which were not at all acceptable to the Congress. Soon after, the Congress President demanded from the Viceroy a copy of Jinnah's letter as well as his reply to Jinnah. The reply contained an assurance that no change in principle in the list of members of the interim government would be made without the approval of both the Congress and the League. The meaning of this was clear. A national Muslim should not be included in the Congress list without the permission of the League. Besides, the selection of the representatives of the minority communities including the Scheduled Castes would also require the approval of the Congress and the League.

In addition to giving this assurance to Jinnah, the Viceroy informed the Congress President on 22nd June that it was not possible to include a national Muslim in its list. Thereupon the Congress Working Committee decided against participation in the interim government subject to this condition. It may be stated that Maulana Azad did not agree with this decision - another instance to show that the difference within the Congress leadership was getting sharper.

The Congress decision against participation in the interim government brought the work of the Cabinet Mission to a deadlock. As the final effort to resolve the crisis, the Mission invited Gandhi and Sardar Patel for a talk. During the talks, differences of opinion between Gandhi and Patel surfaced even on the question of the approach the Mission had adopted in the tal's.

Gandhi emphatically stated that he was suspicious about the Missions long-term and short-term schemes and that he was not in agreement with the acceptance of the schemes. Following, the Working Committee declared its rejection of the Viceroy's proposals with regard to the interim government, but stated at the same time that it accepted the long-term scheme of the Cabinet Mission with its own interpretation.

According to Jinnah, this meant rejection of the Cabinet Mission's long-term scheme by the Congress. Since his Party had accepted the scheme, he expected the formation of an interim government without the Congress. But the Cabinet Mission maintained that if the Congress and the League were not prepared to join the interim government, the entire scheme for Constitution-making would fail. Besides, the Mission interpreted the decisions of the Congress and the League as if both had accepted its proposals unconditionally.

As the Congress has rejected the proposal with regard to the formation of an interim government, the Cabinet Mission decided not to proceed with its scheme and left India leaving the Viceroy to hold discussions on the formation of the interim government and to take steps to form the Constitution-making body. This made the League leadership highly discontented. They demanded that since the question of forming the interim government had been deferred, the steps being taken to form the Constitution-making body also should be put off. When the British Cabinet refused to concede this demand, Jinnah accused to Cabinet of "bad faith". The League also decided to withdraw its acceptance of the Cabinet Mission's scheme and to resort to "direct action", to achieve its objective of Pakistan.

Now it was the first time in the history of the League that it was renouncing the constitutional method of struggle and contemplating direct action. This had far-reaching consequences in Indian politics. Here it is worth noticing the fact that hitherto only one section of the Indian bourgeois leadership (i.e., the Congress) had resorted to the method of open mass agitation as an integral part of the politics of bargain.

For the Congress, the final form of direct action was reached in 1942. They were now engaged in the final stage of the bargain making use of the popular support they had gained in the 1942 struggle. It was at this stage that another section of the bourgeois leadership (i.e., League) was resorting to the method of direct action. While the Congress had been engaged in direct action to achieve swaraj, the League was now resorting to direct action to achieve Pakistan. The League also decided to observe 16th August as 'Direct Action day which together with the events that followed the observance the Day changed the entire course of the political history of India.

Kashmir

While the Congress and the League leaders were engaged in discussions with the Cabinet Mission, the problem of the place of the princely states in the future Constitution of India had started coming to the fore. The attitude of the British government towards this problem was thoroughly undemocratic. The relationship between 'British India' and the princely stales was governed by a treaty entered into between them. Consequently, in the event of the British relinguishing power in India, the princely states would become free. The British government had been maintaining that the states had the right to decide their own future.

The League had never openly expressed an opinion about it. Their only concern was the place of the Muslims as a community in India's future constitutional set-up. The attitude of the Congress was different. They wanted to establish democratic rule in the princely states as well as in British India. This was not merely because they were more committed to democracy than the League; establishment of democracy in the princely states was essential for them to keep in their proper place those forces which were opposed to them in the future constitutional set-up of the Indian Union. If the representatives of the Maharajas of the states happened to go to the Central Assembly and the Cabinet, there was a possibility of them joining hands with the representatives of communal and caste politics facilitating the British vested interests to continue their dominance in a new form. It was therefore natural for the Congress to extend its support to the demand for ending the autocratic rules in the states.

However, the Congress was never prepared to help without reservation the struggles for responsible governments in the princely states and to give these struggle a revolutionary character. In the earlier days, the Congress kept away from these struggles in accordance with the policy of "non-interference in the internal affairs of the princely slates". Later, when organisations like Praja Mandals and state Congress started emerging in the states, Congressmen came forward to occupy leadership positions in these organisations. However, they looked upon the mass agitations in the states as a mean to bargain with the rulers of the states.

The discussion on India's future constitutional set-up which started with the First Shimla Conference gave an added strength to the agitations for responsible governments in the princely states. The movements in certain states like Travancore, Cochin, Hyderabad and certain states in Orissa were under the leadership of leftists. Even in those stales where they were not in leading positions, their influence in the movement was evident. Particular mention must be mode in this connection of Kashmir in which a majority of the population was Muslim and the Maharaja a Hindu. Consequently, the early form of the movement for responsible government in Kashmir had the characteristics of Muslim politics. Started in the name of 'Kashmir Muslim Conference', the movement transformed itself into 'National Conference', via 'Muslim Conference'.

Its leaders like Sheikh Abdullah and G. M. Sadiq came under the influence of left-wing nationalism and socialist-communist ideologies. They engaged themselves in the task of rallying the people irrespective of their religious affiliations against autocracy and landlordism. Thus, the National Conference became part of the left front comprising communists, socialists and left-wing Congressmen in British India.

These developments before and during the war influenced the post-war politics in Kashmir, strengthening the movement for responsible government there. Following the slogan of 'Quit India', the National Conference raised the slogan of 'Quit Kashmir', meaning thereby that the Maharaja should quit Kashmir and transfer power to the people.

The democratic movements is no other Indian state had raised such a radical slogan with far-reaching consequences. The demand raised in most other states was confined to the establishment of a government responsible to an elected legislative body with the Maharaja remaining as the formal head of the state. The significance of Kashmir was that, as distinct from this, a native organisation representing bourgeois nationalism came forward to raise the demand of ending the rights of the Maharaja.

An equally significant feature of Kashmir was the communal character of the leadership of the National Conference. It was a mass organisation comprising people of all communities with a leadership composed of the representatives of all communities under the overall leadership of Sheikh Abdullah who belonged to the Muslim community. The very existence of such an organisation constituted a challenge to the League's 'two-nations theory'. The only organisation matching to this was the mass movement led by Abdul Ghaffar Khan in the NWI Province, which was a source of constant irritation to the League.

Consequently, the democratic movement in Kashmir appeared as a problem which was in a sense connected with the discussions at the Shimla Conference and with the Cabinet Mission.

The Kashmir problem worsened when the talks with the Cabinet Mission were in progress. "The League leadership made an attempt to get the National Conference merged in the League with a view to strengthen their bargain with the Congress and the Cabinet Mission. Out it did not succeed. Like the Khan Brothers in the NWF Province and the national Muslims elsewhere in the country, the National Conference took a firm stand against Muslim sectarianism. As its slogan was 'Quit Kashmir', the Maharaja and his government started taking actions against it. Leaders of the National Conference, including Sheikh Abdullah, were arrested. The Sheikh was arrested while he was on his way to Delhi to meet and hold discussions with Nehru who was then the president of the All India States People's Conference. This provoked Nehru who proceeded to Kashmir, but he was also arrested on his entry into the state. The situation was brought under control by the intervention of the Viceroy and the Indian government, on the one side, and the Congress Working Committee, on the other.

This was a shining example of the attitude of the British government and that of the rulers of the princely states as well as the leaders of the Congress and the League towards the problems of the states. The Maharaja tried to suppress the democratic movements in the state by putting under arrest even Jawaharlal Nehru who was widely known to become the Prime Minister of the country within the next few necks. Neither the Viceroy nor the British government did anything worthwhile to dissuade the Kashmir government from taking such repressive actions. The Viceroy who suggested the Kashmir government to avoid Nehru's arrest and to postpone the trial of Sheikh Abdullah received a reply from the Maharaja offering to "abdicate and his Prime Minister to resign if the Government of India compelled them to take no action against Jawaharlal". Thereupon the Viceroy withdrew his suggestion. It was only after the arrest of Nehru that the trial of Sheikh Abdullah was adjourned and Nehru brought back to Delhi at the instance of the Viceroy, the Cabinet Mission and the Congress Working Committee.

It is worth noticing that the Muslim League was completely indifferent to the Kashmir issue. The National Conference accepting the general political outlook of the Congress and under the leadership of a national Muslim who had been maintaining relations with Nehru, had been irritating to the League and its leader, Jinnah But they were helpless. They were placed themselves in a position in which they were unable to protest against the actions taken even by a 'Hindu ruler' against such an organisation like the National Conference and Its leaders.

On the other side, the leaders of the Congress which had been characterised by the League as a Hindu political party had been coming forward to protest against the repressive actions of this Hindu ruler. Although this was contrary to the 'two-nations theory of the League, it could not have taken any other stand in the background *of* the bargain with the British and the Congress in which it had been engaged.

On the other hand, although the Congress and Nehru acted in a manner helpful to the National Conference, they found that the only way to solve the Kashmir problem was through consultations with the Viceroy and the Cabinet Mission. Nehru's biographer has stated that on hearing the news of the arrest of the Sheik "his (Nehru's) first impulse was to leave Shimla to Kashmir to support his friends, but he curbed himself so as to give the Viceroy a chance to intervene and not to worsen the situation by disobeying any restraining order which might be served on him... By the middle of June. Jawaharlal felt he had waited long enough and decided to enter the State..." He added that "it was the adjournment *of* the trial of Sheikh Abdullah and the insistence of the Working Committee which led Jawaharlal to return to Delhi on the clear understanding that he would be back in Kashmir".

The Kashmir incident was only one of the events which had been taking place in the princely states, all over India. Following the efforts made by the leftist organisations to link the mighty struggles of workers, peasants, government employees and other sections of the people that were going on across *the* country with the people's movements in the princely states, these movements had begun to take a revolutionary form. Some of these movements took a still higher form as that of Pannapra-Vayalar and Telangana.

The movement in Kashmir under the leadership of the National Conference also had taken a revolutionary form. The 'Naya Kashmir' programme formulated by the National Conference had been considerably influenced by the ideologies of communism and socialism. However, the partition of India and the developments that followed caused the democratic movement in Kashmir to deviate from this path and made it a problem preparing the ground for disintegration of India. The British rulers, the Muslim League (later the rulers of Pakistan) and the Hindu communalists all alike utilised the democratic movement based on secularism and the 'Naya Kashmir' programme as part of the Hindu-Muslim problem which was later turned into an India-Pakistan problem.

The Congress, though it had adopted an approach relatively more democratic and secular, regarded, on the other hand, the problems of the princely states, including that of Kashmir, as a part of its bargain with the government and the Muslim League. The dreadful results of this attitude adversely affected the future not only of Kashmir, and other princely states but also of the entire country.

Before and after the Calcutta Riots

We have noted earlier that the League had unconditionally accepted the long-term scheme of the Cabinet Mission. They regarded the provision contained in the scheme to group the provinces into sections with the right to every section to decide by majority votes the future of the provinces included in the respective sections would lead to the formation of Pakistan. The Congress, on the other hand, accepted the long-term scheme subject to its own interpretation of this provision. The League leaders maintained that the acceptance of the scheme by the Congress with interpretation was, in fact, a rejection of the scheme and accused the Cabinet Mission of hiding this fact.

As we know, the essence of the short-term scheme of the Cabinet Mission was the formation of an interim government at the Centre with the representatives of the parties accepting the long-term scheme. Thus, the leaders of the Muslim League thought that the interim government would be formed including the representatives of the league which had accepted the long-term scheme but excluding the Congress which had rejected the scheme. I have also thought they would be able to utilise such a political situation to strengthen their activities for the formation of Pakistan. But the Cabinet Mission's declaration that both the Congress and the League had accepted its long-term scheme believed their hope.

When the problem of the formation of interim government came up, it became necessary for the Congress to introduce certain changes in the organisation. Nehru took over the presidentship from Azad. Subsequently, the AICC which met at Bombay in July ratified the Working Committee's resolution accepting the long-term scheme of the Cabinet Mission with the interpretation that the provinces irrespective of which section they were placed in would have the right of autonomy.

Besides, in the speech he made as the Congress President, Nehru rejected League's interpretation and declared that neither the British government nor the Cabinet Mission had the right to impose limitations on the sovereignty of the Constituent Assembly. This angered the League leaders. The efforts made by the British government to appease them also failed. The Council of the League which met at Bombay on 27th July decided to resort to the method of 'direct action' in protest against the attitudes of the Congress and the British government.

A resolution adopted by the Council called upon the Muslims to renounce forthwith the titles conferred upon them by the "align government". In the words of Jinnah, "never have we in the whole history of the League done anything except by constitutional methods and by constitutionalism. But now we are obliged and forced into this position. This day we did goodbye to constitutional methods." Jinnah said that the British and the Congress had been holding pistols in their hands, the former the pistol of authority and arms and the latter that of mass struggle and non-cooperation. "Today we have also forged a pistol and are in a position to use it."

The council directed the lower units of the League to organise processions and public meetings as part of the observation of the 'Direct Action Day* on 16th August to explain the League stand on the scheme of the Cabinet Mission. Although it was suggested that the observance of the Protest Day should be peaceful, it tamed out to be the beginning of terrible the events (Hindu-Muslim riots) to come.

Meanwhile, certain developments took place before the observation of the Direct Action Day, which agave it an added impetus. The Viceroy had been taking steps with regard to the formation of an interim government in accordance with the short-term scheme of the Cabinet Mission. He presented before the Congress president Nehru and the League President Jinnah a proposal to forma M-member interim government with six Congress members (including one Scheduled Castes member), five League members and three representatives of other minority communities including one Sikh.

But since the League had withdrawn its acceptance of the long-term scheme of the Cabinet Mission when it decided to resort to direct action and also since the Congress had already declared acceptance of it, the British government had taken a decision to form the interim government without the representation of the League. Accordingly, the Viceroy sent a letter to the Congress President Nehru inviting him to form an interim government.

In the same letter the Viceroy indicated that he would appreciate Nehru reaching an agreement with Jinnah and asked him to consider whether he should discuss the matter with Jinnah before submitting his proposals in this regard.

In reply to this Nehru stated that he would approach the League and urge their cooperation if a public announcement was made to the effect that he bad been invited to constitute an interim government and that he bad accepted the invitation. Accordingly, an announcement was made on 22nd August.

This announcement naturally angered the League leaders. Consequently they carried out vigorously the observation of the Direct Action Day. The observation of the Day in Calcutta deserves particular mention. The League government of Bengal declared 16th August a holiday. In the background of extremely provocative speeches and other forms of agitation adopted by the League, the action of the provincial government created a situation of great tension in Calcutta. The observation of 'Direct Action Day' culminated in mass killings and other acts of violence. Although an accurate account is not available, it has been generally admitted that about 5,000 people were killed and 15,000 seriously injured. Human corpses piled and blood spilled all over the streets. Among the killed were women and children. Hindus, Muslims and Sikhs were all among the victims of violence.

Even while these brutal acts were going on, the provincial government did not take any action to put down the violence. The Governor who was particularly responsible for the maintenance of law and order did not move either. He stuck to the attitude that he would not do anything unless asked by his ministers. The military was called in only after the massacre which lasted for about 48 hours. And within a few hours after that all violent activities were stopped and the situation brought under control.

This brief description of events clearly demonstrates the role played by the Muslim League and the British authorities in the outbreak of the Calcutta riots. Through the "direction action day" observation, the League tried to create the impression that it was capable of creating the kind of 'mass force' that the Congress was able to forge through consistent efforts made during the past quarter of a century. And the League ministry of Bengal tried to convert it into the beginning of the politics of communal riots. The British Governor was not prepared either to dissuade them from this or to curb the riots with the help of the military. It was a warning to the effect that, like the Congress, the League also was capable of forging the weapon of 'direct action' and that if the League ventured to do it, the entire country would be thrown into a civil war.

The League organised these riots against the Hindus and the Congress. At that stage, the victims were mostly the Hindus. As it was found that the ministers and the Governor who were responsible for patting down the riots were not acting in that way, the Hindus and the Sikhs also started resorting to violence. Among those who were killed and injured at the stage, there were many Muslims. The riots spread to other places too. In Noakhali (now in Bangladesh) the victims of the riots were the Hindus, while in Bihar and other places the victims were the Muslims. Thus, the Calcutta riots led to a series of communal riots in many parts of the country.

These riots were reflected in the moves being made to form the interim government. The Viceroy who had taken steps to form an interim government under the leadership of Nehru, now started exerting pressures on him to reach an agreement with Jinnah with a view to bring the League in the interim government. He reminded Nehru that the exclusion of the League from the interim government would only help to spread the communal riots all over the country.

Meanwhile, a new ministry (Executive Council) had taken office on 2nd September. On the very next day. Sir Shafaat Ahmad Khan, a member of the Cabinet, was stabbed. The attack on him was an expression of wrath of the followers of the League for allowing his name to be included in the list of Congress members in the proposed ministry. This further worsened the situation and also helped the Viceroy to exert more pressure on Nehru to placate the League and change the composition of the ministry. Finally, on 15th October. Sharat Chandra Bose, Shafaat Ahmad Khan and Syed Ali Zaheer resigned from the ministry to make room for the League nominees in the ministry. Subsequently Liaquat Ali Khan, Chundrigar. Abdur Rab Nishtar, Ghaffar Ali Khan, and Jogendra Nath Mandal joined the ministry representing the League. Mandal, belonging to the Scheduled Castes figured in the League quota because Azad Ali, a Muslim, was included among the Congress nominees in the ministry! Thus, the entry of the League in the ministry sharpened the Congress-League quarrel.

The explanation offered by the League for deciding to join the ministry is significant to note. They considered that the entire Central administration remaining under the control of the Congress was detrimental to the interests of the Muslim and other communities. Further, the presence of certain individuals in the ministry who did not command the confidence and respect of the Muslim community would have serious repurcussions. Jinnah wrote to the viceroy that the League was joining the ministry to avoid these problems.

In other words, the entry of the League in the ministry was a continuation of the communal riots raging on the streets of Calcutta and in the villages in Noakhali, Bihar and other places. Two mutually competing parties in the government and two communities cutting the throat of each other in the streets and in the fields—this was the situation. The entire Indian politics had entered a new and more dangerous stage.

The Greatest Test

The Conflicts that occurred inside the interim government as well as those outside before its formation marked the beginning of the process of partition, India. All these won known to the public. Certain other developments also were of taking place not so publicly during the same period. Although most people could not perceive the significance these developments at that time, they had a lot to do with the politics of Indian Union which emerged out of the partition.

We have noted earlier that Nehru had taken over the Congress presidentship from Azad while the discussions with Cabinet Mission were in progress. Consequently the Viceroy invited Nehru as the Congress President to form the interim government. However, evidence had come to light later to indicate that things might have developed in a different way. J. B. Kripalani, then the General Secretary of the Congress, stated:

> The Working Committee meeting held in Calcutta from December 7 to 11.1945 decided to hold the session of the Congress *in* the first week of April 1946. Proposals were invited by the AICC office for the election of the president...Three names were duly proposed by the provinces— those of Sardar Patel, Pattabhi and mine. Jawaharlal's name had not been proposed.
>
> Gandhiji had earlier expressed a wish that at that juncture Jawaharlal should be the President. What reasons impelled Gandhiji to recommend his name were not mentioned, so far as I remember. The final date of the proposals to be received by the AICC was drawing near. Only fifteen members of the All India Congress Committee are required to propose the name of the President. A meeting of the Working Committee was being held in Delhi a few days earlier. I sent a paper round, proposing the name of Jawaharlal. The

> members of the Working Committee signed it and also some local members of the AICC. It was thus that the name of Jawaharlal was proposed for the presidentship. The others thereupon withdrew their names. It was certain that if Jawaharlal's name had not been proposed, the Sardar would have been elected as the President. The Sardar did not like my intervention. I have since wondered if as the General Secretary, I should have been instrumental in proposing Jawaharlal's name in deference to Gandhiji's wishes in the matter. But I did not think that the matter was of very great importance. The President of the Congress is the Chairman of the Working Committee. He is first among the equals. No important issue can be decided except by the Working Committee. Also. I do not think that independence, in whatever form it might come, was round the corner. I thought that we had many more struggles ahead. But who can forecast the future? On such seemingly trivial accidents depend the fate of men and even of nations.

Kripalani indicates that if he had not proposed Nehru's name to the presidentship at the instance of Gandhi. Sardar Patel would have been called upon to form the interim government as the Congress President. Although Patel and other members of the Working Committee, as the loyal colleagues of Gandhi, approved of Nehru outwardly as the head of the interim governments, they were unable to approve of this choice at heart. As the League ministers left the interim government following the partition, the friction between Nehru and Patel became intense. It continued till the death of Patel.

This was hardly a problem of rivalry between Nehru and Patel alone; it was the beginning of factionalism and conflicts at the top level of the Congress. The faction fight appeared again when a new president had to be elected following the resignation of Nehru as the president consequent upon his selection as the bead of the ministry in the interim government. Azad Pattabhi Sitaramayya and Kripalani were the candidates to fill the post of the president. When it appeared that Kripalani was most likely to get elected to the liking of Gandhi and Patel many Congress leaders, including Nehru, approached Gandhi requesting him not to approve of Kripalani's candidature. Nevertheless. Kripalani was elected president of the Congress.

Briefly speaking, while a wild controversy was raging between the Congress and the league on the question of India's partition, a serious factional fight was developing within the Congress itself. The contents of both these conflicts were of the same nature. The main question underlying the Congress-League conflict was whether India should be kept united or should be divided into two in order to share the political power which was going to be obtained in the near future. The conflict within the Congress, on the other band, was over the question of who should occupy the top position in the Congress which was going to wield political power.

Although this was a new development at the Central leadership level in the Congress, it was not a new phenomenon in the Congress organisation taken as a whole. Right in 1937 when Congress ministries took office in the different provinces, disputes started at the provincial level over berth in the ministries.

The war and the Quit India struggle pat an end to these disputes for the time being. But when the Congress ministries again came to power in the provinces following the elections in 1946, the disputes reappeared in the provinces. When the gulf between the ministerial and organisational wings widened on the one side, disputes arose on the other side as to who should be the leader of each of the two wings. The developments that took place in the second half of 1945 only showed that this dispute spread to the Central leadership when the time came to form the interim government.

These developments naturally perturbed Gandhi. But more perturbing developments were taking place in the different parts of the country. The communal riots which started in Calcutta spread to Noakhali and from there to Bihar. Details of the attack on the members of the minority Hindu community in eastern Bengal bad been coming in. In one of his prayer meetings, Gandhi announced that Congress President Kripalani would go to Noakhali and stated that if necessary h(himself would visit Noakhali and die there. Accordingly, Kripalani accompanied by his wife. Sucheta Kripalani and a group of Congress leaders left for Noakhali. They collected details or the ghastly happenings and consoled the victims of these acts and rendered them different kinds of assistance. Following. Gandhi himself left for Noakhali.

Meanwhile communal riots had sprouted to the Hindu majority province of Bihar. While the Noakhali killings were organised to avenge the attack on the Muslims at a certain stage during the Calcutta riots, the attack on the Muslim minority in Bihar was organised to avenge the attack on the Hindu minority in Noakhali. Pained deeply by these happenings, Gandhi wrote to Patel: "My non-violence is being tested here in a way it has never been tested before."

As reports from Bihar started pouring in, Gandhi felt the desire to leave Noakhali and go to Bihar. He felt that being a Hindu it was his duty to leave Noakhali where the Hindus were being attacked and go to Bihar where the Muslims were facing the same fate. However, certain Muslim leaders, advised him that his presence in Bihar was not an urgent necessity since other leaden from Delhi had arrived there and that it would be better if he continued his work in Noakhali. So, he stayed back.

This was the beginning of the activities in which he was going to engage himself in the next several months. Gandhi had been staying in the capital city of Delhi to assist other Congress leaders in their discussions with the British authorities on the transfer of power. He felt deeply disturbed by the fact that the Congress leaders who were considered to be his loyal disciples were not working according to his advice. He saw for himself that Nehru. Patel, Rajagopalachari and other top leaders were eager to get hold of power by any means. Further, they were fighting among themselves over the sharing of the political power after its transfer to the Congress. Above all, there was the problem of the country-wide communal riots. He described this as "the most complex and difficult problem which he had to face in his life."

The (Congress) organisation which he was able to build through consistent efforts for a quarter of a century had begun to crack. The leaders who had been engaged in selfless service to the people had now begun to engage themselves in factional struggles over the sharing of power. On the other side, the Hindu and Muslim communities were brutally attacking each other in such a way as it appeared impossible to ever realise the goal of Hindu-Muslim unity and friendship which he bad been consistently advocating.

In the circumstance, Gandhi thought that his place of activities was not the capital city but in the villages of East Bengal and Bihar where people belonging to the two communities were killing each other and that his work was not to advise and assist the Congress leaders in their discussions with the British government on the transfer of power, but to solace and assist those who fell victim to communal riots. Thus, while Nehru, Patel, Rajagopalachari and other disciples of Gandhi began to wield power as ministers. Gandhi took up the work of saving the people from the horror of communal riots as the last mission of his life.

The gulf between Gandhi and the leaders who were known to be his disciples was widening. Two groups were emerging: a ministerial group playing all kinds of tactics with a view to acquire political power as early as possible, on one side, and Gandhi and his closest associates feeling disturbed by the sight of these manoeuvres and engaged themselves in implementing constructive programmes, including communal unity.

How did this happen? How did the Congress which was considered to have been built on the principles of non-violence and selfless service to the people turn itself into a centre of rivalries for political power"? How did the ideology of communal unity ceaselessly propagated for about a quarter of a century get destroyed in this manner? Gandhi was unable to find answers to these questions. But he had recognised the truth that such a situation had emerged. This was what distinguished him from other Congress leaders.

Strikes and Peasant Struggles

The arguments and counter-arguments centring around the formation of the interim government and the communal riots that followed did not complete the picture of Indian politics in the later half of 1946 and in 1947. While the tragic drama of communal riots was being enacted in the different parts of the country, and in parallel to it, certain other developments also were taking place.

We have dealt earlier with the mass upsurge which had emerged throughout the country following the end of the war. Strikes by workers, demonstrations and other forms *of* protest action by workers, students and other sections of the urban masses were widespread in the country. These were linked with political agitations, too. This was how agitations embracing all sections of the people developed against the trial of the INA leaders. It was in the same atmosphere again that people in thousands came out in support of the navel mutiny against imperialist domination.

It was, in fact, to stem the tide of this mass upsurge that the British imperialists devised the evil design to prepare the grounds to intensify the Hindu-Muslim conflicts leading them to communal riots, while, at the same time, creating the impression that efforts were being made to transfer power to Indians. As a result, communal feelings began to get strengthened among the poor sections of the people like workers and peasants leading the less class conscious among them to actively participate in the communal riots. However, the rulers could not completely stem the tide of strikes and peasant struggles as evident from the following.

In August-September 1916, workers of the South Indian Railway went on a strike. The authorities let loose cruel repressions against the striking railwaymen as a result of which nine were killed and more than a hundred injured in the police firing. Over 400 workers were arrested. The AITUC gave a call to observe 18th September as a day of solidarity with the striking railwaymen. In response to this call, rallies and demonstrations were held in the different parts of the country and funds collected to help the workers on strike. The strike which brought the railway traffic to a standstill for about a month was withdrawn only after Asaf Ali the Minister of Railways in the interim government, gave assurances to the workers on their demands.

Workers of the North Eastern Railway also launched a strike almost during the same period. As was the case with the strike in the South Indian Railway, communists and the AITUC were in the forefront of this strike. Although there was a union led by the Muslim League in the NW Railway, the union led by the Communists was able to surge ahead of all other unions, including the one led by the League. Later, workers under its leadership courageously fought against the communal riots in the north western region until the partition of the country.

Among the strikes launched in other sectors during the 1946-47 period, the strikes of the textile workers in Bombay, Nagpur and Kanpur and those *of* the worker, of the coal mines in Giridih in Bihar, workers of the Kolar gold mines in Mysore, the port workers of Calcutta deserve particular mention. In many of these strikes several workers were killed and several more injured in police firing.

A notable feature of the series of strikes launched during the post-war years was that a large section of middle class employees including government servants had entered in the strike movement. The country-wide strike of the employees of the Post and Telegraph Department was, in fact, the forerunner of the strikes of the government employees in Madras and in other provinces. Neither the trade union workers nor the government employees bad ever thought that it was possible to link the agitations and struggles of the government employees with those of the organised working class. The special feature of the 1946-47 strike movement was that it marked the beginning of the efforts in that direction.

It was an upsurge of the working class embracing the movements in the princely states more extensively than ever before. The strikes which were launched by the working class in the stales like Travancore, Hyderabad. Mysore, Indore, etc., were linked with the political movements being conducted by the democrats in the respective states. Working class struggles in Travancore and Hyderabad had played significant roles in the development of the movements of Punnapra-Vayalar and Telangana respectively, which represented the highest form of the people's struggles in the princely states.

A revolutionary upsurge was witnessed also among the peasantry during the same period. In April 1945, immediately before the end of the war in Europe, a conference of the All India Kisan Sabha was held in the Netra Kona Village in the Mymansingh district of East Bengal (now in Bangladesh). In the conference and also in the meetings of the Kisan Council that followed, the problems affecting the peasants as well as the common problems affecting the people were discussed elaborately and a call was given to build a broad based mass movement with a view to find solutions to these problems. These developments prepared the ground for mass based peasant struggles in all the provinces side by side the working class strikes.

Even before the Netra Kona session of the Kisan Sabha, the peasants in Bengal had been raising the slogan of reducing the share of the landowners (jotedars) to one-third instead of the existing one-half of the crops raised by the cultivating peasants (sharecroppers). The resulting movement known by the generic name of the Tebhaga movement received a new impetus from the Kisan conference. Thus, while the discussions with the Cabinet Mission and other political developments were taking place, the tide of the Tebhaga movements in Bengal was rising high.

Peasant struggles based on similar partial, immediate demands of the peasantry were going on in many other provinces. But the Tebhaga movement was distinct from the peasant movements in other parts of the country on two counts. First, in all other provinces the peasant movement was confined to certain regions, whereas in Bengal the movement was spread all over the province. For example, in Kerala the movement of the peasants to establish their right to pay the rent to the landlord in cash was confined to the northern part of the erstwhile Malabar district. Similarly, in Andhra, the peasant movement (except the Telangana movement) was largely confined to the Krishna. Guntur and Godavari districts. Again, in Maharashtra the peasant movement was purely confined to the centres of the Warli peasants embracing one or two taluks.

Second, peasants in both the Muslim majority East Bengal and the Hindu majority West Bengal equally participated in the straggle, it may even be slated that the movement in the East was somewhat more powerful than in the West. It may be noted that the entire peasantry, irrespective of religious affiliations, were fighting against the jotedars in the Muslim majority region of a province in which a political party (the Muslim League) functioning on the basis of the argument that the Muslims are a separate nation, was in power. And it was the Muslim League ministry which resorted to repressive actions against these struggles with a determination to suppress them. The Hindu and Muslim jotedars who were quarrelling with each be on the issues of future Constitution and the interim government extended full support to these repressive action of the League government.

The Tebhaga movement and the Kisan Sabha played a unique role in resisting the communal riots in Bengal and Bihar it may be specifically noted that the riots did not break out in those areas in the Noakhali-Tippcra districts of Bengal in which the Kisan Sabha had considerable influence. In such areas the Kisan Sabha and the activists of the Tebhaga movement organised relief camps for the refugees from the riot affected neighbouring areas. Similarly, in Moghpur in the Monghyr district of Bihar, the Communist Party. Kisan Sabha and other mass organisations organised relief activities to protect the people in the riot stricken areas and to provide relief to the victims of the communal riots. In the urban areas, the trade unions and students organisations were active in the relief operations. Both in the rural and urban areas the Communist Party was in the forefront in giving leadership to these activities.

This and the activities of Gandhi in Noakhali were apparently the same. Both were pained by the sight of people, who ought to have lived as brethren, cutting each other's throat and both expressed their intense desire to stop it. However, they were poles apart on the answer to the question as to how such a situation came about and how to get out of it. The Communist Party regarded that the way to stop all quarrels and to forge unity among the different communities was to wage an uncompromising struggle against the British rulers and organised struggles of workers and peasants against capitalists and landlords based on their grievances and demands. Gandhi on the other hand, had been engaged in giving advice and directions to the Congress leaders in their negotiations for a compromise with the British government. He had no sympathy towards workers' and peasants' struggle.

But the atmosphere of communal riots did not cease to exist, as desired by Gandhi and the Communist Party; on the contrary the conflicts were getting sharper day by day. Finally, in the midst of the worst kind of human tragedy, two independent countries, Indian Union and Pakistan, emerged.

Could this have been avoided? It is difficult to answer this question. But the Communist Party, one among those which tried to avoid it, was not powerful enough to effectively challenge the policies pursued by the leaders of the Congress and the League. Gandhi without being conscious of the need to challenge these policies was, on the other hand, blessing the politics of compromise of the Congress leaders. The political approach of the top bourgeois leadership of the Congress and the League, including Gandhi, and the policy of disintegration pursued by the League leadership together with the efforts made by the British rulers to utilise both these factors to preserve their dominance made Indian partition and the widespread communal riots inevitable.

Gandhi could not do anything other than feeling pained to have to sec the mission of his life failing. The Communist Party, on the other hand, was not strong enough to bring into action what it thought correct and clear. Thus, Indian politics which had been the plaything of the British rulers as well as of the leaders of the Congress and the League moved from one crisis to another.

Punnapra-vayalar and Telangana

The struggles in Punnapra-Vayalar in Travancore and in Telangana in Hyderabad represented the highest from of the post-war revolutionary struggles. In many respects, these struggles were similar in nature. *For* example, both Travancore and Hyderabad were princely states and in both the states agitations for responsible government were making great strides. In both the states there was a developed Communist Party. The princely rulers of both the states were striving to safeguard their status in the background of the discussions being held among the representatives of the British government, the Congress and the league. The Communist Party which bad been playing a decisive role in developing popular agitations against these manoeuvres had been able to enhance its influence among the non-communist democrats in both the states.

In many other respects these struggles were also dissimilar. In Travancore, the ruler and a majority of the population were Hindus whereas in Hyderabad the ruler was a Muslim and a majority of the population were Hindus. The Muslim League bad been trying to include Hyderabad in Pakistan in the event of Indian partition. Whether it joined Pakistan or it was maintained us an independent state, a state of Hyderabad which was not part of India would constitute a danger to the security of India. Therefore, the Congress wanted to make Hyderabad a part of India. That is. Hyderabad occupied a vital place in the conflicts between the Congress and the League. As for Travancore, there was no question of joining Pakistan. But the rulers declared their intention to remain an 'independent' country' without joining Hindustan, either. Based on this, an "Independent Travancore" movement and come into existence their. Besides, in place of the democratic demand of a responsible government in the sense that it should be responsible to an elected legislature, the rulers of Travancore raised the issue of establishing a constitutional system with a government not responsible to a legislature which may be an elected one. Since the contemplated system was on the model of the presidential system of America, it was named "American Model".

If the contemplated system of "Independent Travancore" in the "American Model" was to come into force, it would be extremely dangerous to the entire bourgeois democratic movement, for the "American Model" was a negation of the democratic objective which the freedom movement had been upholding from its very inception. In addition, the existence of an-independent country with a long sea coast at one end of India would bring danger to India's security. Therefore, a state-wide agitation arose against the ideas of 'Independent Travancore' and 'American Model' with the Communist Party in the forefront.

Another factor which distinguished Travancore and Hyderabad from one another relates to the social organisations and class relations existing in the two states. In Travancore, there was a fairly organised working class. Right from the agitations for responsible government in 1938, the working class had effectively used general strike, a weapon characteristic of that class. As the strike helped the agitation for responsible government, the agitation in turn helped the growth of the working class. In Travancore, the Communist Party was born in the background in which democratic struggles of the people and the independent workers' struggles were helping and relying on each other. Consequently the

Communist Party in Travancore was the political party of the working class as well as the vanguard of the democratic movement in the full sense.

That was not the position in Hyderabad. True, there was a kind of trade union developed in the capital city of Hyderabad and there were militant strikes immediately before the beginning of the Telangana struggle. But the Communist Party had no influence in the trade union movement to any considerable extent. The main strongholds of the Party were in the rural areas and that, too, in the Telugu speaking Telangana region. Although there were democratic movements against the princely rule in the Marathi and Kannada speaking regions in the state, these movements were under bourgeois leadership. The influence of the Communist Party was weak in these movements. Thus, the Party in Hyderabad was confined to the Telugu speaking region of Telangana relying mainly on the peasantry. The peasant unions and the Andhra Mahasabha were the mass organisations involved in the Telangana struggle.

The distinction between Travancore and Telangana in regard to the class relations that had existed amongst the people and the mass base of the Communist Party may be found reflected in the nature and development of the Punnapra-Vayalar and Telangana struggles. The coir workers in the Ambalappuzha and Sherthalai taluks with a fighting tradition of over a decade and their fighting organisations together with the repressive actions taken by the rulers to suppress the workers constituted the political background which led to the Punnapra-Vayalar struggle. In Hyderabad, on the other hand, the discontent of the Telugu speaking peasantry towards the feudal elements, called the Deshmukhs, and the aspirations of the Andhra nationality led to the Telangana struggle.

Although the workers in Alleppey and the Communist Party in the whole of Kerala bad taken part in the mass upsurge against the feudal elements in the Ambalappuzha-Sherthalai taluks only weeks before the outbreak of the Punnapra-Vayalar struggle, the Communist Party there could not rise to the position of the leader of the peasant masses. (In Kerala, the peasant movement emerged and peasant struggles fought in the erstwhile Malabar district of Madras and its influence did not extend to Travancore).

In contrast to this, the working class had no direct role in the Telangana movement, although the communist movement there, like elsewhere, was based on working class ideologies and outlook.

There was also a difference in the course of these two struggles. The Tunnapra-Vayalar struggle developed rapidly into a conflict between the armed volunteers of the working class and the state army and got suppressed—all in the matter of a few weeks. The Telangana struggle, on the other hand, was a peasant revolutionary struggle lasting for about five years during which more than 4000 communists and peasant activists were killed and over 10,000 communists and workers of mass movements were thrown behind the bars for long periods. As a result of this long drawn out struggle, 'Gram Raj' was established in 3000 villages covering an area of 10,000 square miles with a population of about three million. The people's organisations and the volunteer force seized about a million acres of land from the landlords and distributed them among the peasants Minimum wage of agricultural workers was fixed and they were liberated from the social-feudal oppressions. Such a long drawn out revolutionary movement with far-reaching effects of this kind had never taken place anywhere in India before.

What was expressed in these two struggles was the efforts made by the princely rulers of these states to sustain their autocratic rule in the background on... the future Constitution being carried on by the leaders of the Congress and the League and the protests of the democratic minded people against these efforts. Consequently, the impact of the Punnapra-Vayalar struggle remained in the politics of Travancore even after it was suppressed. Although the armed conflict bad ended, the democratic minded people in the state, inspired by the struggle, continued their political struggles raising the slogans of "End the Dewan Rule". "Dump Independent Travancore and the American Model in the Arabian Sea", etc. Until the rulers, isolated from the people, retraced their steps, the politics of Punnapra-Vayalar remained relevant in the state.

The rulers of Hyderabad held on for about another year after the establishment of a responsible government in Travancore. Finally, the Indian army had to intervene to force the rulers to surrender, following which Hyderabad joined the Indian Union and a responsible government established there. The political situation changed after these developments. As the bourgeois democrats withdrew their support to the movement following these developments, the Telangana movement lost the popular support of an important section which had remained behind the movement until the surrender of the Nizam.

From this brief description, it will be clear that Punnapra-Vayalar and the Telangana struggles formed an integral part of the post-war revolutionary upsurge in India. Therefore, as the Indian political situation which formed the basis of this revolutionary upsurge underwent a fundamental change with the establishment of a bourgeois democratic system at the centre and in the provinces including the princely states, the political base of these straggles disappeared.

Since the Communist Party had been playing a leading role in both these struggles, the match to the revolutionary future as visualised by the Party became more unhindered. The bourgeois parliamentary elections held after these two struggles demonstrated the premier position of the Communist Party in the Andhra districts including the Telangana region and in the districts of Kerala including the Ambalappuzha-Shethalai taluks. It became clear that the Communist Party was one of the foremost political parties that emerged in the post-independent Indian political scene.

We have explained earlier the circumstance which led to the suppression of the naval mutiny of February 1946. The same can be applied to the Punnapra-Vayalar and Telangana struggles as well. The different streams of people's actions and feelings like the discontent among the ranks of the British Indian armed forces, the widespread workers strikes and peasant struggles of 1945-46, the agitations of the people in the princely states throughout the length and breadth of the country and the preparedness of the people to carry on armed struggles as witnessed in the Punnapra-Vayalar and in Telangana— each of these streams passed through little channels and finally petered out, rather than joining together to make up a mighty turbulent river of revolution. Each of these struggles was isolated and suppressed as and when it occurred.

The leftist parties including the Communist Party were not strong enough to unify them and convert them into a single comprehensive revolutionary upsurge. The burgeois leadership of the independence movement, on the other hand, adopted the course of bargain and compromise, instead of revolutionary struggles. The result? The British rulers could convert the popular feelings into Hindu-Muslim riots.

Crises in the Interim Government

For over six months after the formation of the interim government, Wavell remained as the Viceroy. This period was as marked by constant conflicts between the Congress and the League, on the one hand, and between the Congress and the British authorities, on the other. As a result, the functioning of the interim government often came to a standstill. The events that took place during this period were such that everyone was convinced that a united independent India was impossible to realise.

At the provincial level, in Sindh and Bengal where League ministers were in power, the Viceroy and the Governors were in full cooperation with the provincial ministries and the ruling party, whereas in the provinces ruled by the Congress, they were indifferent if not hostile to the ministries. The Viceroy even ventured to prevent Nehru's protest note being forwarded to the Secretary of State and openly defended the Governors of the League-ruled provinces. A mote important incident was the attempt made by the British authorities to prevent Nehru's visit to the NWF Province after the formation of the interim government.

The subject of tribal affairs in the interim government was directly under Nehru and the NWF Province was ridden with tribal problems. As such, no one could object to his visiting the province. But his visit to the NWF Province had a political significance, Although the Muslims constitute 97 per cent of the population of the NWF Province, the League was polled less than 30 per cent of the votes. In the circumstance, his visit to the province would not remain purely official; it would change into a political visit challenging the claims made by the League. Therefore, the Governor himself proceeded to Delhi to request Nehru to defer his plan to visit the province, When this became of no avail, the British officials encouraged the League in organising anti-Nehru demonstrations during his visit. Later, in a letter to

Mountbatten, Governor Olaf Caroe blamed Nehru's holding the portfolio of tribal affairs for the whole trouble.

This was by no means an isolated incident. This and similar other incidents were part of the scheme consciously devised by the British authorities to put as much obstructions as possible before the Congress after the formation of the interim government. They fully utilised the anti-Congress feelings of the League for this purpose.

With the entry of the league in the interim government, the problem of distribution of portfolios came up. Wavell supported the League in its claim either to external affairs or to home, which were being handled by Nehru and Patel, respectively. When the Congress refused to part with either of these subjects, it was feared at one stage that the entire plan of Wavell would break down. Finally the League had to be contented with the finance portfolio. What prevented the interim government from breaking up at that stage was the thinking among the League leaders that to have a share in the government was far more important than getting hold of this or that portfolio, lest the Congress be the sole ruling party in the country.

When the league joined the government, the Congress-League conflicts were extended to the level of administration also, providing opportunity for the Viceroy to act as an arbiter. In order to avoid it, it was suggested that the ministers meet informally and arrive at an understanding and based on this understanding take decisions formally at the Cabinet meeting. But this arrangement did not work. Instead, the Congress and League ministers met separately in groups. It may be noted that the ministers who did not belong to either of the parties attended the Congress group meetings. Thus, the interim government turned into a scene of conflicts between these two camps. The Viceroy got the opportunity to sharpen the conflicts between the Congress and the League by functioning as an arbiter between the two.

The League had made it clear earlier that they were joining the interim government as it would facilitate the formation of Pakistan. And they adopted an approach towards the Constituent Assembly suited to service this purpose. They argued that the members elected to the Constituent Assembly from the west should be grouped into two sections and the members in these two sections should frame the Constitution for their respective' sections and that the provinces belonging to these sections would be bound by the decisions taken by the sections by a majority vote. According to the League, this was the essence of the scheme prepared by the Cabinet Mission.

This was not acceptable to the Congress. They demanded that each province belonging to these sections should have the right to decide its own future. They further demanded that any dispute arising out of this should be referred to the Federal Court for its decision.

Since the two parties could not reach an agreement on this issue, the Viceroy had not called for the Constituent Assembly to meet. Finally, under the pressure from Nehru, he called for the session of the Assembly. The League strongly protested against this.

The first session of the Constituent Assembly was scheduled to be held on 9th December. But it was made clear that the League would not participate in it. It had also become clear that even if the League did not participate, the work of the Constituent Assembly would proceed with the participation of all the non-League members of the Assembly. The dispute between the Congress and the League on this issue led to a political deadlock. Outside the government and the Assembly, the people who had rallied behind these parties had begun to move in the direction of communal riots.

The British government once again intervened in the Indian affairs. Prime Minister Attlee invited the leaders of the Congress and the League to London for a discussion. The Sikh minister Sardar Baldev Sing was also invited to join the talks. Jinnah and Liaquat Ali Khan went to London to participate in the discussions representing the League. The Congress first declined the invitation, but later agreed to participate in the talks in London.

The talks in London did not help solve the problem. The British government made a declaration accepting the interpretation given by the League with regard to the provisions of section meetings contained in the scheme of the Cabinet Mission. As an attempt to solace the Congress, the British government further declared that any dispute over interpretations on this issue could be referred to the Federal Court. This decision naturally left the Congress dissatisfied.

The situations in India began to deteriorate again. The AICC met in January 1947 and adopted a resolution to the effect that there should be no compulsion on a province to join a section and that the rights of the Sikhs in Punjab should not be endangered. The resolution also declared that if there was an attempt to compel a province to join a section, then a province or a part of a province should have the right to take whatever action as required to give effect to the wishes of the people concerned.

Following, a meeting of the Working Committee of the League was held and adopted a resolution stating that the Congress had now openly rejected the scheme of the Cabinet Mission and demanding dissolution of the Constituent Assembly constituted in accordance with the scheme of the Cabinet Mission which had been rejected by the Congress as well as the Sikhs and the Scheduled Castes who stood with the-Congress. The Congress, on the other hand, demanded removal from the interim government the ministers of the League who not only refused to attend the Constituent Assembly but also demanded its dissolution. The Congress raised the complaint that the Viceroy and other British officials were rendering all kinds of assistance to the League. As a protest against this attitude of the British authorities, the non-League ministers threatened to resign from the interim government. The Congress leaders tactfully suggested to the British government the removal of Wavell from the viceregal position.

While the Congress and League leaders were in London in December, certain moves were made by the British government to change the Viceroy. Here, it may be noted that the Viceroy came to realise that things in India were not moving the way he wished. He had thought that after the formation of the interim government first without the League and later with League's participation, he would be able to control the situation by acting an arbiter between the two contending panics. That hope had now belied.

On the contrary, it became obvious now that the policy of 'divide and rule' which the British authorities, including himself, had been pursuing might lead to a civil strife in India. He feared that the responsibility for such a situation would rest solely upon the British authorities. In order to avoid it. Wavell formulated a plan to phase out the British forces from India.

The British government, however, rejected his plan thinking that it would constitute an admission of defeat. They came to the conclusion that it was essential to formulate a new approach towards India and to have a new Viceroy capable of functioning in accordance with it.

Wavell and Mountbatten

The announcement made by Prime Minister Attlee on 20th February. 1947 was in recognition of the need to adopt a new approach to find a solution to the problems arising out of the rapidly deteriorating situations in India. The announcement which was often considered '"historic"' expressed their "definite intension to leave India" by a date not later than June 1948 handing over power to a Central government formed on the basis of a Constitution agreed upon by the parties concerned or in the absence of it, to "some form of Central Government" as a whole or "in some areas to the existing Provincial Governments...." Attlee also announced the appointment of Lord Mountbatten, the Supreme Allied Commander in the South-East Asia, as the new Viceroy.

The news media had from the beginning tried hard to build the image of Mountbatten as a person lacking the faults which Wavell had and possessing the merits which he lacked. The admirers of Mountbatten have praised the "unusual abilities" of Mountbatten and Lady Mountbatten, the pan played by the new Viceroy in the British efforts to "free India" as a whole, if possible, otherwise in two pans, etc. Conscious efforts have been made to create the impression that "Freedom at Midnight" became a reality because the "unimaginative" Wavell was replaced by the "imaginative" Mountbatten as the Viceroy. This was reinforced by the fact that the Congress requested Mountbatten to continue as the first Governor-General of Free India.

It is not true to state that Wavell was against the idea of Britain leaving India handing over power to the Indians. It many be recalled that Wavell had placed the proposal before the Secretary of State for India that since it would be futile to attempt to bring about an agreement between the Congress and the League, the British should be ready to leave India in a phased manner. Although different in form and details, the same idea was contained in the announcement made by Attlee. It is thus clear that the "imaginative" Mountbatten and Attlee and the "unimaginative" Wavell alike recognised the fact that the British rulers would not be able to hold on to power in India for long.

It was widely propagated that Wavell was inimical to the Congress and friendly to the League, while Mountbatten was the other way round. This was baseless. For, it was Wavell who took the initiative to form the interim government under the leadership of the Congress but excluding the League and also convened the Constituent Assembly on the face of opposition from the League. At the same time, it was the British government that made an announcement in favour of the League when the dispute arose between the Congress and the League over the right of the provinces grouped in the different sections in accordance with the scheme of the Cabinet Mission. Mountbatten was in fact, appointed Viceroy to implement the decision taken in favour of the League.

All this, however, does not mean that there was no distinction between Wavell and Mountbatten or between Wavell and Attlee. Nor does it mean that differences in personalities and their approaches did not affect political developments. There were, however, certain approaches of fundamental nature adopted by the ruling classes of Britain above personal characteristics and approaches. Wavell, Mountbatten, Attlee, Cripps, Pethick-Lawrence and all others, including the out and out conservative Winston Churchill, were handling the Indian question subject to this fundamental approach of the ruling classes. None could deviate from this approach.

The central point of this approach was that the British would not be able to hold on to power for long after the war. How to get out of India was the only question over which they had differed from one another. Wavell was of the opinion that it was futile to hold negotiations with Indian political leaders and that Britain, should withdraw from India in a phased manner. Attlee and his colleagues who did not agree with this thought that Britain should consult with Indian political leaders and leave

India with their consent. In taking the decision to change the Viceroy, they were led by the understanding that Wavell was incapable of getting their consent by negotiating with them in accordance with this new approach, whereas Mountbatten would be able to do it.

The British rulers were unanimous in the opinion that in the event of the British leaving India, power should be handed over to a coalition government of the Congress and the League by bringing about an agreement between them, or, if this was not possible, to two governments by dividing India into two.

Some among the British rulers like Attlee, Cripps and Mountbatten had closer relations with Nehru and certain other Congress leaders. For that reason, the League leaders looked upon them with suspicion. All the schemes formulated by the British beginning from the *1942* Cripps Mission contained the dichotomy of Hindu India and Muslim India. Autonomy to the Muslim majority provinces and the right to form groups constituted the common factor of all these schemes. The League had the hope and the Congress the fear that this would lead to the realisation of the League's objective of Pakistan, The Cripps Mission and other schemes formulated by the British government reinforced this feeling. Further, as we have repeatedly stated, the central point of dispute between the Congress and the League since the formation of the interim government was the problems relating to the 'sections' and the rights of the provinces grouped into these sections. The judgement awarded by the British government on this dispute went in favour of the League.

In other words, the British rulers were unanimous in the view that they would not be able to hang on to power in India for long and that in the event of their leaving India, no Muslim majority province should be allowed to opt out of Pakistan even if it decides that way. The difference of opinion among them was over the question of how to hand over power to the Congress and the Muslim League. Here Mountbatten had certain advantages over Wavell.

First, Mountbatten was a new comer to Indian politics and government. Unlike Wavell who had to deal with the Congress during the Quit India struggle as the Commander-in-chief of the

British forces in India, Mountbatten was free from being the object of people's prejudice. His appointment as the Viceroy at the juncture helped him to create the impression as 'an administrator to implement a new policy".

Second, his relation with the British royal family, the stories that got around about his experience of leadership in a vital area during the war and his ability to deal with people had raised expectation that he would be able to face complex political situation in India. The personal behaviour of Lady Mountbatten added strength to this expectation.

Third, the friendship which had developed between Nehru and Mountbatten while he was the Supreme Commander stationed at Singapore had helped the conduct of negotiations latter, when he became the Viceroy.

Finally and more importantly, perhaps, he did not attract the hatred of Jinnah as the personal friend of Nehru. This was mainly because Jinnah was conscious of the nature of the scheme Mountbatten was going to implement. Jinnah was certain that whatever Mountbatten might do while maintaining friendship with Nehru, he would be able to rum it in his favour. Both before and after the arrival of Mountbatten, Jinnah acted as a lawyer-politician proficient in negotiations. Consequently, Mountbatten was able to adopt an approach based on the friendship with Nehru and avoiding confrontations with Jinnah.

It must, however, be started that these personal qualities and capabilities might not have shone but for the political situation prevailing then. The Congress leaders had accepted the partition of India as a reality. They had accepted the sections system contained in the long-term scheme of the Cabinet Mission. They had only instated that the provinces which are grouped into the different sections should not be forcibly merged either in India or Pakistan, They had also recognised the reality that India would have to be divided as a logical extension of the operation of this provision. They now only insisted that just like the division of India, the provinces of Punjab, Bengal and Assam should also be divided.

In other words, while opposing Jinnah's slogan of 'Divide India and Quit', the Congress bed adopted the state of mind in effect to bring this slogan in force. Mountbatten had only to accomplish the task of determining the details of Indian partition which was being realised through bargains between the Congress and the League.

Scheme of Partition

Mountbatten was sworn in as Viceroy as 24th March 1947. For more than a month after taking office, he held separate discussions with leaders of the various political parties, analysed their opinions and communicated his conclusions to the British government in early May. Based on an amended version of Mountbatten's report, on 3rd June, the British government made an announcement which formed the basis for the establishment of two independent sovereign countries. India and Pakistan, on 15th August 1947.

Based on a vast body of documents comprising notes and letters giving the details of the discussions which Mountbatten had held with Indian leaders in this brief period, many books have been written, some of which, like Freedom at Midnight, have been highly controversial. At any rate, these documents indicated that the question being discussed at that stage was not whether India should be divided or not, but how should India be divided.

The Congress demanded that, like India, the provinces of Punjab and Bengal should also be divided and the League demanded division of Assam also. The Akalis, on the other hand, wanted a separate Sikh state comprising areas in both wings of Punjab. Different sections put forward different proposals in this manner before the Viceroy.

Top leaders of the Congress which was supposed to oppose partition, like Nehru. Patel, Rajagopalachari, Rajendra Prasad, Azad and Kripalani proposed, though individually, in one voice to the Viceroy that since the partition of India had become inevitable, the Hindu majority areas of Punjab and Bengal should not be included in Pakistan. Jinnah, on the other hand, argued that these two provinces should "wholesale" become part of Pakistan. If there was justification in the demand for the division of India, what was unjust in the demand for the division of Punjab and Bengal? Jinnah had no answer to this question. He requested Mountbatten not to render Pakistan unviable. At the same time, he insisted on the point that the Muslims must get a separate state, however small and weak it might be. His only request now was that like Punjab and Bengal, the Muslim majority areas of Assam should be made part of Pakistan.

These discussions revealed one thing which is of importance for students of the history of freedom struggle. This was the fact that Gandhi, the undisputed and supreme leader of the Congress for over a quarter of a century remained isolated from his colleagues. Pyarelal, a close associate and secretary of Gandhi, has described an incident which revealed his state of mind in those days. Pyarelal writes:

> On... the 1st June (1947), mistaking the hands of his watch, he (Gandhi) woke up earlier than usual. As there was still half an hour before prayer, he remained lying in bed and began to muse in a low voice: 'The purity of my striving will be put to test only now. Today I find myself alone. Even the Sardar and Jawaharlal think that my reading of the situation is wrong and peace is sure to return if partition is agreed upon... They did not like my telling the Viceroy that even if there was to be a partition, it should not be through British intervention or under the British rule... They wonder if I have not deteriorated with age. Never-the-less. I must speak as I feel... I see clearly that we are setting about this business the wrong way. We may not feel the full effect immediately, but I can see clearly that the future independence gained at this price is going to be dark.

In the midst of spreading the message of communal amity in Bihar, Gandhi reached Delhi on the invitation of Mountbatten. In his first interview with the Viceroy, Gandhi repeated his earlier suggestion to hand over power to a new government headed by Jinnah in order to solve the complex communal problems. This suggestion, however, was not acceptable to Nehru, Patel and other Congress leaders who told the Viceroy that it was an impracticable proposal. Nor was it acceptable to Jinnah who wished to establish a separate state for the Muslims, and not to become the Prime Minister of a Hindu majority country.

Meanwhile, a serious difference of opinion arose between Jinnah and certain League leaders in Bengal. The latter thought that a separate undivided Bengal would be better than dividing Bengal and presented this opinion before the Viceroy. Reacting to this, Jinnah said that there was no wonder if they did not like a Bengal without Calcutta. But soon they gave up the position and favoured a Muslim Bengal within Pakistan.

Thus, the Congress decided, unhappily though, to divide India, and the League to divide Punjab and Bengal. The future of the Congress majority NWF Province and that of the Muslim majority areas of Assam had to be determined. Similarly, the choice of the personnel of the Indian armed forces had to be made as to which country they would like to go.

Actions had to be taken to solve these problems through mutual discussions. These and other matters were contained in the 3rd June announcement of the British government. Before that we have to find answers to a number of questions. Specifically, why did Gandhi, the supreme leader of the Congress for a quarter of a century, remained isolated? Why did the league leaders in Bengal try even at the last moment to avoid the division of Bengal? Why did their efforts fail?

The Indian bourgeoisie which began to emerge in the later half of the 19th century steadily gained strength in the 20th century. A Muslim section also gradually emerged within the same class. The British tried to safeguard their own interests making use of the competition and conflicts between these two sections within the Indian bourgeoisie.

Thus the Congress worked for the realisation of the demand of independence for the whole of India and the Muslim League for an independent Muslim state along with Indian independence. The masses rallied themselves behind both the sections of the bourgeoisie.

Gandhi's personality as well as the programme of struggle he formulated were beneficial to the bourgeoisie in rallying the masses in the movement for India's independence. Gandhi's method of struggle strengthened them enormously in their efforts to bargain with the British on the economic and political planes. The strict adherence to non-violence in Gandhi's method of struggle provided guarantee to the effect that the anti-British struggles of the people did not turn against the interests of their (the bourgeoisie and their feudal allies) interests. Consequently they were thrilled by the leadership of Gandhi in the continuous struggles and negotiations.

The situation as a whole changed by 1946-47. As a result of the straggles launched under the leadership of Gandhi as well as the development that took place at the international level, it appeared possible for the bourgeoisie to establish their regime in India comprising at least the Hindu majority regions and take the country along the path of capitalism by utilising the new political power that was going to be acquired.

It may be recalled that the leading section of the bourgeoisie bad already formulated a plan, known as the Tata-Birla plan, even before the end of the war. The bourgeoisie also had started entering in the field of international relations as evident from the Asian Relations Conference conceived by Nehru in 1945 and held at Delhi in March-April 1947. In the circumstances, it was unthinkable for the bourgeoise to launch another national struggle to win freedom maintaining the integrity of India as proposed by Gandhi. Thus, the Indian bourgeoise ignored Gandhi, the 'impractical dreamer' and stood firm behind the Nehru-Patel wing of the leadership handling 'practical politics'.

It was during the war time that the Muslim bourgeoisie achieved the most notable development. Calcutta was one of their principal strongholds. As a Bengal, and for that matter a Pakistan, without Calcutta was unthinkable for them, they made a last minute attempt to retain a united undivided Bengal comprising the Hindu majority west and the Muslim majority east. Jinnah who understood this 'sentiment' did not stand in their way, either.

But the campaign of 'two-nations theory launched throughout the country for about a decade and the communal riots that followed had altered the very thought processes of the people belonging to the two communities. Although an undivided Bengal had continued to remain a dream for the Calcutta-based Muslim bourgeoisie, ordinary Muslims throughout the eastern part of Bengal including Calcutta had started thinking in terms of forming Pakistan even with a divided Bengal.

It is interesting to note that the leader of the Congress Parliamentary Party, Kiron Sankar Roy had lent support to the efforts of the League leaders in Bengal to maintain the unity of Bengal. Thus, when he had held discussions with the Viceroy the proposal of undivided Bengal had the support of both the ruling and opposition parties in the Bengal legislature. On further discussing the proposal with his colleagues after his return to Calcutta, he realised that the idea was not going to work. Thereupon, the idea of an undivided Bengal was abandoned.

Whatever the differences in details, the contents of all the proposals initiated by the British government from the 1942 Cripps proposals to the 1947 Mountbatten Plan were the same. The essence of all these proposals was that power would not be transferred exclusively to the Congress and that if the Congress was prepared to accept a Central government to the satisfaction of the League, and agreed to partition India under its aegis; it would obtain power: otherwise independence would be postponed indefinitely.

The Congress was not prepared to accept this position in 1942. But after five years it became eager to accept it and to get hold of power. All the Congress leaders except Gandhi were united on this issue, leaving Gandhi a solitary traveller.

E.M.S' Address at a Public Meeting

The modern State of Kerala has also introduced a series of interesting protective social security measures that attempt to provide pensions and other payments to working people in the so-called "informal" sector, and to destitute and physically handicapped persons. Kerala is the only State in India where there is mass literacy (and near-total literacy among adolescents and youth), and is also the State with the lowest proportion of child workers in India. Nutrition levels have improved in Kerala after the 1970s, and, according to official data, household consumption levels were higher than the Indian average by the late 1980s. The public food distribution system, the best among India's States, gives basic nutritional support to the people of Kerala.

Kerala's accomplishment shows that the well-being of the people can be improved, and social, political and cultural conditions transformed, when there is theoretical clarity and determined public action. In the transformation that has taken place in the State, the most important agency of change since the late 1930s has been the Left movement in the State. The Communist Party, and the organisations of workers, peasants, agricultural labourers, students, teachers, youth and women under its leadership, have been the major organisers and leaders of mass political movements in Kerala since the end of the 1930s, and have been the major agents of the politicisation of the mass of Kerala's people.

Radical Left-minded individuals in Travancore began to make an impact on intellectual life in Kerala from the early part of the century; the Communist movement, however, began in Malabar. There is a stimulating scholarly literature and there are memoirs by leading participants, and novels as well, on the Left movement in Malabar in the 1930s and 1940s, which deal with the events of the time and with the people who lived and died in its cause. The number and quality of the extraordinary mass organisers and leaders for which the Communist movement in Malabar is famous are remarkable. Selfless, enlightened, and acutely sensitive to injustice, the Communist organisers of Malabar faced extraordinary repression by the ruling classes in order to achieve a better future for the people of Kerala and of India.

The Communist movement in Kerala was led, from its inception, by three extraordinary individuals - P. Krishna Pillai, a genius of organisation; A.K. Gopalan, an unsurpassed mass leader; and E.M.S. Namboodiripad, thinker, theoretician and active revolutionary and politician. The three were recruited by P. Sundarayya in the 1930s to the Communist Party from the radical section of the Congress movement, and their joint contribution has been the foundation of the Left movement in the State. It is clear that the movement in Kerala today still bears their stamp.

E.M.S. himself had been active in the movement for social reform among Namboodiris, particularly in the movement against the oppression and seclusion of women of the caste. He came to the freedom movement through the Congress in Malabar district. In an interview with me in 1992, E.M.S. spoke of the roots struck by the Congress in rural Malabar in the 1930s and of his own entry into the freedom movement:

As far as the freedom movement is concerned, it had reached the villages even in the days of the non-cooperation movement. You remember the Malabar rebellion of 1921. Even before that, the district of Malabar had a series of Congress and Khilafat committees, almost every village would have one Congress Committee and one Khilafat Committee. Although that was suppressed after the rebellion, its roots continued. An organised liberation movement of this sort dates back to the 1920s - in fact, I am a child of that movement.

E.M.S. rose quickly to a position of leadership in the Kerala Pradesh Congress Committee, and the forms of organisation of the Congress in rural Malabar initiated by him were unique.

As soon as we started work in the Congress, that is, in the mid-1930s, we started to organise night schools and reading rooms. When I was first elected the organising secretary of the KPCC - that is, in 1937 - our effort was to have, in every village, a village Congress Committee and, attached to it, a reading room and a night school.

Through his writings and practice, E.M.S. guided the Communist movement towards assimilating the most progressive features of diverse local socio-political movements and giving them new philosophical and political direction. These different movements in Kerala included the freedom movement, the radical and anti-caste sections of the social reform movement, the movement against landlordism, the movement against autocracy and monarchy, the movement for the linguistic reorganisation of the region and for the establishment of a unified Kerala, and, of course, the modern movement of workers, peasants and radical intellectuals. Communists were among the early organisers of mass political organisations of women in the State.

They played a leading part in the literary movement and in the cultural movement (including the theatre movement) in Kerala. School teachers were key activists and mass organisers of the national movement and the Communist Party; they were the first organisers of the *granthashala* (library) movement and the movement for literacy in Malabar. In the 1970s and 1980s, activists of the Left movement were the main activists in the popular science movement led by the Kerala Shastra Sahitya Parishad, and in the Total Literacy Campaign of 1989 to 1991.

It is no exaggeration to say that the political-theoretical line formulated by E.M.S. laid the basis for the far-reaching changes brought about by public action in the State of Kerala after it was formed in 1956. (Indeed, E.M.S. was one of the first to articulate clearly the demand for an *Aikya Keralam* - united Kerala - based on the linguistic principle and bringing within it the princely states of Travancore and Kochi and the Malabar district of the Madras Presidency.)

He was active in the peasant movement in Malabar, he helped to formulate the demands of the peasantry, and was really the architect of India's first land reform. (His Note of Dissent to the Malabar Tenancy Bill in the late 1930s was a landmark document of its time.) He was active in the movement for the public distribution of food and was instrumental in formulating a food policy for post-1957 Kerala.

His writings on history, society, culture and literature played no small part in public discussion and activism in these spheres. His understanding of the position to be taken by a Communist Party towards the anti-*savarna* movements was crucial to the Left's advance in Kerala. T.M. Thomas Isaac, a leading scholar of the Left movement in Kerala, characterises the attitude of the Communists in Kerala towards caste reform movements in this way:

While supporting and actively participating in the social reform movements in various communities, particularly the anti-*savarna movements* of the oppressed castes, the Communists (also) sought to build class and mass organisations irrespective of caste, and raised caste reform slogans as part of their anti-feudal democratic struggle. The Communists carried forward the radical legacy of the social reform movement and won over a large part of the masses in these movements, while the elites within these castes began to confine themselves to sectarian demands and withdraw into casteist organisational shells.

Elections were held to Kerala's first Legislative Assembly in 1957. Of all the political forces in the State, only the Communists had a coherent vision for Kerala's future; they knew what they were going to do and how they would go about it. In June 1956, the Communist Party in Kerala met in Thrissur to discuss a policy framework for Party activity in Kerala, and the document that emerged from the meeting, "Communist Proposal for Building a Democratic and Prosperous Kerala", provided the basis for the Communist election manifesto of 1957, and, indeed for future public policy in the State.

The first Government of Kerala was a Communist Government, and there was, of course, no doubt about who would lead it. E.M.S. Namboodiripad was sworn in as the first Chief Minister of the State on April 5, 1957. The major features of the agenda of the new Government and of later Communist ministries in the State were, among other things, land reform, health, education and strengthening the system of public distribution of food and other essential commodities.

Land reform and the public distribution system are recognised as unmistakably Communist projects; it is noteworthy that the E.M.S. Government's first Ordinance on land reform was promulgated on April 11, just six days after the Ministry was formed. Communist-led governments also worked on policies that helped bridge the gap between regions, they drafted early legislation on local self-government, and the ministry of 1987-1991 provided administrative and institutional support to the Total Literacy Campaign.

A major feature of political reality in Kerala today is that the Left has been successful in making many parts of its agenda part of the broad social consensus in the State.

For all this, E.M.S. was far from being complacent, or uncritical of the course that change has taken in Kerala. In his view, reflected sharply in his writings and interviews on Kerala in the 1990s, the concentration on development in the social sectors of Kerala's economy had led it into something of an impasse, characterised above all by the contemporary crisis in the spheres of employment and material production in the State.

He had no patience with scholars who attempted to romanticise a "Kerala Model" of development. For him, the very high rates of unemployment in Kerala and the low rate of growth of its economy were politically and socially unviable, and he saw the task of transforming the conditions and levels of production in the State's economy as among the topmost items on the Left agenda.

Those who shall take on the task of building the Kerala of the future that E.M.S. envisaged shall have special historical resources on which to draw, including basic land reform, an educated, skilled and politically conscious working class and unique achievements in the fields of health and education.

To the making of all of these, the contribution of E.M.S. Namboodiripad - Communist, freedom fighter, Marxist thinker, political activist, administrator, historian and social theorist - is immeasurable. E.M.S. was, as President K.R. Narayanan said in his condolence message, *sui generis*.

9

Golden Words of EMS

- We are proud of our Republican Constitution
- We are supposed to be people, who have no faith in the democratic process
- Loyalty to the basic tenets of Marxism – Leninism is supposed to be inconsistent with loyalty to the principles and process of parliamentary democracy.
- Marxism – Leninism does not take a rigid or dogmatic stand on the particular mode of bringing about social transformations
- Force is the midwife of the new society
- Nobody can dispute the wide gulf between the expectations with which the people greeted the attainment of independence and their subsequent experience
- The State Structure, built as per the provisions of the Constitution requires thorough overhauling
- The supreme power in the State must be vested entirely in the people's representatives.

10

Great Life at a Glance

1909, Jun. 13: Elamkulam Manakkal Sankaran Namboodiripad (E.M.S.) was born in an Aristocratic and orthodox family in Palakkad district.

1935: Jan. 9: "Prabhatham" (The dawn), started on 9th January 1935 at Shorannur near Trichur, under the Editorship of E.M.S. Namboodiripad, considered to be the harbinger of Deshabhimani.

—***Apr.:*** N.G. Ranga and E.M.S. Namboodiripad, the secretary and joint- secretary respectively of South Indian Federation of Peasants and Agricultural Labour, suggested the formation of an All India Kisan body.

1949, Jul. 1: Travancore-Cochin state was formed. While the Aikya Kerala movement considered this as a first step towards formation of a United Kerala, E.M.S. Namboodiripad viewed this as a step away from a United Kerala.

1956, Nov. 1: The Government of India's November 1, 1956 States Reorganisation Act inaugurated the new state, Kerala incorporating Malabar District, Travancore-Cochin, and the taluk of Kasargod and South Kanara. A new Legislative Assembly was created, these resulted in a communist-led government, headed by E.M.S. Namboodiripad.

1957: The Communist party won control of Kerala in elections in February, 1957. The state government was headed by E.M.S. Namboodiripad.

— ***Apr. 5:*** A Kerala created history when for the first time a Communist government headed by E.M.S. Namboodiripad was sworn in.

— ***Oct. 2:*** A Kerala School came up in the premises of the Kerala House, New Delhi with a student strength of 17 only.

1959, Aug: E.M.S. Namboodiripad, ministry was dismissed from office in Trivandrum.

1964, Apr. 11: Compromise formula was worked out for maintaining the Unity of Communist Party, by keeping SA Dange (rightist fraction) as the party chairman (a new position) and E.M.S. Namboodiripad (leftist fraction) as its general secretary.

1970: E.M.S. Namboodiripad, the then Chief Minister of Kerala was held guilty of contempt and sentenced for saying that the judiciary was class biased. He had proclaimed that "Marx and Engels considered the judiciary an instrument of oppression and even today...it continues to be so". He had said, "Judges are guided and dominated by class hatred, class interests and class prejudices. And where the evidence is balanced between a well-dressed, pot-bellied rich man and a poor ill".

1998, Mar 19: E.M.S. Namboodiripad died.

Appendix

[Agrarian Reforms (the Marxist Angle)]

Second Five Year Plan: a Milestone (A Case Study)

Every patriotic Indian recognises with satisfaction that the Second Five Year Plan was a step in the right direction. The various targets fixed in the Plan, as it finally emerged out of the several-month-long discussions, were such as take our national economy along the path of industrialisation, modernisation of agriculture and the overcoming of social and cultural backwardness.

But none of us can remain satisfied with the advance visualised in the Plan. For, however satisfactory this advance was when compared with the present position of our economy, it is totally inadequate to deal with the acute problems which we were facing.

Plan and Unemployment

We cannot, for example, help being concerned with the total inadequacy of the Plan in relation to the most important issue facing the common people in our cities, smaller towns and rural areas—the problem of unemployment. The Plan poses the problem thus:

> "A review of data relating to the first plan period shows that unemployment began to show a marked upward trend when the first plan was half way

> through. During the first plan period the number on the live registers continued to increase from 3.37 lakhs in March, 1951 to 5.22 lakhs in December, 1953 and further to 7.05 lakhs in March, 1956."
>
> *(Second Five Year Plan).*

It then goes on to interpret these statistics in the light of the results of a preliminary survey of urban unemployment undertaken at the suggestion of the Planning Commission.

> "According to the survey, it was estimated that about 25 per cent of the unemployed register themselves with the exchanges. On this basis the magnitude of urban unemployment at present might be of the order of 2.8 millions. This estimate appears to be broadly confirmed by the results of some other surveys recently carried out in urban areas in different parts of the country. Allowing for frictional unemployment, which is inevitable in a growing economy, it is possible to suggest that the backlog of urban unemployment may be of the order 2.5 millions."

To this "backlog of urban unemployment" should be added (i) the number of new entrants to the urban labour force and (ii) the unemployed and underemployed people, as well as new entrants to the labour force in rural areas. The Plan calculates the former at about 3.8 million persons for the Second Plan period. As for the matter, it is extremely difficult, if not totally impossible, to make any calculations. But, basing itself on the enquiry recently undertaken into the question of agricultural labour, the Plan calculates 2.8 millions as the figure of the totally unemployed in rural areas. To this should be added the new entrants to the rural labour force which is calculated at 6.2 millions for the Plan period. This adds up to 9 millions (6.2+2.8) of additional jobs to be created in rural areas during the Plan period. In other words, making no calculation at all for the underemployed people in rural and urban areas, employment opportunities for 6.3 million in urban areas and 9.0 million in rural areas, or 15.3 million in the whole country, should be created "if unemployment is to be eradicated during the Second Plan period."

In reality, however, the additional employment envisaged for the five-year period, as calculated in the Plan, comes only to 79.03 lakhs, or roughly 8 millions, i.e., just above half of what is required for liquidating "the backlog of unemployment" and for absorbing all the new entrants into the labour force.

If the Planning Commission felt compelled to admit this much the reality may be even more serious. The calculations made by independent students of the problem show that the Commission's estimates err in two directions: they underestimate the extent of unemployment, particularly rural unemployment: they also overestimate the extent of new employment opportunities which will be created during the Plan period. Rut let us disregard these controversies with regard to calculations: let us stick to the calculations made by the Planning Commission itself. Even that would convince any patriotic Indian that his satisfaction at the advances visualised in the Plan should be tempered with sobriety. It will make him realise that, at least with regard to the question of unemployment, the position at the end of the Plan period will be worse, not better than at its beginning.

Planners' Dilemma

This would naturally raise the question: Are the targets of industrialisation, development of agriculture and other advances adequate ? Is it possible for us to improve upon then: ? Or, is the advance visualised in the Plan all that we can hope for under the present circumstances?

These, however, are not the questions which have been raised by influential elements in the ruling classes. The questions they raise are of an opposite character. They ask: Is it possible for our economy to bear the burdens involved in the advance visualised in the Plan ? Influential persons in the country's economic and political life have warned the Government and the Planning Commission that the undertaking of a Plan of such a magnitude is beset with serious difficulties and risks. The validity of these words of warning has been recognised by the Planning Commission itself in the following words:

> "Sri K. C. Neogy has specially stressed that in view of the magnitude of the Plan it will be difficult to implement it in a period of five years and that deficit

> financing on an excessive scale may prove dangerous to the economy and may cause hardship to certain sections of the population. He has also drawn particular attention to the need for balanced development of transport and production generally. We agree that these considerations are important and should be constantly kept in view in carrying out the Plan." *(Ibid.)*.

We therefore come to the conclusion that, though the magnitude of the Plan is totally inadequate to meet the requirements of the situation, it is impossible to go beyond the targets fixed in it; they are the utmost limit to which our economy can go. While the implementation of the Plan will by no means solve the most important socio-economic problem of national life the problem of unemployment- it will very likely further aggravate another serious problem of national life the problem of inflation which will inevitably follow the policy of deficit financing.

Such is the dilemma which the Planning Commission and the Government have placed before us. Is there a way out of it?

The Communist Party is firmly of the opinion that there is a way out. It is of opinion that: firstly, the magnitude of development can be raised beyond what has been visualised in the Plan as it has finally emerged; secondly, such a raising of its magnitude need not be accompanied by the risks of deficit financing and inflation even to the extent to which the Plan in its present form threatens to do. It is to this end that our Party proposed a series of measures as early as June 1955. (cf. Communist Party and Problems of National Reconstruction).

The Party's proposals in connection with the Second Five Year Plan cover all aspects of planning—industrial policy, agrarian policy, taxation, foreign trade, social and cultural activities, etc. It is not the purpose of this booklet to examine all these aspects of planning—how the incorrect approach of the Government prevents the formulation of correct national policies and how the adoption of a correct approach advocated by the Communist Party would on the contrary, help the evolving of practical and popular national policies.

Two Approaches

However, before proceeding to examine Government policies and the policies advocated by the Communist Party, let us state what these policies are:

> The Broad Objective with regard to Agrarian and Peasant Question. The Communist Party keeps before itself and before the country the objective of complete elimination of landlordism, taking over of the land of landlords without compensation and distributing it gratis among landless and land-hungry peasants. The Congress accepts (in words) the necessity for "abolition of intermediaries" and that too with compensation.

This distinction between "abolition of landlordism" and "abolition of intermediaries" is not an exercise in verbal gymnastics. For, when the Communist Party speaks of abolishing landlordism, it means that the rights of all those owners of land who do not themselves do manual work in the process of cultivation should be ended. The Congress, on the other hand, includes in the term "intermediaries" only certain types of landlords who are statutorily recognised as people who stand between the State and the tiller.

Thus, for example, non-cultivating landlords in the statutorily ryotwari areas (such as the jenmies of Kerala, mirasdars of Tamilnad, etc.) and non-statutory landlords in the zamindari areas (the jotedars of Bengal, etc.) are not included among the "intermediaries" as defined by the Congress. The result is that the process of "abolition of intermediaries" has not made any change at all in the agrarian situation in these States.

Add to this the fact that even for the abolition of "intermediaries" as defined by the Congress (which does not affect even one-fourth of the landlords in the whole country), the Congress proposes to pay over Rs. 500 crores as compensation — Rs. 500 crores whose burden will continue to be borne by the peasants for years to come.

Taking Over and Distributing Surplus and Waste Lands. The Communist Party demands that (i) a ceiling should be fixed on the ownership and possession of lands by any person. (ii) surplus lands (lands above the ceiling) held by anybody should be taken over and distributed and (iii) waste lands, held either by the Government or by private owners should similarly be taken over and distributed among the landless and land-hungry people in rural areas.

The Congress Government and the Planning Commission accept this programme "in principle." But they hedge this acceptance of the "principle of land distribution" by a series of conditions, each of which will help the landlords to keep as much land as possible for themselves, and deprive the landless and land-hungry people of as much land as the landlords keep for themselves.

They, for example, try to keep the ceiling at an impossibly high level: having thus fixed a high level of ceiling, they go on to make so many ridiculous "exemptions" from the provision of ceiling; they also facilitate several devices for by passing the provisions of ceiling such as bogus "transfers *of* land," division of family property among different individuals so that each can keep land up to the ceiling, etc.; above all, there is the machinery of land management, manned by persons who are either landlords themselves or can be very seriously influenced by them. All this makes it extremely difficult, if not impossible, for the peasants to use the provisions of whatever legislation is enacted to lake over and distribute surplus and waste lands.

Tenancy Reforms. The Communist Party takes a very serious view of the eviction drive launched by the landlords and want a total ban to be put on these evictions; it also wants that a review of the recent eviction proceedings be made with a view to restoring the evicted tenants to the lands which they had formerly been holding; it wants, further, that the provisions made in the various tenancy legislations allowing landlords to evict their tenants in the name of "resuming their lands for personal cultivation" should be drastically revised: as regards the rates of rent levied by the landlords, it wants them to be fixed at levels within the reach of the large mass of tenants. These demands are so reasonable that even the Land Reform Panel of the Planning Commission accepted them and made its recommendations to the Commission on the above lines. However, neither the Planning Commission nor the Congress government has accepted them; the Planning

Commission made such "modifications" in the proposals made by the Land Reform Panel that it is now left to the State governments to do as they please with tenancy reforms. So far as the latter are concerned, they have proved by action that they would to their utmost to evade any serious legislation conferring any real rights on the large mass of tenants.

Rural Indebtedness and Credits. Next only to the landlord in the matter of dominating the countryside and exploiting the rural poor is the moneylender. He happens, in a large number of cases, to be not only the moneylender, but also the landlord and the trader, and, besides, is personally connected with the officials and the leaders of the ruling party. The reality of his grip over the mass of the rural poor has been well brought out in the Report of the All India Rural Credit Survey conducted under the auspices of the Reserve Bank of India.

The conclusions arrived at in the Report lend us to only one conclusion—that serious and effective steps should immediately be taken to release the hold of the moneylender on the rural poor It is to this end that the Communist Party proposes such measures as immediate declaration of a moratorium on the rural debts; legislative measures for the liquidation of the usurers' debts within the period of the moratorium: rigorous measures to check the activities of the usurers: and provision of alternative credit by the State to the extent of Rs. 750 crores in order that the rural poor need not depend on the usurers for their credit requirements. The Congress, however is not prepared to take such effective measures; it is only tinkering with the problem by providing small amounts for the granting of rural credits. Since these small amounts are provided in an economy in which the power of the moneylenders and their allies in the rural areas continues, the very credit provided in the name of the rural poor is likely to be grabbed by these rural exploiters.

Prices: An equally important problem is that of prices. The peasantry require and demand, on the one hand, that they should get fair prices for their produce and on the other hand, that they should get timely, adequate and cheap supplies of such goods as they require. The realisation of this demand is prevented by the iron grip which the profiteering wholesale trader has over the rural economy. The problem is aggravated by the fact that it is the foreign monopolists who control the foreign markets of all the exportable agricultural products of India: it is again they who control the mechanism of importing commodities for our use. It is this grip of the profiteering wholesale traders, led by the foreign monopolists, that prevents the peasantry from securing a fair price for their products and makes essential commodities extremely costly. The Communist Party, therefore, demands that the State should effectively intervene in this respect, curb the activities of the profiteering wholesale traders and protect the mass of the rural poor from their greed. The State can well do this if it takes over, for example, the entire foreign trade of our country, and puts effective check on the internal wholesale trade (including, in the case of some commodities which are of key importance, the nationalisation of the wholesale internal trade). The Congress, however, refused to take such effective measures against wholesale traders, thus leaving the mass of the rural poor at the mercy of these exploiting classes.

Taxation: The Communist Party holds that the levels of taxation as now fixed by the Government are too burdensome for the peasants: it is particularly against the proposed increases in the direct taxes on land and peasantry (increase in land revenue, imposition of irrigation charges and development or betterment levy, etc.) as well as the Planning Commission's proposals to collect a major part of the finances required for the Plan through the imposition of indirect taxes (sales tax excise duties) on articles of personal consumption for the mass of the people. It at the same time points out that there are other avenues of taxation, such as steeply graded income and agricultural income taxes, heavy death duties on the higher income groups, taxes on profits and capital gains, etc. These measures of taxation, together with the confiscation of the properties of the ex-rulers of Indian States, nationalisation of foreign capital, or at least stoppage of the export of profits by foreign capitalists, fixation of a maximum limit to the distribution of profits by all capitalists, etc., will help the Government to get the resources for carrying out of the various developmental plans and projects. This approach to taxation, however, is in sharp contrast with the approach made by the Planing Commission and the Government.

Agrarian Reorganisation: Basic changes in the land system are only the precondition for arousing the initiative and resourcefulness of the large mass of the rural poor. Once this objective of unleashing the initiative and resourcefulness of the rural poor has been attained, there will still remain problems of reorganising the social, economic and cultural life of the rural people. It is in this context that, according to the Communist Party, such problems as consolidation of holdings, land management, development of the cooperative movement and organisation of village panchayats, are to be seen. The Party gives central place in connection with all these problems to the peasants, the agricultural labourers, the artisans and other sections of the rural poor. The Party, therefore, puts utmost emphasis on the principle of voluntariness with regard to these questions: it is not from the standpoint of which particular plan or measure is good in itself, but from the point of view of which is acceptable to the mass of peasants, agricultural labourers and artisans that the Party views every such problem. This view is, however, opposed by the Planning Commission and the Government.

Take, for example, the proposals made in the Plan with regard to schemes of resettlement and cooperative farming. The Plan proposes that

> "In the settlement of lands acquired as a consequence of the application of ceilings, tenants displaced as a result of resumption of land for personal cultivation, farmers with uneconomic holdings and landless workers should receive preference. Settlements should be made as far as possible on cooperative lines. Farmers with uneconomic holdings below the basic level should be admitted into cooperatives constituted with surplus lands, if they also agree to pool their lands. In such cases, the tenants should not have the right to claim partition of the surplus lands which are allotted to cooperatives." *(Ibid., pp. 197-8).*

Again,

> "Holdings which are below the basic or the floor limit constitute one of the most difficult problems in the

> reorganisation of agriculture. If these holdings are grouped into larger units of operation through cooperative activity, the economics and advantages of large-scale organisation become available, larger financial resources for agricultural development can be provided and the volume of employment can be increased. The general aim should be to bring below basic holdings increasingly into cooperative pools."
>
> *(Ibid.)*

It is thus clear that the Plan attempts to put all kinds of pressures on the poor peasants (those who have below basic holdings) to join the cooperatives.

The same approach is made when the Commission makes its proposals with regard to land management practices, consolidation of holdings, etc. On every one of these questions the attempt is for the State first to fix what is good (and hence should be done), and then to put pressure on the mass of poor peasants to accept it.

The Communist Party is opposed to this approach. The Party is, of course, for the organisation of cooperatives, for consolidation of holdings and for the adoption of new and improved land management practices, since all these help the development of agriculture. It is however opposed to any measure which even to the slightest extent puts pressure on the mass of the peasantry; it is through a conscious process of education that the peasantry has to be brought to accept the advantages of cooperative farming consolidation of holdings and new standards and practices of land managements.

Furthermore, the Party takes a realistic view of present day rural life. It recognises the fact that the landlords and exploiting classes are still dominant and are in a position to influence the functioning of the cooperative and other rural organisations. There is, therefore, every likelihood of these (cooperative farming and other) organisations being turned into instruments in the hands of these exploiting classes to bring the peasantry under their iron grip.

The Party therefore demands that, instead of proceeding to the compulsory organisation of cooperatives, consolidation of holdings, the Government should encourage and facilitate the organised activity of the rural poor through their own elected leaders. The Party also demands that effective steps be taken to bring about the democratisation of the cooperatives, village panchayats and other rural organisations with a view to completely eliminate the influence of the power of the landlords and other exploiting classes.

Such are the two approaches to the agrarian and peasant question—the approach of the Communist Party and other democratic parties and the approach of the Planning Commission and the Government; the approach according to which the major task is to eliminate the influence and power of landlords and other rural exploiting classes, and the approach according to which the influence and power of these classes are not such a dangerous factor. Anybody can see that the first approach alone will help the nation to proceed To build up an economy which is not only democratic but will rapidly develop in the direction of socialism.

The Communist Party, however, urges the acceptance of this approach not only from this long-term perspective of building a socialist economy; but also because it is the only correct and possible approach which will help the nation to find solutions for the problems which it has to face in the short-term period of the Second Five Year Plan. It is the absence of this approach that obstructs the Planning Commission in its efforts to find practical solutions for the twin problems of planning mentioned at the beginning of this booklet — the problems of unemployment and finance.

Land Reforms and Employment

Let us take the question of unemployment. Is it possible to evolve a method through which the problem of unemployment and underemployment can be solved better than is being proposed at present? Or, has the Second Plan in it present form gone to the furthest limit in the matter of creating employment opportunities?

Let us admit, for the sake of the argument, that the 8 million new jobs visualised in the Plan are the maximum that can be created under the present circumstances. That will leave over 7 million job-seekers who will remain unemployed during the Plan period. This, it may be recalled, is over and above the unspecified number of millions of underemployed in the rural areas.

All these people can obviously be fully absorbed in useful jobs only if the level of development in the industrial and other fields is raised over that at present visualised. The absorption of these millions of unemployed and underemployed people is therefore a question of accelerating development in the industrial and other fields. Since our initial assumption is that developments cannot be further accelerated, we have to sec whether there is any way of giving them employment, or rather lessening the degree of their unemployment and underemployment, without accelerating the development itself.

The Planning Commission and the Government deny the possibility of this. They assume that additional employment can be created, and underemployment reduced, only if further development takes place in the industrial and agricultural fields. There is, according to them, nothing radically wrong in the present mode of utilisation of the nation's material resources and of its human labour power. They do not think it at all possible that the problem of unemployment and underemployment can be tackled through a better distribution and more rational utilisation of the material and human labour resources of the nation.

This basic assumption of the Planning Commission and the Government, however, will not stand close scrutiny. Any impartial observer can see that a better distribution of the most important material resources of the nation-land-and vast labour power, can offer a better, though partial solution to the problem of unemployment and underemployment. Even supposing that the construction plans are incapable of creating a single additional job above the 8 million target visualised by the Planning Commission, even then the problem of unemployment can be mitigated through measures of radical agrarian reforms proposed by the Communist Party.

It is a characteristic feature of our rural life that, while there are millions and millions of people who remain unemployed all through the year, there are millions of acres of land which are being left waste or follow, either by the Government or by the landlords. It is also a reality or rural life that while there are millions of people who are either totally unemployed or seriously underemployed, there are big landlords who own thousands of acres of land and get them cultivated, either through their heavily rack-renter tenants or heavily underpaid wage labourers. Such an unequal distribution of the material and human labour resources of rural India is not only unjust from a moral sense of the term; it is also injurious to national interests from a severely practical, economic point of view. For, it is this that lies at the root of the acuteness of the problem of unemployment and underemployment in the rural areas.

It is in this context that the proposals with regard to the fixation of ceilings on landholdings, taking over of surplus, lands and distributing them, together with waste lands owned by the Government or by the landlords, should be seen. It is pure common sense that such a distribution of lakhs of acres of waste and surplus lands among the poorest sections of the people—agricultural labourers, poor peasants and unemployed or underemployed artisans—will, at least partially, mitigate the problem of unemployment and underemployment facing them today.

It is necessary, in this connection, to make a reference to the usual pedantic argument about the "uneconomic holdings" which will be created through the distribution of surplus and waste lands. It is argued (with all the pomposity characteristic of so-called "experts" who have no living relation with the actual conditions of the mass of the people) that, if the surplus and waste lands that can be made available are distributed among the landless and land-hungry people, each of them will get only a few cents of land and that each of them will therefore be holding an "uneconomically small" patch of land.

These "experts" forget that it is far more "economic" for the millions of people who have not a cent of land, who do not get a single day's work, to get at least a few cents of land which will enable then) to secure gainful employment at least for a few weeks in the year, than to legally abolish "uneconomic holdings'". They forget that their conception of "economic holding" will inevitably perpetuate a state of affairs in which there are a small number of "above-economic" holdings and a large number of "economic" holdings, together with millions of people whose very existence is "uneconomic". The millions of small holdings which will be created through land distribution will not meet the tests of "economic holding" laid down by these "experts"; but they will certainly meet the most important single economic test which should be laid down by anybody who has the interest of the nation at heart—the test of mitigating the sufferings of the millions of unemployed and underemployed people in the rural areas.

This, however, is not all. The proposals for agrarian reform which the Communist Party advances help the solution of unemployment and underemployment in two other respects:

First, the total ban on evictions and other measures for securing complete fixity of tenure for the tenants will prevent the transformation of today's peasants into tomorrow's landless labourers. As a matter of fact, the Planning Commission and the Government, in their approach to the problem of tenancy reforms, miss the fact that the countrywide eviction drive launched by the landlords has enormously aggravated the problem of unemployment and underemployment in the rural areas: the hundreds of thousands of peasants who have been evicted even during the First Five Year Plan have, to that extent, swelled the army of unemployed and underemployed people in the rural areas. This is a fact whose significance has been totally missed by the Planning Commission both in its assessment of the gravity of the problem of unemployment as well as in its proposals for tenancy reform.

Secondly, rent reduction, reduction in the rates of interest and in the extent of rural indebtendess, reduction in the direct and indirect taxes levied on the *mass* of the rural poor—all these are steps which have a bearing (though indirect) on the problem of underemployment. For any reduction in these burdens on the rural poor would mean that a corresponding addition is made to their income. For example, a peasant who pays 50 per cent of the produce to the landlord as his rent and has enough land to give him employment for four months in the year would have his income doubled if his rent is reduced to 25 per cent; this would actually be equivalent to the period of his employment being raised to the level of 8 months in the year from its present four months.

It may once again be repeated that the above-mentioned impact of agrarian reforms on the problem of unemployment and underemployment takes no account of the possibilities for the creation of new employment opportunities by expanding the scope of development itself.

For we have assumed in the above discussion that possibilities for the creation of employment opportunities through the various plans and projects of construction as visualised in the Plan, are the utmost possible. What we have here tried to do is to point out that, even if this assumption is correct, the adoption of agrarian reforms as proposed by the Communist Party and other democratic parties and elements will help (i) to absorb the "backlog of unemployed", as well as to provide employment to the new entrants into the labour force in the rural area and (ii) to provide greater employment opportunities, or alternatively to secure higher returns, for those who are underemployed today. These measures of agrarian reform therefore have their significance for the planning of our national economy as a whole.

Vicious Circles of the Plan

Let us now pass on to the next important problem of national planning—finance for the Plan. The seriousness of this problem is recognised by the Planning Commission itself when it says:

> "It is obvious that the second five year plan will strain the financial resources of the country. A measure of strain is implicit in any development plan, for, by definition, a plan is an attempt to raise the rate of investment above what it would otherwise have been. It follows that correspondingly larger effort is necessary to secure the resources needed." (Ibid.)

It is as part of such a "larger effort" that the Commission suggests various measures such as additional taxation, market borrowings, small savings and deficit financing. All these measures are justified on the ground that the people should make sacrifices in the interest of developing national economy.

This, of course, is a national and patriotic appeal which will be warmly responded to by every patriotic Indian. We all know that, just as in the case of ending colonial rule and winning national freedom, so in the case of consolidating freedom and making it full and real in the sense of economic advance, we have to make immense sacrifices. Our people will, therefore, cheerfully bear all the burdens that are proposed to be imposed on them, provided they help the cause that is dear to their hearts—the cause of national development.

There are, however, certain important questions: Are the measures of financing the Plan proposed by the Planning Commission, such as help the advancement of the national economy? Are the particular forms of sacrifice imposed on the common people necessary and correct in order that resources are found for the development of the national economy?

Furthermore, is the Planning Commission, which exhorts the common people to make sacrifices in the interest of national development, imposing corresponding burdens on that small minority of people who can afford to bear these burdens—the small minority composed of the ex-rulers of princely States, big landlords. Indian and foreign capitalists, etc.? The common people have a right to expect answers to all these questions.

It is, however impossible for the Planning Commission to give satisfactory answers to these questions. For the burdens that our common people are asked to bear are not only unjust and inequitous from the point of view of their capacity to bear these burdens, they are also detrimental to the cause of developing the national economy on the lines of industrialisation, modernisation and development of agriculture, expansion of trade and commerce, etc.

The burdens imposed upon them are also unjust and inequitous in the sense that, while the small minority of those who can afford to bear such burdens are allowed to go virtually free, the vast mass of working people are asked to bear huge, unbearable burdens.

The fundamental basis which guides the Planning Commission in financing the Plan is stated as follows: "Basically, the issue is whether and how domestic savings to the requisite extent can be mobilised in the aggregate. This depends on a judgement not only as to the desirability of limiting consumption beyond a point, but also of the suitability, in the given economic and social set-up, of the means or techniques to be used for the purpose." (Ibid., Emphasis added.)

It is as specific "means or techniques to be used for the purpose" of limiting consumption that the Plan proposes taxation, market borrowings, small savings and deficit financing.

> "All these [market borrowings, small savings and deficit financing] are devices for diverting private savings either voluntary or forced through price rises, to the public exchequer." *(Ibid.)*

This need for limiting consumption in an economy which requires large capital resources is supposed to be nothing but common sense. How can you get resources for the Plan, it is asked, unless the people are prepared to limit their own personal consumption? This, however, is an oversimplified and therefore totally incorrect position.

Unduly limiting personal consumption on the part of the mass of our people gives rise to another serious problem of economic development the problem of a shrinking home market. The more the economy advances, the higher goes the level of production, the greater in the need for expanding the home market; in other words, an expanding economy requires for its basis an expanding level of consumption by the mass of our people. Absence of a proper balance between expansion in production and expansion in consumption will lead to a crisis of overproduction.

That this is no idle imagination has amply been proved by the experience of what happened during the First Five Year Plan. The Second Plan states as follows in its review of the progress of the First Plan in relation to industries:

> "In one group of industries, shortfalls in production were on account of lack of adequate domestic demand. These include some of the light engineering industries such as diesel engines and pumps, radios, batteries, electric lamps and hurricane lanterns. In some industries, production remained below target levels on account of reduced export demand (jute manufactures) or low demand from indigenous industries which cater for exports (plywood for tea chests). Production of superphosphate scarcely exceeded 50 per cent of the planned output." *(Ibid.).*

Nor can we forget the lessons of two very serious falls in the prices of agricultural commodities which took place during the First Plan period—those of 1952 and 1954.

It is true that the crisis of overproduction is not today an immediate threat, either in relation to the industrial or to the agricultural sector. The position today is just the opposite: it is not any catastrophic fall in the prices of industrial or agricultural products, but a serious rise in the prices of several important commodities, that we are faced with. But there are two factors which require our attention and study.

Firstly, limitation of consumption as a basic policy is inconsistent with the strategy of planning according to which production will steadily grow from year to year: it is not limitation of consumption, but its expansion, that is required in a plan which looks forward to an enormous expansion in production. Failure to note this essential point threatens the whole future of planning. It is this reality that was clearly revealed during the First Five Year Plan. Its lessons should therefore be never forgotten even though such a prospect does not appear to threaten our economy at the moment.

Secondly, the Planning Commission seems to discount the possibility of such a crisis of overproduction on the assumption that deficit financing will offset the impact of putting limits on consumption, since the new money that is injected into the economy will generate additional domestic demand. This is fraught with serious consequences. Even supposing that it is in a sense beneficial since it generates additional domestic demand, deficit financing has dangerous implications: the price inflation that is likely to follow the large-scale injection of additional money into the economic system will completely upset the calculations with regard to the cost of production and thus lead to the raising of the levels of resources required for the fulfilment of the Plan. It will also upset the relations between employers and employees and thus lead to industrial unrest which, in its turn, will have serious consequences for the implementation of the Plan.

All these consequences, it may be noted, follow deficit financing even if it is completely controlled and works according to the optimistic calculations made by the Planning Commission. An it is by no means certain that it will work according to such calculations. The possibility is that deficit financing, followed as it will be by inflation, will be taken advantage of by the landlords and capitalists in order to indulge in speculative activities, thus leading the economy to still more catastrophic convulsions.

The basic strategy of financing the Plan as evolved by the Planning Commission is thus one of choosing between two evils. Basing itself alternately on limiting consumption through the "means or techniques" of additional taxation, market borrowings and small savings) and deficit financing, the Planning Commission leads the economy into dangerous channels. The dangerous character of this strategy is frankly recognised by the Commission itself. It says:

> "No amount of prudence in financial management can by itself eliminate completely the risk of inflation in an economy attempting to develop rapidly. The best defence against inflation is in a sense, to keep clear of it, hut a policy of 'playing safe' is not always conducive to development. A measure of risk has to be undertaken..." *(Ibid.)*

The commission thus proposes to draw the economy into a vicious circle: limitation on consumption in order that capital resources may be discovered; this, in its turn, leads to contraction of the home market; attempts are made to meet this situation by the injection of more money into the system; more money into the system leads to inflation; inflation creates additional demand but creates shortages which can be met only by the production of more commodities and what is more, inflation makes production more costly and thus makes it necessary to get more financial resources; this in its turn makes it necessary to put further limits on consumption; so on and so forth.

Communist Strategy for Financing the Plan

It is to break out of this vicious circle that the Communist Party proposes another strategy—the strategy of (a) not limiting, but expanding, the personal consumption of the mass of our people, thus creating the basic prerequisite of an expanding economy—an expanding domestic market; (b) limiting the luxurious personal consumption of the small minority of the wealthy sections of society; (c) mobilising of the financial resources that lie untapped, or are extravagantly or unproductively utilised, by the wealthy sections of society. This is a strategy which will enable the State of find the resources that are necessary for the development of the national economy without in the least restricting, but actually expanding, the personal consumption of the mass of our people and, therefore, the domestic market.

It is this strategy of finding the resources for national economic development without restricting consumption that forms the basis of the proposals made by the Communist Party in its publication, The Communist Party and the Problems of National Reconstruction. It is not the purpose of this booklet to examine and explain all the proposals made by the Party in this connection. What is proposed here is only to point out how the policies and measures advocated by the Party with regard to the agrarian and peasant question have a bearing on this aspect of our national economic planning.

The agrarian reforms advocated by the Communist Party have two crucial aspects:

Firstly, they lead to a more rational utilisation of the resources of the nation in the form of land and human labour power in the rural areas. (How this is to be organised and how it helps the solution of the problem of unemployment and underemployment in the rural areas has already been explained).

Secondly, they help the process of relieving the mass of peasantry of the huge burdens which they are today bearing the burdens of rent, interest and taxes. Whether there is total abolition of landlordism (in which case the burden of rent payable to landlords is totally eliminated), or whether there is only the more modest programme of rent reduction, the peasants will be in a position to keep the greater part of their produce with themselves. The same result will follow measures of relief from rural indebtedness, reduction in the rates of interest on debts and recasting of the structure of rural taxation.

These measures would undoubtedly lead to the expansion of the domestic market. They would do something more: the peasantry will be enabled to allocate a certain proportion of the additional incomes, which they receive through these measures of agrarian reform, for the improvement of their own technique of production; they will be able to invest a part of their additional income on digging wells, constructing bunds, using more and better manures, buying and maintaining more efficient tools and cattle, etc. All this means that, to that extent, capital resources required for agricultural expansion and development are generated within the agricultural sector itself.

Landlordism: an Obstacle for Using Financial Resources

But the most important consequence of the measures of agrarian reform as they affect national planning is that the vast amounts that are today wastefully used in the agricultural sector—the amounts that are used for the purchase of land-will be productively used. This is an aspect of national planning which perhaps requires to be examined in greater detail.

A study of the statistics collected by the registration departments of the various States of India will show that several hundreds of crores of rupees are "invested" every year on land—"invested" not on developing land, but simply in buying it. These "investments" are made between several categories of people. There are, for example, transactions between peasant and another; there are also transactions between a peasant on the one hand and a moneylender or landlord or trader on the other; there are, again, transactions between a peasant and a small employee or a small merchant who has made some savings and wants to take to cultivation and therefore wants to buy land; transactions take place also between persons who are not peasants at all—two people who are selling and buying the land which neither of them cultivates nor intends to cultivate, but the land from which one of them collects today, and the other expects to collect tomorrow, a part of its produce either as rent or interest.

Such a variety and multiplicity of the types of sellers and purchasers of land conceals the fact that what is bought and sold is not the land itself but an existing legal right on the land or, what is in essence the same: an existing legal right to collect a part of the produce of land as rent or interest. It is this right of collecting a part of the produce as rent or interest which is bought and sold. This is true not only of transactions between two landlords, or two moneylenders, or between a landlord and a moneylender,—between two people who do not cultivate land but collect rent or interest; it is true also of transactions between two peasants. Even in the latter, what is sold and bought is the right to cultivate the land as well as the right not to cultivate but to collect rent instead, if the owner so pleases.

The fundamental basis on which this legal "right" has come into existence is the assumption that the land belongs not to those who cultivate it but to certain people who "own" it without cultivating. The right of these "owners" to collect a part of the produce as rent from those who cultivate but do not own it—it is this "right ownership" which is bought and sold. It is this right of ownership, as distinct from the right of cultivation, that is bought and sold even when the purchaser and the seller are peasants.

It is this separation between right of ownership and right of cultivation that is sought to be ended by the slogan "Land to the Tiller". It is this separation that is ended when landlordism is abolished without compensation, i.e., the right of landlords to receive rent from their tenants is ended: a definite limit, or ceiling, is put on the holding which anybody may keep; and surplus land over and above this holding, together with all the waste lands, art distributed among landless and land-hungry peasants. These reforms would make it impossible for anybody to become a non-cultivating "owner" and then to make his right of non-cultivating "ownership" a commodity that can be bought and sold. It will put an end to the "investment" of crores and crores of rupees by landlords, moneylenders, traders and other wealthy people in "buying land." It will make it impossible for the small employee or the small merchant, who has made some savings, to "invest" his savings in "buying land"; it will make it necessary for him to use his savings in more useful ways.

The only type of transactions in land which will be permitted under the new pattern of agrarian relations will be that between one cultivator who wants to give up his cultivation and take to other occupations, and another who is either a cultivator already or proposes to become one. Even in the case of such transactions, the new pattern of land relations will make it unnecessary for crores and crores of rupees to be "invested" in the purchase of land. For it will be a matter of planning and organisation on the part of village panchayats, or other machinery for land management, whose job it will be to facilitate the transfer of land from those who want to give up cultivation to those who want to take to cultivation.

This will mean that the vast amounts that are today being utilised even by cultivators in purchasing land, i.e., in doing nothing but taking physical possession of it, will not be necessary; the major part of these amounts can, therefore, be used as real productive capital: capital invested in digging wells, constructing bunds, improving the tools, buying livestock, etc.

Vast amounts have to be spent on purchasing land and relatively smaller amounts are thus left with cultivators for improving and developing it. Precisely because the land is "owned" by certain people who can get returns on it without doing any work on it; precisely because these "owners" who are not cultivators will not part with their land unless they get the capitalised value of the rent which they are getting today. The ending of this right of "ownership" as distinct from the right of cultivation, will make it unnecessary for the peasant to pay, as "price of land," the capitalised value of the rent which is today collected by the non-cultivating "owner."

Being relieved of this necessity of paying the "price of land," the peasant will be able to invest all his capital in further improving and developing his land. At the same time, the landlord, the moneylender and other non-cultivating classes too will be force to invest their capital productively, i.e. invest it as real productive capital in industry and commerce since they are being deprived of the "right" to "buy land" by "paying its price."

It is, of course, impossible for us to make even a rough calculation of the amounts which are today being paid by the peasants as rent to the landlords, or the amounts that are unproductively "invested" every year in the purchase of land. For, the statistics that have so far been collected by the various departments of the Government and such agencies as the Reserve Bank of India, do not give us even an inkling as to how much of the produce of the land goes every years to landlords as rent; nor are there All India figures to show the extent to which the financial resources of the nation are squandered by the landlords and moneylenders in real or speculative purchases and sales of land. There is, however, no doubt that, if the Planning Commission and the Government, together with the Reserve Bank of India, seriously set about the task of collecting these figures, it will be found that the right of "ownership" of land without the obligation to perform manual labour on it (with its twin consequences of payment of huge amounts every year as rent to the landlord and the 'investment" of still more huge amounts in the purchase of land) is a serious obstacle to the solution of the problem of finding capital resources without restricting the domestic market.

As an example of the conclusions which may emerge out of such a study, I may cite certain facts revealed to me 16 years ago, when I had occasion to study the rural economy of Malabar. These facts have been analysed in detail in ray Minute of Dissent to the Malabar Tenancy Committee, submitted in 1940. I am here giving only the salient facts and the conclusions to be drawn therefrom:

- Out of the Rs. 7 crores worth of agricultural produce, just over Rs. 3 crores goes to the landlords as rent. Deducting the land revenue to be paid by the landlords (Rs. 45 lakhs) out of the rents realised by them, they get over Rs. 260 lakhs net. In other words, the peasant is allowed to keep less than 4/7 of the value of the product of his labour, while nearly 40 per cent of the produce of the land goes to the landlords who do not labour on land.
- Out of the less than Rs. 4 crores (which the peasants keen after paying landlords' rent) has to go the interest on debts which they have to pay to the moneylender. It is difficult to calculate the amount so paid, since the debt owed by the peasants and non-cultivating owners are mixed up. But the total burden of indebtedness which falls on the rural economy of Malabar is about Rs. 15 crores. Interest on this at the moderate rate of 10 per cent comes to Rs. 1.5 crores. Even supposing that only half this is the debt owed by the peasants (the other half being that owed by the non-cultivating owners), the annual burden

of interest on debt which falls on the shoulders of the peasants comes to Rs. 75 lakhs. This plus the burden of rent to the landlords (over Rs. 3 crores) make up a total of Rs. 4 crores. In other words 4/7 of the value of the agricultural produce goes to the landlord, the moneylender and the Government. It is clear that, if other taxes are also added to this, the proportion will go still higher.

- Reduction of this huge burden which now falls on the shoulders of the peasantry will enable them not only to raise own standard of living (which, in its turn, will facilitate the process of industrialisation by expanding the domestic market); it will be possible for them also to use part of their additional income as capital for the expansion and improvement of agriculture (thus partly solving the nation's problem of financial resources required for economic advancement).
- The value of the sale and mortgage deeds registered in Malabar stood at that time at Rs. 160 lakhs per year. Part of these transactions in land is, of course, done among peasants themselves—one peasant selling and another buying land. But another part (the bigger pan from the point of view of the amount involved in the transactions) is carried on among the non-cultivating land "owners." If at least the latter could be stopped by putting an end to the ownership of land by non-cultivating classes, a major part of the amount involved in the sales and mortgages of land can be as productive capital for the nation as a whole.

Agrarian Reform—a National Need

The above study of the impact of agrarian reforms on two most important aspects of national economic planning—on unemployment and on the financial resources for the Plan— shows that the agrarian reforms proposed by the Communist Party are not "doctrinaire," "visionary," "impractical", etc., as is claimed by the opponents of agrarian reform. It is not out of the so-called "ideological considerations," but out of severely practical considerations of the necessity for economic planning, that it is proposed to abolish landlordism without compensation, relieve the peasantry of the huge burdens of rent, interest and taxes which they are bearing today, and to distribute surplus and waste lands among the landless and land-hungry people. It shows that, by championing the cause of agrarian reform, the Communists are championing not merely the cause of peasants, agricultural labourers and other sections of the rural poor; they are championing the cause of developing the national economy as a whole. On the other hand those who oppose the agrarian reforms are injuring not only the peasants, agricultural labourers and other sections of the rural poor but the entire national economy.

Yet it is these agrarian reforms that are denounced by the spokesmen of the ruling classes (including the leaders of the ruling party, the Congress) as "violence," "negation of democracy," etc. It is the right of ownership, as distinct from the right of cultivation, that is defended by these spokesmen of the ruling classes as "democracy" and "free enterprise" which, it is claimed, will be violated if the reforms advocated by the Communist Party are carried out.

It is not violation of "democracy" and "free enterprise" in the eyes of these gentlemen if tens of thousands are every year turned out of their land and even homes. But it is a "violation of democracy" and "free enterprise" if the landlord is deprived of the right to so turn out the peasants.

It is not violation of "democracy" and "free enterprise" if the landlord has the right to tell the peasant:

> "Give me one half (if not more) of what you produce in the land or starve yourself; I won't give you land for less than that much as my rent." But it is a violation of "democracy" and "free enterprise" if the Government tells the landlord: "You have no right to receive any rent; either you cultivate the land, doing manual labour yourself on the land, or we take over the land and give it free to the peasant."

It is not violation of "democracy" and "free enterprise" for the landlords to own several thousands of acres of land in the very village in which there are hundreds of families with no land at all or at best with a few cents of land. But it is a violation of "democracy" and "free enterprise" if the Government enacts a law according to which these thousands of acres of land owned by the landlords are taken over and distributed among the landless labourers, poor peasants and other sections of the rural poor.

This, however, was not the attitude taken by the leaders of the present ruling party when they were struggling for power. There was a time when the Indian National Congress looked upon the agrarian and peasant problem as a very important part of the problem of freedom and democracy. The well-known resolutions adopted by the Congress at its Karachi (1931). Lucknow (1936) and Faizpur (1937) sessions had made it clear that the "removal of British imperialistic exploitation" was closely connected with "a radical change in the antiquated and repressive land tenure and revenue systems." The Faizpur resolution had also added "that the deepening crisis (reference here is to the economic crisis of the 1930s) has made the burden on the peasantry an intolerable one and immediate relief is urgently called for." The Faizpur resolution therefore advanced the following immediate demands in connection with the agrarian problem; it was on the basis of these demands of the peasantry, together with similar demands of the working class and middle class employees that the Congress fought the elections and secured majorities in seven Provinces in the 1937 elections.

- Rent and revenue should be readjusted having regard 10 present conditions and there should be substantial reduction in both.
- Uneconomic holdings should be exempted from rent or land tax.
- Agricultural incomes should be assessed to income tax like ail other incomes, on a progressive scale, subject to a prescribed minimum.
- Canal and other irrigation rates should be substantially lowered.
- All feudal dues and levies and forced labour should be abolished, and demands other than rent should be made illegal.

- Fixity of tenure with heritable rights along with the rights to build houses and plant trees should be provided for all tenants.
- An effort should be made to introduce cooperative fanning.
- The crushing burden of rural debt should be removed. Special tribunals should be appointed to enquire into this and all debts, which are unconscionable or beyond the capacity of peasants to pay, should be liquidated. Meanwhile a moratorium should be declared and steps should be taken to provide cheap credit facilities.
- Arrears of rent for previous years should generally be wiped out.
- Common pasture lands should be provided, and the rights of the people in tanks, wells, ponds, forests and the like recognised, and no encroachment on these rights should be permitted.
- Arrears of rents should be recoverable in the same manner as civil debts and not by ejectment.
- There should be statutory provision for securing a living wage and suitable working conditions for agricultural labourers.
- Peasant unions should be recognised.

Ruling Party's Profession and Practice

This democratic approach to agrarian problem was of course, not adhered to by the Congress either in the 1937-39 years (when it was in power in seven Provinces) or in the post-1946 years. It succumbed to the pressure of powerful landlord interests and refused to implement the very moderate demands which it had formulated in its Faizpur resolution: it did not, for example, enact any legislation (either in the 1937-39 or in the post-1946 years) reducing the burden of rent on the peasant to any considerable extent: most of the provisions concerning rent in the legislations enacted by Congress governments did either stabilise rent at the then existing level or made very insignificant reductions: what is more, innumerable loopholes were left which enabled the landlords even to enhance the rates of rent in several cases.

While this was the practice adopted by the Congress government, it however continued to advocate policies which in theory at least were a continuation of the approach made in the Karachi. Lucknow and Faizpur resolutions. For example, the Working Committee of the Congress appointed, in January 1950, an Economic Planning Sub-Committee with Pandit Govind Ballabh Pant as Chairman; in the resolution appointing the Sub-Committee, the Committee pointed out the need for a system which "can provide an alternative to the acquisitive economy of private capitalism" a system which the Committee called the "cooperative commonwealth." The Sub-Committee in its turn, laid down the basic guiding lines on which this new system is to be established. These guiding lines include the following among others:

- "All intermediaries between the tiller and the State should be eliminated":
- "Land should be held for use and as a source of employment. The use of lands of those who are either non-cultivating, landlords or otherwise unable for any period to exercise the right of cultivating them must come to vest in the village cooperative community, subject to the condition that the original lawful holder or his successor will be entitled to come back to the land for genuine cultivation";
- "The maximum size of holdings should be fixed. The surplus land over such a maximum should be acquired and placed at the disposal of the village cooperatives," etc.

The Communist Party does not, of course, consider this approach of the Congress fully satisfactory. There are innumerable inadequacies and imperfections in the approach. Nevertheless, this approach, if seriously and sincerely adhered to and implemented in practice, offers a common ground for action as between the ruling party on the one hand and the parties of the democratic opposition on the other. For, however inadequate and unsatisfactory, the proposals made in the above-mentioned documents of the ruling party enable the peasantry to improve their lot consequently they enable the nation as a whole to lay a sounder basis for improving its economy in a planned way. That was why it was possible for the Land Reform Panel of the Planning

Commission, consisting among others of Sriman Narayan, the General Secretary of the Indian National Congress. Ashoka Mehta, the Praja Socialist M.P., and Prasad Rao, the Communist M.P. and General Secretary of the All India Kisan Sabha, to come to unanimous conclusions on the main guiding lines for agrarian reform to be incorporated in the proposals for the Second Five Year Plan.

Basis for United Action

The opponents of land reforms therefore are fighting not the programme advocated by the Communist Party with regard to agrarian reforms; they are fighting the approach that is common to the entire national democratic movement—the approach that is common to the Communist Party, to the Praja Socialist Party, to other left and democratic parties, even to the Congress officially—the approach which, though not shared by big sections of the influential leaders of the Congress, is shared by the overwhelming majority of Congressmen.

For, though the details with regard to the manner in which the present land system should be replaced by a new one very from party of party, all these democratic parties and elements are agreed on the general approach that land should be owned by those who actually cultivate it. Though the different parties differ as to the manner in which landlordism should be abolished, all of them are agreed that the abolition of landlordism is an inseparable part of the democratic transformations in the social and economic system visualised by every democrat. It is this common approach, rather than the specific details of agrarian reform, that is opposed by powerful elements inside and outside the Congress Party.

The Communist Party, therefore, calls upon the Praja Socialist, other left and democratic parties, Congressmen who are genuinely anxious to get effective and reform measures adopted, and every other individual or group interested in the democratic transformation of our economy, to come together and fight for such urgently needed agrarian reforms as are practicable today. The Party is of opinion that the proposals made by the Land Reform Panel of the Planning Commission offer a basis on which the democratic elements regardless of party affiliations can unite their forces. The Panel's proposals do, of course, contain some important gaps and loopholes which, unless carefully filled up will provide ample opportunities for the landlords to launch their offensive against the peasants. These, however, are aspects of a problem which can be taken up for free and frank discussion among those parties, groups and individuals who are interested in the welfare of the peasants. The Communist Party therefore appeals to all of them to come together and discuss the basis on which they can put up a united struggle for land reforms.

The Party desires in this connection to draw the attention of other democratic parties and individuals to the following

"Platform for Unity" which the All India Kisan Sabha at its recent Amritsar session placed before the country. It is, of course, possible that certain parties, groups and individuals interested in the struggle for the advance of the immediate interests of the peasants have some criticism to offer to one or more of the proposals included in that Platform. These criticisms and suggestions made by other organisations, parties, groups and individuals can and should be freely and frankly discussed among them with a view to arriving at a common basis of unity with regard to the line on which united struggle is to be organised.

- Total ban on evictions for 3 years until comprehensive land laws are enacted safeguarding the interests of the tenants:
- Restoration of tenants to lands from which they have been ejected and all transfers and sales of land to be declared null and void for the purposes of security of tenure;
- Implementation of the proposals of the Second Five Year Plan on rent reduction within one year;
- Fixation of ceiling on all holdings at three family holdings, conferring proprietory rights on the tenants over their tenancies and distribution of the surplus land among agricultural labourers and poor peasants.
- Acquisition of the waste lands (Government and private) and their distribution among agricultural labourers;

- Moratorium on the usurers debts and provision of Rs. 750 crores to meet the requirements of rural credit;
- Lightening of existing tax burdens on the peasants (no tax on agricultural labourers and poor peasants); graded tax on, agricultural income to be enforced: sales tax and indirect tax on essential commodities and services to be abolished;
- Opening up of network of marketing cooperative societies and warehouses to save the peasants from market fluctuations and fixation and guarantee of fair prices of agricultural and industrial commodities;
- Opening up of cheap grain shops;
- Full participation in all government schemes which benefit the peasantry, taking initiative in organising relief, self-help for rural reconstruction:
- Immediate implementation of Minimum Wages Act in rural areas of all States to fix minimum wages for agricultural workers;
- Democratisation of cooperatives, panchayats district boards so as to ensure their democratic functioning and broader and active participation of the people in them. The development schemes to be implemented through the organs of local bodies in order to save administrative expenditure and wastage by ensuring the people's cooperation. Full civil liberties, separation of executive from judiciary, curbing the powers of repressive organs.

Need for Fighting Pro-Landlord Policies

While thus calling upon all the democratic organisations parties, groups and individuals including democratic Congressmen and Congress committees to come together and unitedly fight on the basis of an agreed platform of joint action, the Communist Party has no illusion that the struggle for the realisation of the above platform will be easy. On the contrary, it is conscious of the enormous obstacles which have to be overcome if even the slightest improvement is to be made in the condition of the peasantry.

It is necessary in this connection to recall that the obstacle in the way of real agrarian reform is the policy adopted by the leadership of the ruling party itself. Despite the outwardly attractive proposals and suggestions made in several of the documents adopted by the ruling party (some of which have been referred to above), it is a fact that there are still several States in which no land reform worth the name has been adopted. The way in which land reform has been adopted in some States has been summarised as follows by a keen student of the agrarian question in India, Dr. Daniel Thorner in his book 'The Agrarian Prospect in India':

Rajasthan: "Jagirdari had to be abolished because the jagirdars were 'intermediaries.' But the jagirdars had to live, so they were enabled to acquire khudkasht lands, and thereby to become cultivators. Now, as owners of khudkasht lands, they are to be permitted to have their lands cultivated by tenants, i.e., to become once again intermediaries. Thus, the full circle has been completed: Rajasthan is back where it started."

Madhya Bharat: "The current agrarian position in Madhya Bharat is quite similar to that in Rajasthan."

"Vindhya Pradesh and Mysore, both of which may be classed together with Rajasthan and Madhya Bharat as former jagirdari or inam areas where land reform legislation, such as has been passed, has had little effect on village realities".

West Bengal: "...The post-independence legislature explicitly failed in 1950 to implement the recommendations of the Commission appointed in 1940 under the auspices of the old regime. The specific provisions of the 1950 Act are inconsequential, if not retrograde, as compared, say, with the sections of the Bombay Tenancy Act of 1948, which deal with crop-sharing.

The next land reform measure to be passed in West Bengal was the Estates Acquisition Act of 1953. By the time the State Government brought out this Act. ample experience had accumulated in Bihar and U.P. to make it clear that the introduction of such Bills in the State legislatures spurs the zamindars to enlarge their sir and khudkasht holdings as hastily as possible by evicting the tenants. But nothing was done in West Bengal to forestall this procedure, and only after the inevitable tide of evictions had risen to flood heights was a preventive ordinance perfunctorily issued."

Bihar: "As in Uttar Pradesh, the Bihar Act permitted the zamindars to retain their sir and khudkasht. As a result, it is not difficult to come across estates of 500. 700 or even 1,000 acres in post-reform Bihar. One also finds after zamindari abolition a persistence of the older structure of landowner, occupancy ryot, non-occupancy-ryot, under-ryot and bataidar (eropsharer)... In short, neither zamindary abolition nor Bhoodan persuasion (although Bihar has been the site of the most intensive Bhoodan efforts in the whole of India) has been able to transform rural Bihar. It remains a stronghold of large landholders and hierarchical property rights: leasing, subleasing and evictions are all common."

Orissa, Assam and Himachal Pradesh. "In no one of these three States has there been any significant degree of change."

These and other examples of how Congress ministries in the States have implemented land reform programme, officially adopted by the Congress, show the enormous influence wielded by the landlord elements on the State ministries. They make it clear that it is not a question of all democratic parties, organisations, groups and individuals coming together and demanding certain reforms. The point is for them all to come together to fight for these reforms. Furthermore, it is not a question of the parties of the democratic opposition unitedly fighting the ruling party to secure these reforms nor of the parties of the democratic opposition uniting with the ruling party to have these reforms jointly sponsored. It is, on the other hand, a question of the parties of the democratic opposition, non-party or all-party organisations and democratically-minded Congressmen, jointly fighting the opponents of land reform both within and outside the ruling party. It is for such a united struggle and cooperation.

It is within this general framework of unity of all the organisations, parties, groups and individuals interested in agrarian reforms that the Communist Party looks upon its own tasks in connection with the coming general elections.

There is one basic question which should guide the thinking and activity of all those who are interested in land reform: how best to see that the Central Parliament and the State legislatures which will be elected such than a community agreed platform of agrarian reforms can be sought to be implemented in the next five years. It is this question which guides the thinking and activities of the Communist Party.

Need for Strengthening Democratic Opposition in Legislatures

The answer to this question obviously is that the representation of the Communist Party, the Praja Socialist Party and other parties and elements of the democratic opposition should be increased to the maximum possible extent. For, it is the MPs and MLAs belonging to these parties who will be in a position to put up a consistent, uncompromising struggle for the broadest possible agrarian reforms.

The MPs and MLAs belonging to the democratic opposition would not be, of course, alone in fighting for agrarian reforms. A large and growing number of Congress MPs and MLAs also put up, in their own way, the struggle for agrarian reforms. The Communist Party and other parties and elements of the democratic opposition would certainly be happy if the number of such Congress legislators increases.

But they cannot forget the fact that the Congress MPs and MLAs, however sincere in their desire for agrarian reforms and in their willingness to fight for them, will be restrained by the organisational discipline of their part)' and that within the leadership of their party are powerful landlord elements who would wield the big stick of organisational discipline to restrain their followers from fighting for radical agrarian reforms. As a matter of fact, it has been the experience of the Communist and other parties of the democratic opposition during the last five years than, while there are several Congress legislators who genuinely fight for radical measures, they have been unable to consistently fight for what they think are the right steps.

A powerful group of democratic opposition in each legislature, consistently and uncompromisingly fighting for those very measures on which they and the democratic Congress legislators are agreed, mercilessly exposing the manoeuvres of the champions of the landlord elements (within and outside the ruling party) will, as a matter of fact, be of immense help even to the democratic Congress MPs and MLAs in their own struggle for agrarian reforms inside their own party. The coordination of the struggle waged by the legislators belonging to the democratic opposition with the struggle put up by the democratic Congress legislators is the only guarantee that the manoeuvres resorted to by the pro-landlord elements in the leadership of the ruling party are detected and defeated.

Nor is it a question of merely strengthening the representation of the parties and elements of the democratic opposition in the Parliament and in every State legislature. It is also a question of installing in certain States such governments as will implement the platform of agrarian reforms commonly agreed to by the democratic elements inside and outside the ruling party. Here again, it is not a question of securing some advantage for the parties of the democratic opposition as against advantages for the ruling party. It is a question of advancing the common cause of all those elements that stand for vital reforms in the agrarian structure of the country—a cause in which are interested not only the parties and elements of the democratic opposition but also large sections of Congressmen as well.

Since the latter are as interested as the former in seeing that the platform commonly agreed to is implemented to the utmost possible extent, it will be to their interest that a government is installed in one or two States at least which is pledged to take immediate and energetic steps to put a total ban on evictions, to see that tenants ejected from their lands during recent years are restored to their lands, to reduce rent at least to the level recommended by the Planning Commission, etc. Not only will these measures resorted to by the alternative government formed by the parties of the democratic opposition improve the material condition of the peasants in that particular State; it will give a powerful impetus to the democratic movement in other States as well.

Let us take the concrete of the new State of Kerala. Example It is in this State and in Bengal that the Communist Party has given the call for the formation of an alternative government as its objective in the coming General Elections. Now, Kerala is a State, in a major part of which (the part which was formerly the State of Travancore) no land reform of any kind has been implemented during the last seven years; even the little improvement that was registered in the position of tenants in Malabar under the Malabar Tenancy Act of 1930 has not so far been registered in the case of tenants of corresponding tenures in the Travancore part of Kerala. Successive Congress ministries refused to make any provision with regard to restriction of rent (so much so that the landlord is legally entitled to demand even 100 per cent of the produce as rent) or preventing eviction of tenants. It was during the tenure of office of the PSP Ministry in 1954-55 that certain legislative measures were prepared and introduced. But the moment they were introduced, the Congress saw to it that the PSP Ministry, which took initiative in introducing them, was overthrown.

The installation of an alternative ministry now, followed by legislative measures providing for prevention of eviction, rent reduction, fixation of ceilings, distribution of surplus and waste lands, etc.—measures which are so modest in their character that they do not go beyond what has been agreed to in the Land Reform Panel of the Planning Commission— would help the democratic Congressmen and Congress committees in every State in their struggle for the implementation of those democratic proposals throughout the country.

In other words, the formation of an alternative ministry in this particular State, together with a similar development in West Bengal and greater representation for the parties and elements of the democratic opposition in the Central Parliament and in all other State legislatures, would be a development not directed against the Congress as such but against those elements and trends inside the Congress which are helpful to the landlords. That is why the Communist Party appeals even to democratic Congressmen not to stand in the way of the formation of alternative governments in one or two States where there are possibilities for the same.

Bibliography

A. K. Gopaian: *In the Cause of the People: Reminiscences,* Orient Longmans, Madras, 1973.

Abani Lahiri: *The Peasant and India's Freedom Movement,* Manak, 2001.

All-India Kisan Sabha, & Namboodiripad, E. M. S.: *Kisans on the March for Food & Freedom: Resolutions of the 7th Session of the All-India Kisan Sabha at Bhakna, April 1943,* People's Pub. House, Bombay, 1943.

Aparna Basu: *The Growth of Education and Political Development in India,* Oxford University Press, Delhi, 1974.

B. Rajeevan: 'Cultural Formation of Kerala', *Essays on the Cultural Formation of Kerala,* Trivanjdrum, Kerala Gazetteers Department, 1999.

B.T. Ranadive: *Caste, Class and Property Relations,* National Book Agency, Calcutta, 1982.

Berger, P. and Luckmann, T.: *The Social Construction of Reality.* Penguin Books, Middlesex, 1979.

Bhattacharya, B. K.: *India's Freedom Movement: Legacy of Bipin Chandra Pal,* Deep and Deep, 2007.

Chandra, Bipan: *India's Struggle For Independence,* Penguin Books India (P) Ltd., New Delhi, 1989.

Das, M. K.: *'Kerala's Decentralised Planning: Floundering Experiment',* Economic and Political Weekly, 2000.

Diraviam, Leila: *Diraviam Our Treasure,* Asian Printers, Chennai, 1999.

Dreze, Jean and Amartya Sen: *India: Economic Development and Social Opportunity*, Oxford University Press, Delhi, 1996.

Economic and Political Weekly: *EMS Namboodiripad on Class-caste Relations see his Problems of National Integration*, National Book Agency, Calcutta, 1966.

Economic and Political Weekly: *Kerala Yesterday, Today and Tomorrow*, National Book Agency, Calcutta, 1968.

Economic and Political Weekly: *Selected Writings*, National Book Agency, Calcutta, 1982.

Erwin Neumayer and Christine Schelberger: *Bharat Mata: India's Freedom Movement in Popular Art*, Oxford University Press, 2008.

Franke, Richard W and Barbara H Chasin: *Kerala: Development through Radical Reform*, Institute for Food and Development Policy, San Francisco, 1992.

Gandhi, Rajmohan: *Rajaji, A Life*, Penguin Books India (P) Ltd., New Delhi, 1997.

Ganjoo, S.: *Muslim Freedom Fighters of India*, Anmol, 2002.

Goyal, P. K.: *Battle of India's Freedom Movement*, Vista International, 2005.

Hari Hara Das: *The History of Freedom Movement in India (1857-1947)*, National, 1998.

Hocschild, A.R.: *The Second Shift*, Penguin Books, New York, 2003.

Indu Dave: *Indian Personality in Its Developmental Background*, Himanshu, 1991.

Isaac, Thomas T.M. and Frank, Richard W.: *Local Democracy Development, People's Campaign for Decentralised Planning in Kerala*, Leftword, New Delhi, 2000.

Iyengar, A. S.: *Role of Press and Indian Freedom Struggle: All through the Gandhian Era*, APH, 2001.

Jacob, J.: 'The Fiscal Equilibrium of Kerala: A Diagnosis' in *Dimensions of Economic Development: Spatial and Sectoral Perspectives*, 1997.

Jayaram, Poduval: *Special Interview of K. G. Subramanyan*.

K.N. Ganesh: *Keralathinte Innalekal*, Dept. of Publication, Kerala Government, Trivandrum, 1991.

Kailash Khanna: *History of Indian Freedom Struggle*, Commonwealth Pub, 2004.

Kamat, Jyostna: *The Pioneers: Kamaladevi Chattopadhyaya*, Kamat's, 2003.

Kapoor, A. N. Gupta, V. P. and Mohini Gupta: *An Encyclopaedic Dictionary of Freedom Movement 1757-1947*, Radha, 2004.

Kaushik, A. S.: *Great Freedom Fighters of India*, Indian Pub, 2007.

Khairul Anam, Md.: *Indian Freedom Movement and Murshidabad District 1905-1947*, Bagchi, K. P., 2008.

Klausen, A.M.: *Kerala Fishermen and the Indo-Norwegian Pilot Project*, Universitetsforlaget, Oslo, 1969.

Krishan Mohan: *Indian National Congress and the Freedom Movement*, Book Enclave, 1999.

Krishna, B.: *Indian Freedom Struggle: The Pathfinders From Surendranath Banerjea to Gandhi*, Manohar, 2002

Leonard A. Gordon: *Bengal: The Nationalist Movement 1876-1940*, Columbia University Press, New York, 1974.

Lion Agrawal, M. G.: *Freedom Fighters of India (4 Vols-Set)*, Isha Books, 2008.

Majumdar, R. C.: *History of the Freedom Movement in India (3 Vols-Set)*, Firma KLM, 1997.

Manju Verma: *The Role of Women in the Freedom Movement in Punjab (1919-1947)*, Abhijeet, 2003.

Maulana Syed Mohammad Mian: *The Prisoners of Malta (Asira'n-E-Malta): The Heart-Rending Tale of Muslim Freedom Fighters in British Period*, Manak, 2005.

Mazhar Kibriya: *Gandhi and Indian Freedom Struggle*, APH, 1999.

Mills, C.W.: *The Sociological Imagination*, Oxford University Press, London, 1967.

Mishra S.N., John Beyer: *Cost Benefit Analysis: A Case Study of the Ratnagiri Fisheries Project*, Hindustan Publishing Corporation, 1976.

Muthaiah, S.: *Women Freedom Fighters*, The Hindu, 2004.

Nair, Gopinathan N. D.: *People's Planning in Kerala: A Case study of two Village Panchayats*, Discussion Paper No.16, Thiruvananthapuram: KRPLLD, Centre for Development Studies, 2000.

Namboodiripad, E. M. S.: *Let us Work Together: An Open Letter to Delegates to the Convention of the All India Socialist Party*, People's Pub. House, Bombay, 1952.

Namboodiripad, E. M. S.: *A Short History of the Peasant Movement in Kerala*, People's Pub. House, Bombay, 1943.

Namboodiripad, E. M. S.: *Anti-communist Gang-up in Kerala: Betrayers of U.F. Set up Anti-people Govt.*, Desraj Chadha, Calcutta, 1970.

Namboodiripad, E. M. S.: *Communism and Social Democracy: Is the Gulf Really Wide?*, People's Pub. House, New Delhi, 1957.

Namboodiripad, E. M. S.: *Conflicts and Crisis; Political India: 1974*, Sangam Books, Bombay, 1974.

Namboodiripad, E. M. S.: *Food in Kerala*, People's Pub. House, Bombay, 1944.

Namboodiripad, E. M. S.: *Food: Achilles' Heel of Indian Economy*, People's Pub. House, Bombay, 1952.

Namboodiripad, E. M. S.: *Ill-informed Criticisms against Communist Government Refuted: E.M.S. Replies Congress President Dhebar*, Govt. Press, Trivandrum, 1958.

Namboodiripad, E. M. S.: *On Organisation*, Communist Party of India, Delhi, 1954.

Namboodiripad, E. M. S.: *Peasants meet at Moga*, People's Pub. House, New Delhi, 1954.

Namboodiripad, E. M. S.: *Selected Writings*, National Book Agency, Calcutta, 1982.

Namboodiripad, E. M. S.: *The "Self Criticism" Which Hides the Mistakes: Comment on Dange Group's Kerala Election 'probe'*, Communist Party of India, Calcutta, 1966.

Namboodiripad, E. M. S.: *The Communist Party in Kerala: Six Decades of Struggle and Advance*, National Book Centre, New Delhi, 1994.

Namboodiripad, E. M. S.: *Twenty-eight Months in Kerala*, People's Pub. House, New Delhi, 1959.

Nanda, S. P.: *Freedom Movement and Constitutional Development in India*, Dominant, 2004.

Om Prakash: *Encyclopaedic History of Indian Freedom Movement (12 to 21 Vols)*, Anmol, 2003.

Omesh Saigal: *Shaheed Bhagat Singh: Unique Martyr in Freedom Movement*, Gyan Pub, 2002.

P. Govindapillai: *Kerala Navodhanam Oru Marxist Veekshanam*, Chintha Publishers, Trivandrum, 2003.

P.K. Gopalakrishnan: *Keralathinte Samskarika Charithram* Mal, Bhasa Institute, Kerala, 1994,

Parmanand Parashar: *Kashmir and the Freedom Movement*, Sarup, 2004.

Pradhan, K. B.: *Freedom Movement in India*, Arise Pub, 2007.

Prafulla Kumar Pattanaik: *The First Indian War of Independence: Freedom Movement in Orissa, 1804-1825*, APH, 2005.

Pratik Chakrabarti: *Western Science in Modern India : Metropolitan Methods, Colonial Practices*, Permanent Black, Delhi, 2006.

Rafiya Nisar: *Shaikh-Ul-Hind Maulana Mahmud Hasan and Indian Freedom Movement*, Manak Pub, 2008.

Raj Kumar: *Essays on Indian Freedom Movement*, History and Culture Series, Discovery, 2003.

Ram Sharma, S.: *Education of Women and Freedom Movement*, Discovery, 1996.

Ram, S. and Kumar, R.: *Quit India Movement: 1942-1945*, Commonwealth Pub, 2008.

Ramanathan, K. V.: *The Satyamurti Letters, Vol. II: The Indian Freedom Struggle Through the Eyes of a Parliamentarian*, Dorling Kindersley for Pearson Longman an Imprint of Pearson Education, 2008.

Ramu, P. S.: *Azad Hind Fauj (I.N.A.) and The Freedom Movement*, Freedom Movement Memorial Comm, 1998.

Ratna Ghosh: *Netaji Subhas Chandra Bose and Indian Freedom Struggle (2 Vols-Set)*, Deep and Deep, 2006.

Ravindra Kumar: *Champaran to Quit India Movement*, Mittal, 2002.

S. G. Ghosh: *Decision-Making and Power in the British Conservative Party: a Study of the Indian Problem, 1929-1934,* Oceania Publishing House, Calcutta, 1972.

Shachi Chakravarty: *Quit India Movement: A Study,* New Century Publication, 2002.

Shailesh Chandra: *90 Years of India's Struggle for Independence: 1857-1947,* Alfa Pub, 2008.

Shantinath Gupta: *Great Freedom Fighters of India,* Anmol, 2006.

Sharma, K. K.: *Encyclopaedia of Great Personalities of India (4 Vols-Set),* Book Enclave, 2007.

Sirisa Kumar Shadangi: *The Prisons of South Orissa and the Freedom Fighters in Incarceration, 1900 - 1947,* Punthi Pustak, 2005.

Sumit Sarkar: *Modern India 1885-1947,* Mcmillan India Ltd., Delhi, 1999.

Sundaram, V.: *Great Crusader for Women's Emancipation,* News Today, 2005.

Sundararaja, Saroja: *March to Freedom in Madras Presidency, 1916-1947,* Lalitha Publication, Chennai, 1989.

Surinder Singh: *The Political Memoirs of an Indian Revolutionary: Naina Singh Dhoot (1904-1989),* Manohar, 2005.

Taneja, Anup: *Gandhi, Women and the National Movement, 1920-47,* Har-Anand Publications, Delhi, 2005.

Thapar-Bjorkert, Suruchi: *Women in the Indian Nationalist Movement,* Sage Publication India (P) Ltd., New Delhi, 2006.

Thomas Isaac T M with Richard W Frank: *Local Democracy and Development: People's Campaign for Decentralised Planning in Kerala,* Left Word Books, 2000.

Verma B. R. and Unnikrishnan K.: *Encyclopaedic Biography of Indian Freedom Fighters,* Commonwealth, 2004.

Warrier, Shoba: *Quit India Movement: 60 Years,* Dr. Sarojini Varadappan, 2002.

Index

D

E

L

M

N

P

❑❑❑